GENDER IN ARCHAEOLOGY

Analyzing Power and Prestige

For the men in my life:
Hal, Erik, Mark, Stan, Sam, Chad, and Calvin

GENDER IN ARCHAEOLOGY

Analyzing Power and Prestige

by Sarah Milledge Nelson

AltaMira
PRESS

A Division of Sage Publications, Inc.
Walnut Creek • London • New Delhi

For information contact:

AltaMira Press
A Division of Sage Publications, Inc.
1630 North Main Street, Suite 367
Walnut Creek, California 94596 U.S.A.

Sage Publications Ltd.
6 Bonhill Street
London EC2A 4PU United Kingdom

Sage Publications India Pvt. Ltd.
M-32 Market
Greater Kailash 1
New Delhi 110 048 India

Printed in the United States of America

Library of Congress Cataloging-in-Publication Data

Nelson, Sarah M., 1931–
    Gender in archaeology: analyzing power and prestige / by Sarah Milledge Nelson.
        p. cm.
    Includes bibliographical references and index.
    ISBN 0-7619-9116-6 (pbk: acid-free paper).—ISBN 0-7619-9115-8
    (cloth: acid-free paper)
    1. Feminist archaeology. I. Title
    CC72.4.N45 1997
    930.1—dc21   97-4860
                                                  CIP

Interior Design and Production by Labrecque Publishing Services

Cover Design by Joanna Ebenstein

TABLE OF CONTENTS

About the Author **9**
Acknowledgments **11**

CHAPTER ONE

Introduction **13**
    Gender as a Concept 15
    History of Gender Research in Archaeology 16
    Power and Prestige 17
    The Constructed Past 20
    The Value of Gendered Archaeology 22
    Lens, Mirror, or Prism? 25
    Chapter Organization 27

CHAPTER TWO

The Creation of Power and Prestige **31**
    Exploring Gender in Anthropology 32
    Scientific Outsiders 36
    Women as Archaeologists 39
    The Hairy-Chested and the Hairy-Chinned 42
    Remedies 46
    Conclusions 48

CHAPTER THREE

Interpreting Gender in the Past:
Theories and Strategies **49**
    Gender Implications of Archaeological Theories 49
    Some Principles for Engendering Archaeology 54
    Strategies for Gender Research 56

Resources for Engendering the Past 58
Conclusions 64

CHAPTER FOUR
In the Beginning:
Archaeology, Gender, and Origins **65**
Origins and Evolution 67
Evolution Constructed as Male 70
Women's Responses 72
Primate Research: Our Own Reflection 75
"Early Man" Studies, and the Absence of "Early Woman" 81
Gendering the European Paleolithic 82
Conclusions 84

CHAPTER FIVE
Gender and the Division of Labor **85**
Tool-Makers: The Critique 91
Strategies for Bringing Women's Tool-Making to Light 95
Gathering and Hunting: The Critique 98
Strategies for Engendering Hunting and Gathering 99
Farmers: The Critique 101
Food Preparation: The Critique 103
Food Preparation: Archaeological Examples 104
Potters: The Critique 106
Strategies to Engender Pottery Production 106
Spinners, Weavers, and Tailors 109
Conclusions 111

CHAPTER SIX
Families and Households **113**
Matriarchy, Matrilineality, and Matrilocality 114
Kin Organization: Stylistic Analyses 118
Motherhood 125
Daughters and Sisterhood 127
Wifehood 127
Conclusions 129

CHAPTER SEVEN

The Larger Community 131
   Traders 136
   Healers 136
   Religious Leaders 138
   Warriors and Athletes 139
   Leaders: Big Women, Chiefs, and Queens 141
   Conclusions 148

CHAPTER EIGHT

Ideology and Gender 151
   Female Figurines 154
   Ideology as Mystification 165
   Conclusions 168

CHAPTER NINE

Gender, Evolution, and Muted Voices 169
   Writing Archaeology 170
   Cultural Evolution and Gender 171
   Agency and Values 174
   Toward a Gendered Archaeology 175

Bibliography 177
Name Index 221
Subject Index 227

ABOUT THE AUTHOR

Sarah Milledge Nelson is John Evans Professor of Archaeology at the University of Denver, where she is faculty in the Anthropology Department and Director of Asian Studies. She teaches Archaeology of East Asia and European Prehistory as well as gender issues, origins of agriculture, and other topics. Her research interests are focused on Korea and northeastern China (Manchuria), especially during the Neolithic and Bronze ages, although she has also carried out archaeological projects in Colorado and Utah. She has lectured on most continents, recently including the cities of Rome, London, Sydney, Buenos Aires, Seoul, Fukuoka, Shenyang, Vladivostok, and Petropavlovsk. Altogether she has published about a hundred journal articles, chapters, and books. Some recent books include *The Archaeology of Korea* (1993), *The Archaeology of Northeast China* (ed.) (1995), and *Equity Issues for Women in Archaeology* (1994), edited with Margaret Nelson and Alison Wylie. She holds a B.A. from Wellesley College and M.A. and Ph.D. degrees from the University of Michigan.

ACKNOWLEDGMENTS

The first draft of this book was written at Villa Serbelloni, the Rockefeller Foundation Study and Conference Center in Bellagio, Italy. Our study looked out over the roofs of the village and toward the ferry plying Lake Como. When we got really restless we could zigzag down leg-aching flights of steps to the village, to enjoy the flowers or poke around in the shops. I owe a heartfelt thanks to the Rockefeller Foundation for selecting me for a residency, to the villa staff who are masterful at setting the stage for productive scholarship as well as making a pleasant stay, and to the other scholars and their spouses, with whom we shared the premises for a month. Thanks also to Hal, for going with me, and bringing his own writing to do while we were there.

Special appreciation goes to all those whose work I took with me to absorb and to write about. Their careful and engaging works about gender and about women in the past are the foundation on which this book is built. I have borrowed many stimulating ideas, as the too-long bibliography shows, and I appreciate the difficulties, the struggles, and the courage that lie behind each piece of writing. There wasn't room to cite every single excellent paper that has been written, and I hope the authors of those not cited will not feel slighted. They all affected my thinking.

Students in my classes on Women in Prehistory over the years helped form and sharpen my ideas as well. They have been skeptical or credulous, probing or accepting. Sometimes their incomprehension made me try harder. I owe a special debt to this year's class, whose comments on the draft manuscript were particularly helpful. An early class wrote such good term papers that I tried to get them published, but the time was not ripe. For the title I couldn't decide between "Woman's Discovery of Her Past" and

"Woman Makes Herself," both parodies of Childean titles that might not resonate with current students, though they seemed amusing at the time.

Conversations with many colleagues helped me arrive at the point of view presented in this book. I particularly want to thank Alison Wylie and Alice Kehoe, as well as two anonymous reviewers, for their detailed and careful comments on the first draft. They are not responsible for my stubbornness in failing to take some pieces of their advice, but they certainly made this a better book.

Mitch Allen, my editor at AltaMira Press, who encouraged me and allayed my inevitable angst, deserves gratitude as well. My student assistants were hardworking and patient with my incessant revisions: Kay Winter, who helped me organize the materials to take to Bellagio, and Beth Rudden, whose computer skills made the "inputting" go much faster, and the output more satisfying.

Finally, this book is not only for the women who have taken gender seriously, but for the men, too. This is not just a woman's issue, but a project all can join to create, together, improved interpretations of the past.

CHAPTER ONE

INTRODUCTION

The second wave of the women's movement, begun in the 1960s, has produced an extraordinary outpouring of scholarship and critical thought overturning the received wisdom of many disciplines.
—Helen Longino (1995:20)

The study of gender explodes order, and restores ambiguity, contradiction, diversity, and possibilities to the center of social process.
—Irene Silverblatt (1988:454–455)

Gender has become the latest catchword for feminists, but what does it mean in the context of archaeology? Is it just another approach to finding the women of the past, or is it a better means to interpret the archaeological record? In this book I argue that a gendered archaeology is an *improved* archaeology, one that helps expose the ways in which an emphasis on power and prestige has obscured gender in the past, and one that makes possible a less distorted view. I also suggest that gendered power imbalances in the present among living archaeologists still contribute to obscuring parts of the archaeological record. These intertwining themes may be difficult to tease apart, but untangling them makes the patterns clearer.

Gender in archaeology is no longer a new topic, though it is one still not well understood outside the circle of its practitioners. Among the hard lessons learned within that circle is that "engendering" archaeology is difficult to accomplish and continues to be a struggle, as various researchers strive to devise appropriate theories and methods to engender the past. How, one asks, is gender to be identified from the mute archaeological

13

remains? What problems have been addressed, and how, and what else should be attempted? Is finding women in the past, or even finding women and men in the archaeological record, the same thing as learning about gender relationships of their period? To what extent can we rely on ethnographic analogy and the direct historical approach? Are all attempts to engender archaeology equally effective? These are some of the myriad questions considered in this book.

I will show that some consensus is forming about theory, and that the search for methods to make rigorous a focus on gender has had some successes, with a distance further to go to attain this goal. These attempts in the aggregate have the potential to transform both archaeological theory and method. What follows is not merely a catalog of gendered archaeology, or a stock-taking of the changes that gender research in archaeology has or could have or should have accomplished—though I review some of the recent important challenges to received wisdom about the archaeological past, and examine selected examples of applications of these principles to specific cases. In assembling many of the path-breaking new directions into one extended discussion, I hope to accomplish two fundamental goals. The first is to describe the growth and changes in feminist archaeology, to examine its roots, to consider reasons for the paradigm lag compared to other disciplines, and to ponder what may be still impeding the acceptance of gender as one of the critical areas of archaeological research. The second goal is to convey the possibilities and ferment of gender research, research that has not yet been the leavening agent that it should be, or has the potential to be, in standard archaeological practice and interpretation. Gender research should in my view not be ghettoized into research done by women *about* women, though such has been largely the result so far, with several important exceptions. Most archaeologists, women as well as men, have continued to ignore both the topic of gender and the feminist critique of archaeology. As Margaret Conkey has frankly noted, "feminist thinking in archaeology . . . has not yet had a significant impact; this is no secret" (Conkey 1993:3).

Research on gender in archaeology was muted in its early stages, but today the importance of the topic is recognized more and more widely, and the literature grows almost daily. The time is ripe for an assessment of the ways in which gender in the distant past is being studied, to consider which

14

avenues of research are the most fruitful and productive, and, reciprocally, in what ways the study of past gender constructions is important for other kinds of feminist research, as well as other archaeological theoretical stances.

Gender as a Concept

Gender is not the same as sex (Hanen and Kelley 1992, Kehoe 1990). Sex (or sex class, as it is sometimes called) refers to the biological male or female, while gender is "the social correlate of sex class . . . one learns to behave accordingly, to be masculine or feminine according to the norms of a particular culture" (Wallman 1978:22). In other words, sex is a given, while gender is constructed. Certain roles, activities, or behaviors are assigned to particular people grouped together as a gender. Thus gender is related to sex, but is not the same thing. Constructed gender varies from one culture to another and must be taught. No one "has" a gender at birth. Nothing about gender is genetically inherited.

Given this definition of gender, it follows that a gendered archaeology considers both women and men, and any other culturally constructed genders (for example, berdache). Gender is not a code word for women, and gendered archaeology is *not* another way of finding women in prehistory disguised with a more neutral and inclusive term. Both women and men—people as individuals as well as in groups—become more visible in studying gender. Other constructed roles, activities, and behaviors, such as ethnicity, age, and class, may also become visible in the course of researching gender in archaeology. As Patricia O'Brien (1990:62) has noted, "archaeology itself is 'asexual.' Too many studies not only do not deal with women in the archaeological record, they do not deal with men or even with *people*."

Some feminist archaeologists disagree that gender should be the major focus of the effort, and assert that the study should properly be about women instead of about gender, as indeed some of the early feminist writings were (e.g. Ehrenberg 1989). Women as subjects were claimed by second wave feminism to "recover women's experience and thereby to find ways that we as women could constitute ourselves" (Mascia-Lees et al. 1989). Catherine Roberts argues that "identifying gender as an irreducible element of human life does not necessarily establish the centrality of women to the historical process" (1993:19), suggesting that instead we need "an archaeology that is informed by feminism" (1993:20). While I agree with the latter statement, there is the question of "which" feminism, for feminism is not monolithic. Many feminists feel that "women" is not a viable category. Instead, there are variously situated women (e.g. Alcoff and Potter 1993). Nor is gender itself unproblematic. Although she agrees that the focus should be on gender, Cheryl Claassen (1993) insists that the existence of gender should not be assumed, that the number of genders is not fixed, and that gender might not be more important than other social variables in a given instance. Further discussions among feminist archaeologists relate to the need to consider additional variables, such as ethnicity, sexual orientation, age, and other ways that people are categorized. The tension between white feminists and women of color reflects real differences in the needs and goals of women situated in different ways. Certainly many variables are important, but the focus of this book is on gender. Everything cannot be studied at once.

History of Gender Research in Archaeology

It is true that some of the earliest feminist archaeology was remedial, and some continues to be, asking basic woman-centered questions such as "Where were the women while men were creating humanity?" and "What tasks did women do if men did all the hunting?" In the late 1960s these were forward-looking and brave questions to ask, but after two decades of such explorations it has become evident that such questions, though important, are insufficient—in spite of the fact that some answers were produced and headway was made. Finding women in the past who were overlooked and trivialized is a valid goal, yet deeper questions must be asked, questions that probe the comfortable categories of "women" and "men." The essentialism and universalizing of the underlying questions of what men and women *do* has become problematical in itself. Are the characteristics attributed to women the same everywhere? How can we tell if men's and women's roles are identical, similar, overlapping, or different, in archaeological contexts? If gender relations and gendered work, roles, and behavior are not always the same, if there is no essence of maleness and femaleness, how can archaeological data reveal these varying gender roles and expectations? What can be used to *identify* gender in the past?

Ethnography reveals many possible gender relationships, as well as the varying negotiations between women and men within particular gender arrangements and their gendered contributions to the societies studied

(Wallman 1978). Simply reinserting women as a category into the social and cultural equation fails to accomplish the full range of understanding that relational research may provide, because the categories of male and female themselves need to be reexamined. It may be "obvious" to us what is male and female within our own cultural context, yet we must be careful not to extend these categories to other cultures. Recent research has shown the potential of such gender studies to overturn, rearrange, or otherwise challenge established paradigms, definitions, and emphases of a number of disciplines (e.g. di Leonardo 1991, Longino 1995).

In spite of these areas of contention, we can probably all agree that research on gender in archaeology considers people in the past, especially the relationships of women and men to the social, economic, political, and ideological structures of particular societies. The goal is not to be privileged to make grand statements about *woman's* past, even when juxtaposed against *man's* past, but rather to elicit all the rich variety of experiences, behaviors, and symbolic systems, of social, economic, and political arrangements of many kinds.

Power and Prestige

Although this book centers on gender in archaeology, power and prestige share the title because they have been, and continue to be, important constructs in the study of archaeology. In considering how to structure this book, power and prestige became two key issues for me, putting gender in archaeology into perspective in several ways. The development of powerful state polities, and the prestige associated with ranking, are two recurrent topics of anthropological archaeology. These themes interact with the gendered structure of the discipline of archaeology itself. The first task is to untangle these strands, by understanding how fundamentally the study of the past is influenced by present practices and attitudes.

Where one stands in relation to structures of power and prestige impacts both methods and theories. Standpoint theory helps us perceive how deeply our gendered selves (as well as other attributes of race, ethnicity, class, and so forth) structure our ways of encountering the world, even our scholarship, our science. The structure of archaeology as a discipline has been androcentric in the choice of topics, the methods, and the theories accepted by the mainstream, and it is time for a feminist balance. The fact that, until recently, few women archaeologists deigned to (or dared to) discuss women in the past is a puzzle that does not have an obvious explanation. Are women archaeologists more timid than our colleagues in history, sociology, and cultural anthropology? Could other factors be operating? The answer relates to the nature of the discipline, both as a society of practitioners and as a theoretical enterprise. In particular, it has to do with power and prestige—both the power and prestige of men in archaeology vis-à-vis women in archaeology, and a focus on men's (assumed) activities in the past and the (attributed) greater power and prestige of male activities within our own culture. Thus the consideration of power, critical to feminist thought (Dirks, Eley, and Ortner 1994:32), must likewise be a central focus of feminist archaeology. This strategy represents a shift from focusing on women, as equal to men and worthy of being made visible, to focusing on unequal gender relations—especially power relations in the present as they are projected into the past by that same power.

The power and prestige of the male establishment, which found the study of gender unworthy of its attention, has certainly hindered feminist archaeology, though other causes can be found as well. Alison Wylie asks why, when gender flourished as a subject of inquiry within most other disciplines in the 1970s and 1980s, was it so tardily addressed in archaeology? (Wylie 1991a). She finds that the ecosystem paradigm hinders a focus on gender, both because cultural factors are deemed unimportant and because they are seen as not sufficiently rigorous. Another part of an extended answer is that the topic of women in the prehistoric and proto-historic past was *not* totally ignored (Kehoe 1992a), though it was certainly muted through derision and marginalization. Nor is the only problem that women have been invisible both in the past and present, for much work has been done to make women visible (see Bacus et al. 1993). Finally, the exploration by feminists of the roots of female oppression, which unfortunately resulted in unsophisticated uses of archaeological data, and occasionally overenthusiastic interpretations of the distant past, was also a problem, paradoxically. The naive use of archaeological data does little to advance the cause of learning about gender. Indeed, the appropriation of archaeological data by segments within the women's movement has been found wanting by most archaeologists, both women and men, though more sophisticated analyses are coming forth, in response to a variety of newly posed questions.

The distribution and negotiations of power are clearly feminist concerns. But power, as Wylie has elegantly argued, is often misunderstood and reified. Power is better conceived of as a process than as an entity to be possessed; and prestige may be temporary, just as the systems that support it are ephemeral (Wylie 1992a:52). This perspective allows consideration of the dynamics of power and prestige, not the conditions at a given moment, which are only the results of those dynamics. An androcentric emphasis on power and prestige that assumes them to be permanent and inherent in roles or persons has obscured negotiated power and conditional prestige in past cultures. Sherry Ortner and Harriet Whitehead (1981) point to prestige systems as critical in creating and maintaining the valuation of the genders, or "gender hierarchies," in Barbara Miller's (1993) terminology. Thus the prestige systems of archaeology and the negotiation of power within it affect interpretations of gender in the past. The possibility of a serious study of gender in the past is inseparable from the gender negotiations of the present—and without challenges to androcentric archaeology as it has been practiced, a gendered archaeology would have been impossible.

Forces that impeded the study of gender, power, and prestige have appeared in various guises. Even the paradigm of cultural evolution, so central to anthropological archaeology since the 1960s, is often construed as a way of asking about changes in the amount and distribution of both power and prestige in societies of the prehistoric and the protohistoric past. This emphasis has powerfully affected our ability to consider the effects of gender in the past, both by projecting our present notions of gender hierarchy on the past and by re-creating gender asymmetry among archaeologists. The differential prestige accorded to women and men in our own society has also had a profound effect on our interpretations of the prehistoric past.

One major effect of engendering archaeology is that it causes us to examine the assumptions about women that are found in many reconstructions of the prehistoric past, and asks us to consider the ways that women have often been trivialized and marginalized. Trivializing women may be accomplished even without comment, by dismissing them as without prestige or power, and therefore without interest. Efforts at asking serious questions about gender relationships can be contrasted with those that make assumptions based on western cultures, demonstrating that an engendered archaeology is an improved archaeology, one that opens new possibilities for learning about the prehistoric past.

Examination of the literature suggests that the epistemology of the discipline, the very ways that knowledge is structured and ideas are given legitimacy (e.g. Wylie 1991a, Brumfiel 1992), is crucial to the ability (or inability) to engender archaeology. Diane Gifford-Gonzalez (1997) refers to the phenomenon of "methodological androcentrism," in which the topics considered and the ways we do archaeology are brought into question. The social practices of archaeology also need to be factored in (Gero 1985, 1993, Gero, Lacy, and Blakey 1983, Gibbon 1984, Kelley and Hanen 1988), in order to have a full understanding of both the problems and the solutions (Boye et al. 1984). The way the field is organized and rewarded, the position of women in the current culture, and the structure of archaeological knowledge, all figure prominently in the previous lack of attention to gender. The (usually tacit) definition of that which is male as both powerful *and* prestigious acts as a double barrier, both to women in archaeology and to alternative ways of thinking about prestige and power in the past.

The Constructed Past

Feminist research has sometimes been accused of substituting one set of biases for another. Whether or not that is ever the case, feminist archaeology does not have such a goal, nor is it a new orthodoxy. If not orthodoxy, is the archaeology of gender then a kind of free-for-all with the archaeological record, a license to invent scenarios with women in them in the prehistoric past? Quite the contrary: feminist scrutiny reveals that some of our "knowledge," our cherished archaeological dogmas, has been based on *androcentric* just-so stories, from which women are absent or in which they are at best essentialized or muted. Many studies have demonstrated that better and more accurate "stories" about the past can be told when women *and* men, and perhaps additional genders where appropriate, are considered. As both the feminist critique of science in general and postprocessual archaeologists in particular have noted again and again, our interpretations of the past have included only some possible interpretations among many (Shanks and Tilley 1987:11). Our stories of the past may be "underdetermined" (meaning that they may be interpreted in several ways that are equally consistent with the data), though this awareness does not constitute a license for speculation. Even though we recognize that observation is theory laden, and in turn theories are value laden (Wylie 1997), the available evidence limits interpretations of the prehistoric past more or less severely. Excavations and laboratory analyses can bring surprises that force us to reconsider our assumptions (Wylie 1992b).

An unanticipated discovery can even lead to a whole new line of research. For example, Tomb 98 in Kyongju, South Korea, the largest and richest Silla royal grave of the fifth century A.D., contains sheet gold crowns and belts hung with pendants and jewels. Both these artifact types are thought to belong only to male rulers. However, a belt was inscribed "belt for madame," and the companion mound of the spouse was full of weapons. This discovery raised new questions about the gender of rulership and royalty in Silla society. To make sense of the discovery, it was necessary to reconsider both the historic documents and "kingship" in the light of gender relations. The archaeological evidence makes it clear that this woman was a ruler. The king-lists recorded in their present forms in later centuries include three ruling queens from the seventh and eighth centuries, so the culture definitely allowed for women rulers. But why did later historians fail to include in their work mention of the woman buried in Tomb 98? Possibly because the woman entombed there had a husband (buried in the other half of the mound), to whom the kingship could be attributed, as the three queens listed as "female kings" did not. A reasonable conclusion is that women were eligible to rule as queens in fifth-century Korea, but their titles were expunged by the later Buddhist and Confucian historians, who found women rulers inconsistent with their own views of the way the world "should" have been (Nelson 1991, 1993). Thus, an unexpected circumstance can lead students of the past into entirely new interpretive territory.

This example demonstrates that, though interpretations of the past can be recognized as constructions, which in even the best cases are based on incomplete knowledge, we cannot read anything at all into the archaeological data. The greater danger to archaeological interpretation lies in reading the present into the past, an instinct that is likely to seem so satisfying or familiar that it is not challenged (Nelson 1990:19). In the words of Christopher Tilley, "[I]n reducing the past to a mere stuttering repetition of the present we rob it of its emancipatory force, which must be its difference or otherness" (Tilley 1989:104). It is necessary to be open to the possibility of different pasts, as even noted by Lewis Binford, a staunch defender of "scientific" archaeology: "We as scientists have the opportunity to learn by placing our received and subjective views of the world in jeopardy, by seeking experiences in the external world that are designed to expose the limitations of our ideas" (1986:475). A gendered archaeology asks no less.

The Value of Gendered Archaeology

Gender research in archaeology is increasingly rigorous, and applicable to other archaeological goals as well. The enterprise of researching gender in archaeology began with remedial "finding-the-women" tasks. This work was necessary because previous interpretations of gender in archaeology were widely (though presumably unintentionally) used to reinforce present values and stereotypes of gender roles, whether produced by representations in the popular press or origin stories created by archaeologists. Particularly egregious have been assumptions about women as being constant in all times and places, resulting in only (presumed) male activities being subjects fit for study. Usually this tactic consists of dismissing women altogether from the creation of culture and culture change, using a "false and wide-spread model based on the assumption that important cultural changes always occurred within the male sphere" (Bertelsen et al. 1987:9).

Many examples of subtle and overt bias have been uncovered in the growing literature on the archaeology of gender. But gender bias is complex, not simply a matter of androcentrism—however important a part a male view of the world may play. To create a credible archaeology of gender, we must insist on the constructed character of gender, as well as the constructed character of the past. It is important to begin with the premise that the gendered categories "women" and "men," as we know them, are far from universal. To base archaeological inferences on notions of the essence of "man" or "woman" is to fall into an essentialist trap from which there is no escape.

In recent years, with more women entering the field of archaeology, attention to gender has been increasing. Some of the new work is innovative, hard-hitting scholarship, while some of it is frankly less compelling. Attempts to "find" women archaeologically and retrieve their prehistory are often interesting, though all such ventures are not equally adequate to interpret archaeological data. Some attempts at adding women to the archaeological past have been rejected by establishment archaeologists, both men and women. In these struggles, two kinds of feminist uses of the past may be at odds with each other. One use intends to empower and inspire women with heroic examples of women from the past, while the other is more conscious of the need to adhere to rigorous standards of archaeological interpretation, whether or not women are empowered by the results. Advocates of the second strand are eager to deconstruct the ways in which the study of gender itself has been muted (e.g. Kehoe 1992a, Gero and Conkey 1991), and in general strive for more subtlety and variety in their work, rather than simply universalizing gender roles. Women, after all, are not considered to be a category about whom statements can be made that are applicable to all women in all times and all places. A nuanced understanding of women in the past is thus beset on two sides—first by the thoughtless application of present gender roles to the past, and second by the attempt to invent a glorious past for women, sometimes by misapplying or distorting the archaeological record (Conkey and Tringham 1995).

Archaeology is a discipline that is late in "overturning the received wisdom" with feminist perspectives, as has occurred in other disciplines (Longino 1995:20). This failure came about not because the nature of gender arrangements in the past is seen as unimportant to feminists, or indeed to anyone interested in the development of societies and cultures. Rather, nonarchaeologists rushed in to fill the void left by the silence and inattention of archaeologists themselves. But reconstructions of the past that either reproduce present gender stereotypes or merely invert them are not only inaccurate, they are also dangerous, because they imply that gender roles and behaviors cannot change. Unfortunately, the authority of archaeology lends a specious weight to such pronouncements. Reference to the archaeology of specific cultures can counter any tendency to overgeneralize, universalize, and essentialize women's roles, statuses, and behaviors. Thus, archaeology has an obligation to uncover and discuss all the varieties of gender relationships in the past, in the interest of both presenting more accurate views of the past and combating essentialist views of men and women in society. Why, then, has archaeology until recently ignored gender as an analytical category, at the same time thoughtlessly using present gender relationships to interpret the past? This important topic is complex, but at base it relates to power and prestige.

Attempting to engender the past is an important task because as archaeologists we have an obligation to the society that supports our work. Archaeological discoveries, after all, are avidly consumed by many nonprofessionals. The popular press quotes archaeological "authorities" not merely about their discoveries but also about their interpretations regarding those discoveries, usually without making any distinction between data and interpretation, and the public tends to believe these archaeological "stories" about the past. But in truth the "archaeological record" is only a collection of fragments of the past, derived from excavations and other sources; without a more expansive framework, it can seem dull and colorless. What intrigues the curious public is the narrative, or multiple narratives, woven from and around those fragments. The public (which includes students) tends to understand and relate to the narrative itself better than to fragments that suggest a narrative. Reconstructions of the past that fail to consider gendered archaeology on its own terms can only serve to reinforce present gender stereotypes, and are therefore particularly reprehensible—especially when they carry the cachet of "scientific" explanations.

Furthermore, assumptions about gender—which until recently have been as common in the archaeological literature as has treating gender as a fundamental concept been rare—ordinarily remain utterly unacknowledged. They linger just out of conscious reach, achieving their force through their silence. For example, it is often the case that those roles or characteristics that are associated with men in our culture are represented as having higher prestige value than those associated with women (e.g. Mead 1949:125). This prestige system can be completely unarticulated and unconscious, and still can impact the evaluation of gender roles. This state of affairs, coupled with the fact that the search for prestige itself is a strongly male-associated trait in our culture (whether correctly or incorrectly so ascribed), means that this entire set of ideas about prestige and power needs to be "unpacked" with reference to gender roles.

Finally, an untenable belief that culture (in the anthropological sense) is created by males *for* males often lurks, unexamined, just below the surface (Schlegel 1977:2). What other explanation can there *be* for the assertion by Ian Hodder (1992:287) when discussing the meaning of female figurines,

24

that "it thus seems possible that the culturing or ordering of the female form [in Upper Paleolithic "Venus" figurines] was part of a more general process of controlling the wild and the dangerous." Gendered questions about this interpretation reveal again the androcentric perspective. Why an emphasis on control? Who is implicitly doing the controlling? To whom are women dangerous? Themselves? Other women? Children? Hodder implies that men are in control, because the pertinent anthropological literature regarding women and danger indicates that women are symbolically dangerous only to men. But this implication remains unstated; in fact, the male point of view is presented as the *human* point of view. The possibility that women might find *men* dangerous is not raised, though some men are physically rather than symbolically dangerous to some women in a number of cultures. In fact, the assumption that culture is both by and for men is so deeply buried in the rhetoric of archaeology that it is in danger of passing by unnoticed.

Lens, Mirror, or Prism?

If a feminist perspective can transform archaeology, how shall we understand that transformation? Some metaphors that have been useful to illuminate the changes that occur with feminist research are those of removing a distorting lens, or viewing the past as reflected in a mirror. My preferred metaphor is that of a prism, though, like all metaphors, all three of these provide some useful analogies and revelations.

Sandra Bem (1993) focuses on how feminists in several disciplines learned to see in new ways by finding and naming the "lenses of gender," which she identifies as androcentrism, gender polarization, and biological essentialism. These offer extremely useful perspectives on previous assumptions about women in the past, helping us to understand why it is necessary to set aside these assumptions before one can approach gendered roles in the past or discover their variety. Bem defines androcentrism as the belief that whatever is male is natural, normal, central, and right. Anything else, according to the androcentric lens, is deviant. Whatever women do in any context that is different from what men do is defined as inferior, for men are by definition the standard. The feminist literature that exposes the notion of women as "the other" is vast (e.g. De Beauvoir 1953, Gilligan 1982) and has been an important tool in clearing the way for a more

balanced analysis of gender, one that does not value that which has been gendered male above that which has been gendered female.

Gender polarization, according to Bem, is the assumption that women and men are fundamentally different, and the belief that this difference must run throughout the entire social fabric, rather than representing overlapping and intertwined categories. Consider height as an example of an unproblematic and obvious human dimension. The mean height of men in most human populations is greater than that of women, but not all men are taller than all women; anyone can observe individual women who are taller than individual men. These are not "exceptions," they simply represent normal deviations from the mean. Explanations that focus on means fail to account for substantial spread, together with considerable overlap. Thus, being wary of gender polarization is important for studying gender of the past.

Biological essentialism is another trap, Bem argues. She defines it as the view that insists that biology imposes certain roles or restrictions on women sufficient to explain differences in gender roles that formerly were asserted to be universal. This occurs particularly when "woman" is equated with "mother." But not all women are mothers, nor do women function as mothers of dependent children throughout their own lives. Indeed, in all cultures, women are more than their biology, and they carry out productive as well as reproductive roles—productive roles critical to the economy and the social structure as a whole. The biologizing of women and their roles thus disparages the rich variety of actual women's lives.

It is necessary to be alert to all of these "lenses" of gender in order to perceive men and women from the prehistoric past without the distortions the lenses introduce. These lenses have all been discussed and exposed in the anthropological literature, though, as in other fields, biological essentialism is especially difficult to perceive and overcome.

Alex Barker uses the metaphor of archaeological research as a mirror, in which "held one way we see the dim outlines of past social forms and institutions, held another we see the interplay of culture and environment, or the intricate web of relations spanning domestic and political economies, while yet another way we see ourselves staring back" (Barker 1993:xvi). However, the mirror image suggests that one way to hold the mirror is as good as another, and that whichever way we hold it yields an equally partial truth. I am not convinced that this is so. Some "mirrors," as any trip to a boardwalk fun house will tell you, are more distorting than others, while some may *only* reflect ourselves. So the metaphor of the mirror image may be yet another trap to avoid, or at least a caution.

Researchers in many fields have found that to study gender is to produce changes more profound than merely another way to see, even if the study clears our vision of androcentric distortions. I prefer to think of gender studies as functioning like a prism through which light passes and breaks up into its constituent colors. Light is transformed, disclosing its differing wave lengths, and something new is seen. The colors, present all along, were not visible before they passed through the prism. Gender studies similarly have the power to transform the study of the past, allowing us to perceive characteristics that were not visible before. The details of gender relationships are like the colors revealed by the refracting power of the prism. It is possible, even if difficult, to move beyond distortions of the past and to apprehend infinite variations of gender roles.

Chapter Organization

In this book I draw most of my examples from prehistoric archaeology, though the lines between prehistorians, historic archaeologists, and classicists are not always clear. Many archaeologists from other cultures find these distinctions inapplicable to their situations or unimportant to their goals. Insofar as other archaeological traditions have contributed to an archaeology of gender, they will not be ignored. Indeed, some of the earliest contributions to feminist archaeology were made by historic archaeologists (e.g. Spencer-Wood 1984) and classicists (e.g. Pomeroy 1974), who could use texts to enrich their interpretations and who had sister scholars in closely allied disciplines, such as history and art history, who had already ventured to explore gender questions. Archaeology is thus defined broadly here as the study of earlier peoples and their cultures from their material remains. I have attempted to find worldwide examples, though some regions are severely underrepresented. More important, I believe, the grounding of archaeology in anthropology is critical, both historically and to point the way to future research.

It would have been possible to divide archaeological gender studies into other categories, such as evolutionary stages, temporal divisions, or technological ages, but each of these emphases is problematic in tending to distort gender relations or to render them invisible in standard archaeological works. Another possible organization for the book would have been a regional approach. Examining archaeological gender studies in different areas of the world would reveal uneven coverage, though it would not provide the comparative emphasis that is important at this stage in the development of gender studies in archaeology. The chapter topics used instead include structures in which gender might be particularly visible and important, and in which some explicitly feminist archaeological work has been done.

The following chapter discusses the growth of gender studies in the context of the social relationships of archaeology as a discipline. As is discovered again and again in feminist research, the personal is political, and we cannot reasonably separate the persons who practice archaeology from the interpretations of their research. As is said more and more insistently, facts are theory laden, theories are value laden, and values held relate not only to the larger culture in which a person operates, but also to the particular circumstances of that person—their race, ethnicity, and gender, their size and age: in short, their total standpoint. Researchers themselves are embodied, not disembodied, minds. In considering the roots of feminist archaeology in Chapter 2, I take up several topics: the feminist philosophy of science, feminist anthropology, and the sociology of feminist archaeology.

Chapter 3 turns to archaeological theory and explores the theoretical grounding for feminist archaeology. Ways of understanding gender in the past are considered, and resources and strategies are enumerated. Subsequent chapters examine the specifics of good and bad gender studies. The chapter topics are reflective of particular emphases in anthropology: origins, division of labor, kinship, state formation, and ideology. While these are not exclusive domains in any branch of social science, in archaeological research in particular they often overlap, sometimes in surprising ways that open new avenues of research. In spite of these interconnections it is useful to focus on these topics separately, for they illuminate particular facets of feminist archaeology.

Chapter 4 considers our "western" fascination with the origins of various institutions, especially those considered to be universal or quintessentially human. Origins research was one of the first areas in which the lack of any attention to women, let alone gender, was revealed as distorting our understanding of the prehistoric past in basic and important ways. But, as several examples demonstrate, acknowledging the presence of women in the past is not sufficient by itself. It is also important to realize how little actual archaeological data are involved in many reconstructions of the past. The very emphasis on origins can be seen to essentialize gender roles in interpretations of the archaeological record.

In Chapter 5, which treats the division of labor by gender, the work of women and men is discussed. Women's work in particular has been under-represented in archaeology, yet several recent studies thoughtfully consider what women do, how women's work can be studied, and the ways that much of women's work was overlooked in the past. New avenues of approach to lithics, bone tools, pottery—the basic materials of archaeological analysis—demonstrate that it is possible to go beyond stereotypes of gendered work in the prehistoric past.

Women as members of social systems are the topic of Chapter 6. Since kinship, social structure, and social organization are mainstays of much cultural anthropology, it is important to ponder how it came to be that social systems were left out of "anthropological archaeology" with so little com-ment. Household archaeology is particularly important here, for distribu-tions of features and artifacts in households and public buildings alike can lead to understanding gendered roles in various societies. Mortuary analysis may also reveal the gendered lives of men and women, with differential burial treatment or evidence of different eating habits and diets.

Chapter 7 shifts the focus to women in the public sphere, from which for too long it has been assumed that women were absent, or in which women holding positions of authority either were manipulated by men behind the scenes or were viewed as man-like women, not "really" women. As the "exceptions" pile up they require reexamination of androcentric prejudices. How has authority been gendered male? How can we perceive and under-stand women in positions of authority? Again, burial remains may be helpful, as well as iconography and public architecture.

Women and ideology are examined in Chapter 8. Female images, often construed as goddesses, are central to many analyses of ideology. Their study has led to a vast and varied literature on the meanings of the images, with varying rigor and results. Ideology has been approached in other ways as well, with a number of iconographic and stylistic studies, and these can also be gendered, grossly or with subtlety.

A concluding chapter, Chapter 9, looks to the future of gender research in archaeology.

This book, then, offers an assessment of how far we have come in learning about gender in the past through archaeology, why the effort is worth pursuing, and how future research might extend our understanding of gender in the past. It is a compilation and comparison of many and varied critiques of archaeology as currently practiced, as gendered analysis attempts to invade and enlarge new spaces created by both feminist theory and archaeological theory. Over the course of this book, I will demonstrate that a gendered feminist archaeology has a number of benefits for archaeology:

- Feminist theory treats gender as a process, not as a thing.
- It frees archaeology from false, dichotomizing thought, not only in questions of gender but in other realms as well.
- It enriches archaeology by enlarging the base of available data and posing new questions.
- It improves methods and produces better explanations by requiring more attention to detail.
- It questions a whole suite of assumptions about social life that are thoroughly embedded in our own culture.
- It allows us to develop social theory from archaeological evidence, with much more sophistication and detail than prior "social archaeology" offered.

These benefits will become evident as various specific examples of gendered archaeology are provided in a range of anthropological/archaeological categories.

CHAPTER TWO
THE CREATION OF
POWER AND PRESTIGE

In turn the routine institutional decisions—about awarding
research grants and departmental budgets, allocating equipment
and information, and employing personnel—produce a template
that enables and constrains the knowers and thereby structures the
knowledge they produce.
—Joan Hartman and Ellen Messer-Davidow (1991:6)

Like a Third World person who has been educated at Oxbridge, we
feminist scholars speak at once as the socially constituted "other" and as
speakers within the dominant discourse, never able to place ourselves
wholly or uncritically in either position.
—Francis Mascia-Lees, Patricia Sharpe, and Colleen Cohen (1989:33)

If androcentrism, biological essentialism, and gender polarization can
be rejected, it will be possible to understand gender roles as constructed,
and varying from culture to culture. The premise that gender is culturally constructed requires reexamination of all assumptions about gender in
the past, attempting to refocus the "lenses of power" in the present to ask
serious questions about how our present world came to be, including what
the possible variants are that the past might reveal. The task is difficult
though not impossible.

The present stage of questioning received wisdom did not burst onto
the scene without antecedents: certain work had to be done before the study
of gender in archaeology became a possible goal. Critiques within archaeology of other sorts of bias and of limiting assumptions helped open a space

for feminist critiques, and these are explored in Chapter 3. More explicitly included in the heritage and "toolkit" of the engendering archaeologist are work that has been done in both feminist anthropology and the feminist philosophy of science. These stepping-stones include not only the aware-ness of gender bias and its naming, but also analyses of thought processes that privilege males, especially prestigious and powerful ones. To appreciate the growth of feminist archaeology, it is necessary to make a few excursions into feminist anthropology, feminist issues in the philosophy of science, and the demography of women archaeologists.

Exploring Gender in Anthropology

Anthropology in the 1960s was replete with pronouncements, both obvious and subtle, that declared a lack of interest in women's activities and a belief that women around the world and throughout time were static, while men advanced. Men's roles over the course of history differentiated, the experts proclaimed, and in the process they were able to create forms of power and prestige. For example, Elman Service explained that the title of his book, *The Hunters,* a book about band level society, was selected simply because it sounds more interesting than "Woman's Work," "The Gleaners," or "The Foragers" (Service 1966:10). "More interesting" to whom? Based on what prejudices? Why does Service assume a male readership, or grant privilege to his own male perspective?

The eye-openers for many of us who were trained as anthropological archaeologists, the writings that transformed these "ordinary" assumptions about women into an awareness of androcentrism, were two edited volumes that appeared in the mid-1970s (Reiter 1975, Rosaldo and Lamphere 1974). In retrospect it seems odd that, though the papers in these volumes touched on several topics of direct concern to archaeologists, they had little effect on archaeology itself, though their repercussions in other subdisci-plines of anthropology were dramatic. Looking back at my first attempt to teach a class called "Women in Prehistory" in 1979, I see that my bibliog-raphies were based on abundant publications by primatologists, physical anthropologists, classicists, and historians, but virtually nothing by prehis-toric archaeologists. To demonstrate the lack of attention to women in archaeology, I gave the class an assignment in which they were to locate any archaeological site report that discussed the roles of women. Most of the students searched in vain, and returned to me with tales of woe—but with their object lesson learned. Women and gender were in fact *missing* from archaeological reports.

The Woman-the-Gatherer challenge, which took direct aim at Man-the-Hunter and demonstrated women's extensive subsistence contributions to "hunting" societies, was taken up very effectively by cultural and physical anthropologists (e.g. Dahlberg 1981, Zihlman and Tanner 1978), and even some anthropological textbooks echoed the new critique. Physical anthropology and primatology both responded with more inclusive and better models of the human past, models that showed more awareness of females of primate species if not of gender relationships. The conversion was not absolute, but the feminist critique had an impact far beyond the circle of early feminists.

In sociocultural anthropology, many critiques of the androcentrism of past ethnographies appeared, even (or especially) classics of ethnography (e.g. Annette Weiner on the Trobriand Islanders [1976], Jane Goodale on the north Australian Tiwi [1971]). Origins were critiqued, too, and the Victorian roots of anthropology were found wanting, especially the matriarchy/patriarchy debate (Tiffany 1979). Elizabeth Fee (1974) reexamined matriarchal theories and meticulously brought to light the sexist assumptions of 18th century anthropology, showing that, whether matriarchy or patriarchy, androcentric assumptions and intentions lurked in all evolutionary schemes. Alice Schlegel (1972) questioned the concepts of men's power and authority in matrilineal societies, while other women scientists and writers revisited some of the classic locations of anthropological wisdom, retrieving what women were doing in specific societies and showing the importance of the overlooked women's roles in those societies. Perhaps because by the mid-1980s about half the new degrees conferred in anthropology were conferred on women, these extensions and critiques were well received in the discipline as a whole, and served as ferment in many ways.

In the 1970s and 1980s, it was customary to use the concept of "patriarchy" to describe this androcentrism in anthropological theory, as well as the domination of society by men. Peggy Sanday described two forms of the "patriarchal model": the peripheral position of women in social structures, and the symbolic devaluation of women (Sanday 1988:51). Rosalind Coward titled her book, in which she discusses understandings of women's sexuality, including anthropological views, *Patriarchal Precedents*. "What has been exposed," she writes, "are the absences, the questions not asked, and the answers not heard in these theoretical discussions" (1983:2). The androcentric lenses were being removed, the surgery was successful, and the subject was seen with fresh eyes.

Marxist feminist anthropologists found useful models in Friedrich Engels (e.g. Leacock 1978, Sacks 1979). One consideration was the extent to which some women may have enjoyed forms of equality in various cultures before the impact of European colonialism, and whether they indeed lost power and prestige with the advent of private property. Thus the past was highlighted, in some cases using archaeological evidence (e.g. Rapp 1977, Rohrlich-Leavitt 1976, Barstow 1978)—but, for the most part, archaeologists did not join in. Instead this rich mine was left for historians (Lerner 1986, Boulding 1976, French 1985). This often meant that archaeological data were not treated in satisfactory ways, but the uses made of them were passed over in silence. The major credentialed archaeologist to step into the fray was Marija Gimbutas (1982, 1989, 1991), whose interpretations may have made many archaeologists uncomfortable (e.g. Hayden 1986, Tringham 1991, Fisher 1993), though few seemed willing to say so in print.

Although many of the early papers in feminist anthropology were generalizing, using the concept of patriarchy and asking universal questions about women in all societies, in the next stage feminists began to criticize attempts to make statements about women as a *class*, preferring to consider specific groups of women in particular situations. While it was still important to examine the relative status of women and men, the studies concentrated on concrete cases, and were less concerned with sweeping cross-cultural comparisons. For example, the chapters in *Sex and Gender Hierarchies* (Miller 1993) highlight the variety of women's roles in various cultures, not their sameness. Furthermore, the need to revise the way in which hierarchies are perceived was emphasized. "The early feminist assumption that enough (or too much) is known about men and that to understand women's status we must focus entirely on women errs in a disregard of the standard of measurement: men's status" (Miller 1993:13). The influence of the four-field approach in anthropology (sociocultural anthropology, biophysical anthropology, archaeology, and linguistics) was responsible for the inclusion of archaeology in the 1987 conference on which the book is based, and in the volume itself (Nelson 1993, Cohen and Bennett 1993). Still, most archaeologists and other anthropologists were skeptical that archaeology could provide much insight into past gender relations. For example, Henrietta Moore, in her useful volume *Feminism and Anthropology* (1988), makes no mention of archaeology at all.

Ethnohistorians began to use archaeology and have an effect on it, since they share protohistory with archaeologists. Irene Silverblatt, working on the Inca state in Peru, noted the need to attend to historical differences, rather than evolutionary sameness. "Following their explanatory models, history functions as a laboratory for social science—a showcase of examples to substantiate predictive hypotheses that are, ironically, ahistorical. History becomes the proof of those very relationships" (1991:153). The same could be said of evolutionary archaeology. In contrast, Silverblatt suggests, "the construal of gender relations and of women must be in accord with specific histories and contexts" (1991:155). This direction has been fruitfully followed by gendered archaeology.

In retrospect it seems strange that archaeologists ignored gender, when assumptions about women and their activities were already present (though only implicitly) in many archaeological constructs. For example, the notion of a base camp, whose "key characteristics" are "domestic dwellings, site furniture, specialized utilitarian structures and outdoor work spaces, service centers, diversified tool fabrication and repair, child rearing, diversified food consumption, and so forth" (Thomas 1986:238) has much that implies women and women's work. But these potentially gendered implications usually were not drawn out (an exception is Todd Guenther 1991), for reasons detailed below.

In spite of resistance and inertia, the fact that most American archaeologists were trained in anthropology departments meant that some were exposed to radical new ideas about the roles of women and about gendered relationships in many cultures. Many were also led to the feminist literature through personal experiences of overt discrimination and a perceived "chilly climate" in the profession (Sandler 1986, and see Alison Wylie 1994 for the application of this concept to archaeology), as well as the need to understand events in their own lives in a broader social context. New books with stimulating theory in history, sociology, philosophy, religion, psychology— almost every field *but* archaeology—were available to be discovered. Each of them examined the androcentric roots of their own discipline, and also searched for examples to counter the universalizing opinions about women. As in other fields, "epistemology and politics emerged as two mutually enforcing sides of the same unequal coin" (MacKinnon 1989:xi). Still, archaeology lagged behind.

Scientific Outsiders

The problem of women in science is another strand that must be woven into an understanding of feminism in archaeology, for it helps to explain the backwardness of women in archaeology. Archaeological ambitions to be scientific make the literature on women in science in some ways even more pertinent than the anthropological debates of the 1970s. Evelyn Fox Keller was one of the first to articulate the relationship of women to science in a number of essays. It is perhaps not unexpected that few other women scientists joined immediately in the exploration of women's issues, since such exploration itself was seen as "soft" and unscientific, and therefore unlikely to lead to tenure for academic scientists. No doubt the status of women in other sciences was similar to that of archaeology—their positions may have been marginal, but they were so hard-won that many of those with a secure job and solid achievements were cautious about jeopardizing their status by venturing into questionable territory that might marginalize them further.

Keller confronted gender issues in a biography of Barbara McClintock, a Nobel-prize winner whose pathbreaking work was recognized late in her life. Questioning whether McClintock's unusual and creative approach to science might have stemmed from feminine sensibilities led Keller to ponder more general gender questions. The socialization of women into science took on importance in that regard. Keller saw McClintock not as an outsider to science, certainly, but also not as a total insider (Keller 1983:175). Science, when scrutinized, isn't genderless, she asserted. "To the extent that science is defined by its past and present practitioners, anyone who aspires to membership in that community must conform to its existing code . . . To be a successful scientist, one must first be adequately socialized" (Keller 1983:167). This situation is particularly hard on women, for Keller shows through numerous examples that science is constructed, not just as male, but as antifemale. "Only if she undergoes a radical disidentification from the self can [the woman scientist] share masculine pleasure in mastering a nature cast in the image of woman as passive, inert, and blind" (Keller 1983:174–175). In a later paper, Keller notes that not only is science based on male metaphors and patriarchal imagery, but, more elementally, "modern science is constituted around a set of exclusionary oppositions, in which that which is named feminine is excluded, and that which is excluded—be it feeling, subjectivity or nature—is named female" (Keller 1986:173).

Evelyn Fox Keller also raised questions about the types of problems that the scientific community deemed worthy of addressing, and further examined gender bias in the design of experiments. Through the prism of her feminist gaze she considered the ways that scientists became successful and described how this competition disadvantages women. For example, she pointed out that large laboratories, which women scientists are less likely to select, for a number of reasons, provide a competitive edge. "The number of papers on which the name of a principal investigator appears will, in general, depend directly on the size of the laboratory or group he or she heads" (Keller 1986:233). In addition, this group becomes a "quoting circle," inflating the number of citations—the coin of the realm in the kingdom (there is no "queendom") of academic prestige—leaving those who have chosen smaller labs in a disadvantaged position.

Helen Longino, philosopher of science, sounds the same note, though her perspective is even broader:

> Scientific inquiry takes place in a social, political, and economic context which imposes a variety of institutional obstacles to innovation, let alone to the intellectual working out of oppositional and political commitments. The nature of university career ladders means that one's work must be recognized as meeting certain standards of quality in order that one may be able to continue it. If those standards are intimately bound up with values and assumptions one rejects, incomprehension rather than conversion is likely. (1987:62)

These observations by Keller and Longino are based on a great deal of data collected to detail the experiences of women scientists. Nevertheless, the critique of gender inequities in science has itself been criticized for its lack of "objectivity." This caused several scholars to scrutinize and problematize "objectivity" itself. Philosophers of science have demonstrated that there are no disembedded facts. The data used result from the questions asked and the theories held. Facts are not "out there" waiting to be discovered; what are considered "facts" depends on the theory at hand, thus they are theory laden, and theories are in turn value laden—embedded in the society, not existing in the void. The idea that science is value-free, objective, and uninfluenced by its cultural milieu has been thoroughly debunked (Lloyd 1993, Longino 1987). Longino goes further: "Not all science is value-free and, more importantly, it is not in the nature of science to be value-free" (Longino 1987:56). Scientists are fooling themselves with the chimera of objectivity. This is not a trivial problem. "Constitutive values (i.e., truth-seeking) are not adequate to screen out the influence of contextual values in the very structuring of scientific knowledge" (Longino 1987:56). But if science is not value-free as it has claimed to be, the possibility of "mak[ing] explicit value commitments and still do[ing] 'good' science" is opened up (Wylie 1992b:18). In other words, all scientists have values, science itself has values, and denying that values drive science is a dangerous illusion. Alison Wylie asserts that "politically engaged science is often much more rigorous, self-critical, and responsive to the facts than allegedly neutral science, for which nothing much is at stake" (1992b:18).

How then are we to evaluate facts, theories, and values themselves? Some feminists have suggested that by simply being a woman one can automatically ferret out androcentrism—that the lived experience of being female is sufficient. This seems unlikely, given the recent spate of antifeminist books by women and a few critical works on androcentrism by men (e.g. Reyman 1992). An uncomfortable assumption lurks behind this assertion of innate female knowledge, one that most feminist archaeologists would reject: the notion that there is something about the essence of women that makes us more able to detect "true values." This claim is just as unsupportable as other kinds of essentialism. We need to recognize many kinds of women, in the past as well as in the present, rather than postulating blindly that some feminine essence, or experiences of being a woman, or even a feminist standpoint, provide superior insight. The test of values cannot be whether or not the scientist is female. But this stance does not jeopardize the insight that women may be socialized differently from men in many cultures, and are more likely to perceive discriminatory practices when the discrimination is made on the basis of gender—a fact that is true of any group experiencing discrimination on the basis of their membership in that group.

Women as Archaeologists

Archaeology has been gendered male, and that fact has affected all women who have become archaeologists. Jane Kelley (1992:88–89), though generally disapproving of mixing a science with its sociology, notes that "sociological issues are unusually important in archaeology." As late as 1985 it was possible to refer to "the archaeologist's image of *himself* . . ." (Haag 1986:73), implying that past archaeologists were gendered male, though women have of course been in the field all along (Levine 1991, Mason 1992, and chapters in Parezo 1993a and Claassen 1994). Thomas Patterson notes the presence of women archaeologists from the beginning of American archaeology: "A number of women pursued archaeology as a profession or serious avocation between 1890 and the 1920s; for example, they delivered eight of the thirty-eight papers presented at the general meeting of the Archaeological Institute of America (AIA) in 1923" (1995:48). The percentage of women members of the AIA varied from 37 percent to 40 percent in the years 1935–64 (1995:82). But anthropological archaeology—in general, Americanist archaeology—had relatively fewer women than classical and historic archaeology. In 1956, fewer than 14 percent of the members of the Society for American Archaeology (SAA) were women. In 1969, the percentage had not changed. Thus it was that SAA could be conceived of as a "band of brothers." In spite of the small number of invisible sisters in anthropological archaeology, the numbers of women increased substantially in the 1970s (Patterson 1995:107), and now are quite visible and participatory in all ways in SAA (1991). Lest we become smug about this considerable progress, it is well to note that the program of the annual meeting of SAA as recently as 1993 deliberately excluded "sessions submitted by women and Latin American students" (Patterson 1995:138–139).

Some feminist archaeology did emerge in the 1970s, though it tended to come from the margins of the archaeological enterprise (where women had been able to find jobs), was published in obscure places (if at all), and was largely ignored by other women as well as men (Kehoe 1992a). That women of equivalent credentials found "lesser" positions than men, or none at all, was documented by Carol Kramer and Miriam Stark (1994). Papers refused by mainstream journals were published in smaller journals, or simply circulated (like clandestine samizdat in the former Soviet Union) among those known to be interested, and many were finally published only years later. Some of these early papers are still probably gathering dust in authors' files.

An explicitly feminist archaeology became visible with the publication of Margaret Conkey and Janet Spector's review (1984), though, as has already been noted, it was not the beginning of serious work about women in the past, for the "gray literature" and circulated papers were active, in addition to a few papers that slipped past the gatekeepers and were actually published. What Conkey and Spector accomplished was to begin to make feminist archaeology respectable, by getting their critique published in a highly credible place, *Advances in Archaeological Method and Theory*. The editor of the series, Michael Schiffer, deserves credit for his willingness to publish it when so many editors, even women, were rejecting feminist archaeology. Although many articles published in obscure journals were still overlooked by mainstream archaeology, Conkey and Spector provided a jumping-off point for the dozens of archaeologists, mostly but not entirely women, who were eager to dive into these waters but had been warned off explicitly or implicitly by the circling sharks that could damage their careers or merely bite their legs off.

This beginning did not mean that opportunities to publish feminist archaeology opened immediately. Even later, in the 1980s, an openly feminist perspective meant that one's work was unlikely to be published, and equally unlikely to be accepted for presentation at a national meeting. At a time when several feminist panels in cultural anthropology could be attended at annual meetings of the American Anthropological Association (AAA), there was still scorn for gender topics from many of the archaeologists who screened the archaeology panels. Therefore in 1987, when Alice Kehoe and I decided to assemble some papers about gender in archaeology into a proposed session, we disguised our intentions by calling it "Powers of Observation, Alternative Views in Archaeology," and inviting men with other perspectives to present additional alternative views. Thus feminist papers could be presented in a "respectable" circumstance. The tactic worked, and the session was well accepted and well attended. To our surprise, a volume of these papers was published by the Archeology Division of the AAA, completely legitimizing our covert gender-strategy views (Nelson and Kehoe 1990).

The first time large numbers of women came together to discuss gender in archaeology was at the Chacmool Conference in Canada in 1989, which became the instrument for stimulating such studies and providing them with respectability, as well as uniting the emerging strands of feminist archaeology. Although relatively few attendees at the Chacmool Conference identified themselves as feminists (Wylie 1996, Hanen and Kelley 1992), this lack of identification may have been a response to the male exercise of informal power such as Alison Wylie points to in her paper on social power (1992a), especially given the tenuous position of most women archaeologists in the power field. For many women, feminism was danger-ous even to *think*.

The Chacmool gender conference was so stimulating that it became the kick-off event for most attendees, the venue for serious discussions about gender in the past, and even a catalyst for other meetings. The papers covered many topics, from women's status in the present to women in the archaeological past, and their publication was an important event (Walde and Willows 1991). Roberta Gilchrist (1991:495) divides issues of the type discussed at the Chacmool Conference into political feminism, gender theory, and historical revision. These topics are all related, though an emphasis on equity issues (a part of political feminism) appears to have existed prior to either an explicit interest in the stereotyping of women in the past or more theoretical questions about gender, as Alison Wylie (1996) has documented. Women's experiences as an unwelcome minority had more influence on their interest in gender issues than a knowledge of the anthropological literature, according to Wylie's survey. She notes that "feminist commitments . . . have been instrumental in mobilizing the latent grass-roots interest in these questions. . . . On this account it is, most simply, the experience of women and, more important, the emerging feminist analysis of this experience, which figures as a key catalyst" (Wylie 1992:18).

While this history accounts for the interests of current women in gendered archaeology, it does not yet answer the question of earlier female archaeologists, who had the same experiences and possibly worse (see below), but who did not express interest in gender. The answer is partly that an analysis of androcentrism was not yet well formulated, partly that the systems of power were a disincentive for women, and partly that in archaeology making direct observations of gender is not possible, because inferences are more vulnerable to criticism than observations.

The Hairy-Chested and the Hairy-Chinned

One of the founding fathers of the discipline, Alfred Kidder (1949), is quoted by Linda Cordell (1993) as noting two kinds of archaeologists, the hairy-chested and the hairy-chinned. This partitioning doesn't leave much room in archaeology for women. Many women archaeologists in the earlier part of this century were scorned, ignored, or trivialized. The lack of hair on the chin or chest marked them not as merely different, but as inferior. Their histories are only now being recovered (e.g. Levine 1991, Bender 1991, Cordell 1993, and chapters in Claassen 1994).

The particular metaphors in which this maleness has been expressed are wonderfully revealing and cover more than the distribution of hair. These include the archaeologist as cowboy (Gero 1983); the archaeologist as military strategist, adventurer, or culture hero (Preucel and Joyce 1994); and the excavator as Superman (Rick 1969:1). Appropriate clothing is worn in the field or even in the university to underline these roles. Particularly hilarious are "trowel holsters" (Woodall and Perricone 1981:507), even though much of the behavior is deadly serious and women's careers may be imperiled by failure to appreciate that fact. A masculine ego upheld by cowboy boots and a trowel holster is likely to respond with highly defensive gusto to *any* criticism, whether expressed or even implied.

Alison Wylie reminds us that archaeology is a social and political enterprise. "The problems we choose to work on, the hypotheses we take seriously, the presuppositions about what variables are relevant to consider, even the methods we think appropriate and the standards by which we judge results, are *all* conventions" (Wylie 1991b:21), and these conventions are agreed on by people within disciplines. The conventions in archaeology have not been welcoming to women. Joan Gero (1985:344) suggested that "archaeologists might have responded earlier and, like the socio-cultural anthropologists, participated more actively in the climate of interest in gender had it not been for the profession's traditional structure of concerns and practices, which offer very low or even negative prestige for engaging in such discourse." Nancy Parezo (1993b:335), speaking of pioneer women anthropologists in the American Southwest, more explicitly notes "harsher criticism of their work than that of men," while Roberta Gilchrist (1991:499) sees the same phenomenon in the present as well: "Many observers remain intolerant: they caricature such endeavors [gendered archaeology] as part of the lunatic fringe." Furthermore, "issues which concern women, like gender, still invoke dismissal by all but a few within archaeology" (Arnold et al. 1988:3). Part of the problem is that archaeological topics have been very frankly and overtly gendered male—leading to male concerns, male language, and male prejudices. "The emphasis was on topics like leadership, power, warfare, exchange of women, rights of inheritance, and notions of property [that] can all be cited as issues of special interest to males in particular historic contexts and sociopolitical structures" (Conkey and Spector 1984:4).

It has been suggested that because excavation is the defining characteristic of what makes an archaeologist (Gero 1985, Preucel and Joyce 1994), it has been used as a powerful weapon against women in various ways, such as exclusion from the field, the labeling of laboratory tasks as "women's work," "the housework of archeology" (Gero 1985), and harassment of women when they *do* get to the field. As Linda Cordell notes, "A long-term apprenticeship in the field and diverse field experiences are not only highly valued but required for professional acceptance" (1993:205). This meant that the "facets of machismo, including hard drinking and womanizing" (Woodall and Perricone 1981:506), could become a problem for women if and when they were allowed to venture out into the field. Dena Dincauze notes instances of women being barred from the field because they only wanted to join archaeological crews "to seduce the men" (Dincauze 1992:9). Women on archaeological digs were often ridiculed, treated as sexual objects, or relegated to the laboratory where they could not learn field procedures. And since these behaviors were often perpetrated or instigated by the men in charge, women rarely had an authority figure to appeal to for fairness or change. Cordell reminds us that "until fairly recently (perhaps the late 1960s and early 1970s), mixed-gender digs were unusual" (1993:204). The reason is that, "digging is, after all, a masculine occupation" (letter written in 1987, quoted in Wurtzburg 1994:120).

Another characteristic of archaeology is the emphasis on the overcoming of difficulties in fieldwork, exaggerated or otherwise (Preucel and Joyce 1994). "The mud, the bugs, the heat, and hardships produced our culture heroes, and for most students the message was clearly 'archeology builds men' " (Woodall and Perricone 1981:507). Sometimes extraordinary efforts are made to deter women from the field. On one project, not only were the ubiquity of rattlesnakes and the difficulty of negotiating the dirt roads exaggerated to try to keep the woman principal investigator out of the field, but an alleged threat from a Neo-Nazi group was also introduced through a falsified call to the student newspaper. The attempts were not successful, yet the tactics—though extreme—may not be unique.

Joan Gero and Dolores Root analyzed the *National Geographic* view of archaeology, and found that exploration and treasure-seeking were emphasized. "Masculine" traits were glorified, but the archaeologists depicted were hyperactive and rugged, braving remote and inhospitable locations alone (except, of course, for the photographers necessary to document their solitude). These characteristics show that as archaeologists, "to gain new knowledge you have to get to new places, and to get there first you have to be tough" (1990:33).

While much of the prejudice encountered by women was unconscious and often unstated, not a few examples of overt androcentric thinking have been ferreted out by various women in archaeology. For example, Stanley South delineated how many skills a historic archaeologist needed—all of them clearly defined as male skills. What was needed was an "action man" (South 1969:76). Kent Flannery's distinguished lecture in 1981 reflected male points of view in his imagined conversation among four male archaeologists. He included the much-quoted observation that archaeology is the "most fun you can have with your pants on" (Flannery 1982:278), a view possibly shared by some women but unlikely to be expressed in the same way. It highlights the sexual innuendos that are often directed toward women in the field. Even in 1985, on the occasion of the fiftieth anniversary of the founding of the Society for American Archaeology, Bruce Trigger could emphasize that "prehistoric archaeology . . . originated in a colonial milieu" (1986:187) without drawing out the implications for women or for interpretations of women in the past. He did note that "[o]n the whole American archaeologists were a conservative lot. They remained predominantly male and of Anglo-Saxon origin; which was very different from ethnology, where women and ethnic minorities played a much more significant role" (1986:191).

Analysis of women in other sciences shows how detrimental these attitudes have been for women's careers. Access to the archaeological profession requires membership in a group, and if women are excluded from the "boys' club" their ability to work suffers. Ruth Hubbard (1990:1) reminds us that "making facts is a social enterprise," and this includes the fact making of archaeology. Furthermore, acceptance into the club is far from automatic, even for those with proper credentials. "As scientists, we must follow certain rules of membership and go about our task of fact making in professionally sanctioned ways . . . If we follow proper procedure, we become accredited fact makers" (1990:2–3). Sometimes just being female is not considered proper procedure. "It is a club in which people mutually sit on each-other's decision-making panels. The criteria for access are supposed to be objective and meritocratic, but in practice orthodoxy and conformity count for a lot. Someone whose ideas or personality are out of line is less likely to succeed than 'one of the boys'."

Linda Cordell starkly describes the results for women archaeologists as outsiders. "Although [women archaeologists] have contributed scholarship in the mainstream of their discipline for decades, their work often is not recognized" (1993:220). But for women to adopt male styles was not a viable strategy, either. Although "it was very hard to maintain a professional identity without a job" (Parezo 1993b:343), to succeed, "women had to be independent, unconventional, tenacious, stubborn, and ambitious" (p. 342), all of which could be and were interpreted as strident, unfeminine, and confrontational.

Confrontation as a strategy had particular risks for women, but almost any effort by a woman to stand up for herself was so labeled. "Confrontation involved insisting on being employed, being paid equally, and never allowing others to show or accept discrimination in any form . . . [this] gained one a reputation for being a 'pain in the ass'" (Parezo 1993b:339). The worst of it was that such behavior could not produce the desired results: "A strong feminist confrontational style would have led to ostracism or blacklisting" (p. 340). And there was unlikely to be a community to turn to. "Confrontation is always lonely because people mistrust a fighter" (p. 341).

Men had the means to employ "leveling mechanisms," and many did so. As Judith Stiehm noted regarding her research on acceptance of women students in a military academy, "I failed to appreciate men's assumption that 'runnin' 'em out' is an appropriate way of dealing with persons who are disliked" (Stiehm 1985:388). Many other women have also made this discovery, to our surprise and dismay. And there is no level to which those motivated to "run out" women archaeologists cannot stoop. For example, on one project, a crew chief refused to let a woman in his disfavor keep her nonalcoholic beverages in the "beer refrigerator," though it was the only possible place for her to cool her sodas in the heat of a summer dig. This sort of petty harassment was common in digs at least up through the 1980s, and my students tell me it has not yet disappeared.

Men who are "trying to get ahead and keep ahead in the world" are characterized by "competitiveness, envy, and dependence on recognition and rewards" (Bleier 1986a:5), giving them every reason to want to reduce competition by any means. This is considered fair because, as Sandra Harding chillingly suggests, "part of being a man is to regard whatever women do as inferior, and to expect other men (and women) to share in this evaluation" (1986:64). Luckily, not all men share these attitudes, nor do all men indulge in these behaviors—and some have even been staunch allies of women in the field (Anonymous 1994). It is appalling that this letter praising some men had to be written anonymously.

Women archaeologists were, not surprisingly, cowed by this state of affairs. "By and large the archaeologists who worked before 1960 followed a modified acceptance strategy, working hard yet quietly" (Parezo 1993b:345). The picture before the 1960s was bleak, though a surprising number of women nevertheless persevered in the field. Some had male relatives or spouses to give them support, and all probably had some men willing to aid them. Eventually, federal equal opportunity laws gave women the tools to fight for equality—whether or not they were perceived as a "pain in the ass" for doing so.

Remedies

Mentors are important in all fields, but they are particularly important in archaeology. Jane Kelley (1992) suggests that while "survivorship" of women in archaeology is low, good mentoring can help keep promising women in the field. Mentors "help establish professional networks, instill accepted values and behavior, impart technical expertise, and provide official and/or professional endorsement . . . However, men may not want to invest in female proteges" (B. Garrow, P. Garrow, and Thomas 1994:198). Nancy Parezo notes the other side of the coin: a woman needs a mentor to protect her from "influential target people with strong personalities [who] act as gatekeepers" (1993b:346). Furthermore, "however deserving a woman might be, promotions were gifts from one's colleagues, particularly the powerful ones" (Rossiter 1982, quoted in Parezo 1993b:350). Mentors may save women who otherwise might drop out at difficult points in their careers, and certainly the attrition rate of women is high (S. Nelson and M. Nelson 1994). Dena Dincauze (1992:133) considers "conflicting personal agendas" to be a "matter of varied career styles," but asserts that the institutional barriers must be removed to allow women to have both a career and a personal life.

Quoting circles and peer review provide other hazards for women archaeologists, who may have fewer colleagues and be less well connected than men. It is important to have friends and colleagues to discuss ideas, critique one's work, invite one to conferences, and keep one abreast of the latest fieldwork. "Personal contact between archaeologists has been a vital aspect of communication in the discipline" (Kelley and Hanen 1988:152).

Women may also publish on more topics than men do (Kelley 1992), giving rise to their being criticized for lack of "depth." Dena Dincauze refers to this as a "chicken feed approach, foraging for crumbs among more major research agendas" (1992:34). The notion of "major" here seems somewhat androcentric, since whatever women do has been by definition *not* major. Of course, everyone's career track is to some extent constrained by outside factors, but my own wide interests have been developed partly in response to the challenge posed by the height and breadth of various barriers. For example, both personal and institutional factors prevented me from returning to Korea, the area of my dissertation, for a number of years. This is not so much a "career style" as an adaptation to difficult circumstances. Women have been versatile as a means of survivorship. But perhaps women are also, as Dena Dincauze (1992:34) suggests, less prone to repeat themselves, and more widely curious.

Women are less likely to teach at large research universities, and therefore rarely have adequate resources. When resources are inadequate, it is difficult to do research, for "doing research requires money as well as access" (Stiehm 1985:384). Furthermore, those from "lesser" institutions, or no institution at all, have fewer opportunities to publish, since more time is spent on teaching or otherwise making a living. As noted above, much work on gender in archaeology has been circulated as gray literature, unpublished in professional journals. A compilation of such writings, in addition to new material, was itself created as camera-ready copy on a faculty member's computer, without much institutional help (M. Nelson, S. Nelson, and Wylie 1994), but was criticized for its typos as well as lauded for its content (Cullen 1995). Although I regret the errors, this type of carping indicates a lack of understanding of the substantial handicaps under which women archaeologists still labor, compared to equivalent men. We also lack wives to read over and correct (even perhaps type and edit) our work.

Conclusions

The structure of archaeology as a discipline has not been welcoming to women. But lessons have been learned, and women archaeologists are talking to each other and offering mutual support. Women are networking in new ways, in spite of considerable risk to careers even now (S. Nelson and M. Nelson 1994). Margaret Conkey notes that organizers of women/gender conferences "are to be congratulated for having a vision and for having the professional and personal courage and energy to realize their goals in a still skeptical environment" (1993:3). A few women are secure enough and high enough on the career ladder to offer a leg up to those on the lower rungs, a boost they give willingly. The climate has improved, though not all the problems in the profession are solved. Jonathan Reyman (1992:77) notes that archaeology has "lost valuable people, and . . . overlooked important data or made serious errors of various sorts by ignoring women's contributions." The most hopeful part is the new energy with which gender studies are being pursued in archaeology. Women and men working in this subfield are beginning to form an "invisible college" (Kelley and Hanen 1988:154). The good news is that there are too many women in archaeology for exclusivity, and too much good work to simply be ignored by the patriarchs of the profession, as the following chapters reveal.

CHAPTER THREE

INTERPRETING GENDER
IN THE PAST

Theories and Strategies

The analysis of the past is shaped by the present; our choice of questions, our selection of evidence, our analyses, all are influenced by contemporary concerns. The reconstruction of the past in turn serves present need, as it clarifies or justifies the contours of present reality.
—Elizabeth Fee (1974:86)

I could accept real male power but found ways of rejecting real female power.
—Ian Hodder (1991a:13)

Interpreting the past is done within the framework of theories, and as we have seen the selection of data to bring to bear on our research questions is constrained by our theories. While engendering archaeology has been attempted within all archaeological paradigms, and I think this is proper and effective, some theories are more welcoming to the study of gender than others. Strategies for revealing gender also need to be considered, as well as the principles which guide the strategies, and the resources available to follow the strategies.

Gender Implications of Archaeological Theories

For more than a quarter of a century the dominant archaeological paradigm in the English-speaking world was positivist and materialist. This paradigm, often called processualist archaeology, or sometimes "new" archaeology, has been perhaps the least available to feminist archaeology. Agency and values

49

are particularly important in feminist anthropology (di Leonardo 1991), but both are missing in processualist archaeology. Problems with the lack of space for human agency have been noted more and more insistently. Elizabeth Brumfiel, in describing the limitations of processualist archaeology, stresses that "ecosystem theory focuses on abstract behavior rather than the group of actors that control resources and power" (1992:553). This obscures any sense of who the controllers may be, and allows the assumption that they are exclusively male. George Cowgill critiques processual theory for being 'acutely unsatisfactory about social phenomena . . . because it is excessively materialist and drastically underconceptualizes the individual actors from whose behavior large-scale social phenomena emerge" (1993:551). Although Cowgill is not specifically concerned with gender, his viewpoint is entirely applicable to a gendered approach to archaeology.

The notion that science is value-free has been another stumbling block. We archaeologists, being as steeped in our own cultures as other mortals, reflect cultural values related to personal achievement. Few are immune. It is germane that Bruce Trigger ties nomothetic, or generalizing, goals in prehistoric archaeology to the "desire of American archaeologists to conform to a more prestigious model of scholarly behavior, especially as the National Science Foundation became a major source of funding" (1986:201). Alice Kehoe additionally points out that funding became an individual effort under NSF, rather than the cooperative venture that archaeology had been before. She further notes that "discourse in the mode of science was the discourse of power" (1995:21), an observation particularly relevant to this book. Thus the values of science have influenced the values of archaeology, and of archaeologists as well. It is a serious problem that these values contain certain attitudes that are inimical to feminism, as well as to gender studies.

Research questions framed in terms of subsistence, population, or ecology, while they do efface agency, do not necessarily obscure gender differences, even though in practice they have often done so. In the early days of processual archaeology, explicit gender assumptions were made, such as that women made the pottery and that mothers taught daughters (Hill 1968, Longacre 1966, Deetz 1965). These papers, more than any others of the nascent "new" archaeology, drew fierce criticism of several kinds (Allen and Richardson 1971, Stanislawski 1973), which may have helped to push such topics off the agenda.

One way they were *not* criticized (but should have been by current standards) was for essentializing women's roles.

Not all challenges to the hegemony of the ecosystem paradigm have been feminist. Others have arisen from the application of Marxist theory to archaeology (e.g. Kristiansen 1983) and the insistence on the influence of ideology in the past rather than merely material conditions (e.g. Miller and Tilley 1984, Hodder 1992). Still others have examined the constructedness of our archaeological "reconstructions" (e.g. Shanks and Tilley 1987). These viewpoints are sometimes lumped together along with feminist archaeology as "postprocessualism," though they make strange bedfellows. Postprocessualist archaeologies, with their emphasis on agency, on ideology, on power, and on critiques of scientism in archaeology, may open up a space for an archaeology of gender, but they do not automatically motivate archaeologists to explore that space, nor do they necessarily welcome gender studies. Archaeological theory in all its guises has provided little room for feminist views—or even, as we have seen, for women archaeologists.

Margaret Conkey and Janet Spector (1984) began their pathbreaking article by acknowledging the space created for a feminist perspective by critiques of archaeologies that reinforce national mythologies, especially Mark Leone's work a decade earlier, in which he documented some of the ways in which nationalist views had invaded archaeological writings and understandings of the past (1973). This is important ground on which feminists can also stand, in the same way that other perspectives could build on feminist theory. But many postprocessual theorists fail to acknowledge their debt to feminism, and fail to recognize that gender is central to the issues they raise. Daniel Miller and Christopher Tilley (1984), in a devastating critique of archaeological practices, nevertheless focus on diachronic (extending over time) social change without much attention to half the human species. In a later paper, Tilley acknowledges that "theories of the human subject always tend to be simultaneously theories of the masculine" (1993:22), but he nevertheless misses the point of a gendered archaeology, perhaps due to limited acquaintance. "It is quite disgraceful that there is only one feminist book in existence in archaeology," he goes on to say, ignoring all the other published work that had accumulated by that time. In the same year students at the University of Michigan were able to compile and publish an annotated bibliography of almost two hundred publications relating to gender in archaeology (Bacus et al. 1993). The invisibility and muting of most feminist work in archaeology is all too clear (Kehoe 1992a). The "quoting circles" of all theoretical stripes exclude virtually all gray literature as well as much of what women have managed, against heavy odds, to get into print.

Marxist archaeology, with its interests in "social difference, tension, conflict and negotiation" (Saitta 1992:887), would seem to have much in common with gendered archaeology, and should provide more space for and pay more heed to feminist debate than it has so far. Earlier important exceptions are the papers in *Power Relations and State Formation* (Patterson and Gailey 1987), but for the most part Marxist archaeology has either ignored gender or considered it as another kind of "class." Nevertheless, progress in including gender is evident. "Concrete ethnographic and eth-nohistoric work has established the importance of these variables [power, gender, and ideology] in shaping human behavior" (Saitta 1992:888). Marxist archaeology, as so constructed, is a hopeful avenue of research for gendered archaeology, as it has been for gendered anthropology, but it does not guarantee an interest in gender. In practice, the emphasis on power often crowds out gender.

Marxist frameworks have guided archaeological research, including methodologies and interpretations, in a number of communist countries for half a century and more, including the former Soviet Union (Soffer 1983, Tringham 1991:96), China (Pearson 1983, Nelson 1995), and North Korea (Nelson 1995). Some important methodological breakthroughs resulted from this emphasis, including settlement archaeology and closer attention to technological details. But the lack of questioning implicit in the invariant underlying evolutionary framework is a distinct drawback, which hinders a more subtle engendering of the past. The scheme of matriarchal Neolithic society leading to patriarchal complex society is never argued, only stated as fact, based on 19th century works by Lewis Henry Morgan (1877) by way of Friedrich Engels (1881). Gender attributions made within this paradigm are presented in ways that are simply doctrinaire, and as such are unconvincing. Some attention is paid to gender issues in the Morgan/Engels scenario—but the whole scheme is androcentric, gender polarized, and reductionist, assuming simplistic worldwide gender relationships at each stage. Thus Marxist theory in its several forms does not by itself provide a method for engendering archaeology

Middle Range Theory (MRT) is the name given to a body of ideas for translating contemporary observations about the archaeological record into inferences about past social dynamics. Ethnoarchaeology, experimental archaeology, and other "actualistic" studies are the arenas for building MRT. Researchers with various theoretical orientations have found MRT useful. This "source-side" work (Wylie 1989) helps choose between alternative explanations (Tschauner 1996), but to whatever extent these studies are based on distorted gender assumptions, or ignore gender altogether, they will not advance an understanding of gender in the past. Studies that consider specific types of relationships are needed. MRT could be used in ideological research, as well, to produce a "MRT of the mind" (Cowgill 1993). Application of this suggestion may turn out to be an important avenue for feminist archaeology to pursue, but it is important to avoid universalizing and essentializing gender roles in the process. Feminist archaeologists need to develop our *own* MRT.

While the postprocessualist debate would seem to resonate with the point being made here, for the most part the discussion has not taken androcentrism into account. For example, Ian Hodder (1982) failed to acknowledge feminism as an important source of postprocessual archaeology, though he rectified this oversight in a later publication (1992:84). And in spite of the general inattention to developing feminism, some of the feminist challenges find resonances elsewhere. For example, a direct critique of the role of power and prestige in the archaeological profession contains a statement of a situation known all too well to women: "We want archaeologists to recognise that charisma and social context play far more important a role in academic discourse than is usually acknowledged" (Johnson and Coleman 1990:16). Women archaeologists have been all too aware of this fact, and have discussed it in print (see chapters in M. Nelson, S. Nelson, and Wylie 1994), but the gender issue remains unacknowledged in Johnson and Coleman's paper.

Ecological, scientistic, Marxist, postprocessual, and other archaeological theories have of course been critiqued, often by women. In spite of this, more women in the field, and more attention to gender by some archaeologists, has not made gender a central issue in the discipline; it is still marginalized. The tables of contents of recent collections of theoretical papers in archaeology—at least those edited by men—show that few women archaeologists are included, with little or only passing reference to gender. In a collection of papers titled *American Archaeology Past and Future: A Celebration of the Society for American Archaeology 1935–1985* (Meltzer, Fowler, and Sabloff, eds. 1986), only one author (Watson 1986) even references Conkey and Spector (1984), seen as one of the pathbreaking papers by feminist archaeologists (Watson 1986). In that same volume Patty Jo Watson also cites Gero (1985), another classic paper in feminist archaeology, and again she is the only author in the volume to do so. Even Watson lumps these papers with "critical theorists" who believe that "the past is inaccessible unless we can analyze adequately, and then neutralize or circumvent, the social and political ideologies that bias and shape our understanding of it" (1986:444). While the postprocessualist critique opened possibilities, as noted above, gender issues were not specifically raised.

In *Archaeological Theory: Who Sets the Agenda?*, Norman Yoffee and Andrew Sherratt (1993) published three out of eleven papers by women, thus acknowledging the growing numbers of influential women in the field, but none of the papers address women or gender in the past (though the papers may be grounded in feminist perspectives). Even a book published as recently as 1995 (compiled from a conference that took place in 1992) contained no mention of gender, though it is entitled *Theory in Archaeology: A World Perspective* (Ucko 1995). It is clear that the archaeological male majority worldwide has taken little notice of the feminist revolution, though updated editions of a few archaeology texts show increasing awareness of gender (e.g. Patterson 1993, Thomas 1989). The "lenses" of androcentrism are thus mostly still present, regardless of the archaeological paradigm. If other disciplines have been transformed by feminism, why is archaeology so recalcitrant?

Some Principles for Engendering Archaeology

As noted by several authors (Gifford-Gonzalez 1997, Conkey and Spector 1984), the problem is not that archaeology has been unaware of gender, but that gender arrangements of the present have been universalized and read back into the past. Therefore, I would like to paraphrase what I have written elsewhere (1997) about some basic requirements for a thoughtfully gendered archaeology. These topics are elaborated in subsequent chapters, but it is useful to list them together here as a basis for further discussion.

Essentialism

Gendered archaeology must be firmly based on the notion that differences among gender arrangements are what research should focus on, and we must abandon all attempts to explain gender in the past with reference to "universals" of women's biology or women's experiences. While it is true that all human groups, in order to continue, needed to reproduce, to make women's role in reproduction the centerpiece of an explanation for women's other roles in society is to ignore the variation in those roles. In my judgment, neither biological nor psychological essentialism is a productive place to begin understanding women's roles in the past.

Division of Labor

A related point is that the division of labor by gender should not be taken for granted. It may not have existed in all societies. Division of labor by gender needs to be demonstrated for a given society, and then considered critically. Are all activities, locations, and artifacts allocated to a particular gender? Where is there comparability, overlap, or flexibility in gender roles?

The Public/Private Dichotomy

The tendency to create opposites such as public versus private may inhere in Indo-European languages, but it is not wired into our brains, and it is important to begin any search for gender in the past without preconceived notions about women in the household and men in the public arena. Ethnographic examples of women assuming a variety of public roles should open our eyes to the androcentrism inherent in this dichotomy. Instead we should ask what roles were open to both women and men, and which were ungendered roles, and *why*.

Homogenizing the Men and Women of a Culture

It is important not to begin with the premise that all the women of a given culture or all the men fill the same roles and do the same things. Finding gender does not mean that other categories of difference are not also meaningful or important for separating people into groups for work, rituals, or social events.

Strategies for Gender Research

Producing real archaeological results is the challenge of current feminist archaeologists. Ian Hodder (1992:1) notes the need to combine theory and practice, and suggests that academic prestige systems have been responsible for the separation between method and theory (p. 3). Alison Wylie (1992a) challenges us to produce useful examples. Several strategies and resources have been noted by Mary Whelan (1995) and Cathy Costin (1996), which are considered and added to here. Strategies such as critiques of androcentrism, ethnographic analogy, and the direct historical approach are necessary first steps in arriving at a gendered archaeology.

Critiques of Androcentrism

Basic work in becoming aware of the unconscious gendering of the past was necessary in order to begin afresh with *conscious* gendering of that past. While of course it is necessary to go beyond them in finding ways to engender the past that are neither androcentric nor ethnocentric, many topics still need to be critiqued and their biases explicitly exposed before we can move on. For example, my publication on the Upper Paleolithic female figurines pointed out biases based on the way men perceive women in our own culture, as well as in cultural attitudes toward breasts, nudity, and other characteristics of the figurines (1990a). Joan Gero (1993) draws attention to androcentric biases that underlie the study of Paleoindians in the Americas. These kinds of studies are useful for providing a level playing field for future studies of these topics.

Ethnographic Analogy

Many cautions about the use of ethnographic analogy have been raised (see Duke and Wilson 1995:5–6 for a recent critique of the "tyranny of the ethnographic record")—and rightly so. Awareness of the effects of colonialism, of the bias of the ethnographer, of environmental change, and so forth, is critical, if the ethnographic record is to be of use to archaeologists. We must avoid assuming that past or recent cultures are relics of a stagnant or pristine past, as pointed out by Edwin Wilmsen (1989). However, wide-ranging citations from ethnographies on a particular topic (e.g. Wadley 1997 on women hunters) can open a variety of new possibilities for interpreting archaeological sites. Lyn Wadley found that what is considered "hunting" varies considerably from culture to culture, and that women's contributions to the endeavor are very widely recognized. Examinations of cultures in similar relevant circumstances (for example, environment, population density, or continuous warfare) can similarly provide models for understanding the past.

Mary Whelan (1995), specifically considering the North American plains, points out the androcentric nature of Plains Indian ethnography, which was also documented in *The Hidden Half* (Albers and Medicine 1993). Whelan shows, too, that a new discovery, such as fragments of net in a Late Paleoindian site in Wyoming (Frison et al. 1986), require rethinking the standard notions of hunting as exclusively gendered male.

Cathy Costin (1996) notes that we need to be aware of the ethnographic data in craft production, but also to *beware* of it. "Perhaps our most relevant lesson from the ethnographic data is that craft production is gendered in largely idiosyncratic, historically contingent ways, making sweeping generalizations and general analogies problematic in many cases" (1996:116).

Thus, ethnographies help us to see alternative possibilities for interpreting archaeological sites, but they should never be applied without careful argument about why it is an appropriate analogy for that particular site.

The Direct Historical Approach

Following cultures from their early encounters with western researchers into the archaeological past (which presumably contains the remains of their own ancestors) avoids some of the pitfalls of ethnographic analogy from unrelated studies, though it is not without analogous problems. The first accounts of contact might well have been androcentric, and the group could have been significantly changed by contact with colonizers, traders, and missionaries, or even by indirect contact. The reasons hypothesized that a particular part of the culture is believed to have persisted require specific argument.

Ethnoarchaeology

Asking specifically gendered questions about artifacts and their distribution on archaeological sites is an important step in gendered site interpretation. Susan Kent (1995) has shown how risky some of our assumptions about space and tool use turn out to be. Many ethnoarchaeological studies that purport to explain archaeological patterns may be flawed by pertaining only to one gender. Lewis Binford's (1986) study of men's disposal of artifacts in a hunting camp may reflect different behavior than disposal when women are along, or in other situations such as long-term occupation of a site. A cartoon by Laurent (1965) speaks to this point: a woman sweeping up in the cave explains to a man that she is preparing a stratigraphical problem.

Resources for Engendering the Past

Although it may be possible to use any archaeological data to understand gender in the past, some types of data are more easily adapted to this purpose. These include depictions of humans, documents, burials, artifacts, and spatial arrangements of home sites and so forth. Furthermore, any argument is improved by having multiple lines of evidence. The more the following types of evidence can be weighed in the analysis, the more convincing and secure will be the results.

Depictions of Women and Men

Archaeology is rich in representations of people in many media. They may be in three-dimensional form (portable or not), and made from many materials, painted on ceramics, or painted and pecked on larger surfaces. These are valuable traces of the past, but this rich lode cannot be treated as straightforward records of the past. Chapters in *The Role of Gender in Precolumbian Art and Architecture* (Miller 1988), for example, demonstrate a variety of ways to use such material. The relative attention given to women and men may demonstrate cultural emphasis by gender, while the activities portrayed can be assumed to have been significant in some way for that culture. A common problem of interpretation is that figures for which the gender is not clearly depicted are often assumed to be male (Whelan 1995, Levy 1995), so this potential pitfall must be avoided.

Written Documents

The usual cautions apply in regard to texts, which cannot be used uncritically. Yet they may provide a wealth of information about details of a culture that can be combined with the archaeological record to learn about gender relationships. Rita Wright (1996) uses texts regarding weavers in the Ur III period in Mesopotamia in the late third millennium B.C. She is able to compare temple policies with those of the state as they impact weaving workshops and the gendering of this technology. She finds that this was a deeply stratified society, in which social strata were related to occupation. Weavers existed in large numbers to make cloth for both state and temple needs. They were semifree or slaves, and they were all women. Textiles were a major export commodity (also see Barber 1994). The product was highly valued, the producers were not. The fact that textiles were central to the economy worked against women weavers. Class differences among women are thus highlighted with attention to weaving.

Cathy Costin (1996) also suggests the uses of "texts," which she defines broadly as including oral literature, censuses, myths, and so forth. These sources naturally have their difficulties, and can never be used without considering their contexts. Further, women's voices are often absent from them. Nevertheless, Costin points out, the texts are useful for parts of culture that have no obvious material correlates.

Burials and Human Remains

Analysis of human remains is yet another avenue through which to research gender in the past. DNA analysis has barely begun, but it is now being applied to mummies in both Egypt and the dry western deserts of China's Xinjiang region, and results are eagerly awaited. Through other sorts of skeletal analysis it is possible to learn about differential gender treatment, as well. Changing sex differentials in workload, physical risk, disease, nutrition, reproductive patterns, childhood stress, and mortality have all been inferred from burials. Trauma is recorded in bones as well, and not only can much be learned from the distribution of traumatic injuries by age and sex, but also work in finding patterns (such as which bones are more commonly broken) can reveal models of activities and the distribution of gender-related violence. Increase in warfare may be reflected in wounds made by weapons. Increased trauma to women may indicate wife-battering, implying men's rights over women and a concomitant decrease in status and autonomy, though other explanations are possible. Physical stress and workload may appear in the remains as degenerative arthritis, or as more robust bones. Infection and disease can leave traces in the skeleton, and indications of nutrition in childhood and adulthood are retrievable from bones. All these types of studies can lead to a better understanding of specific gender arrangements (Cohen and Bennett 1993).

Mary Whelan (1995) suggests looking at artifact categories in burials *before* considering the sex of those buried, to avoid the unconscious re-creating of present gender arrangements in the past. She uses Blackdog Cemetery from southern Minnesota as an example (Whelan, Withrow, and O'Connell 1989, Whelan 1991) of a burial ground in use in the first half of the 19th century. Artifact distributions in burials did not suggest a division of labor by sex, though artifact patterning nevertheless was found. Ritual equipment was found clustered, buried with six men and one woman. This suggests that it was possible but less common for women to be ritual specialists. Another artifact distribution that claimed attention was the unequal number of artifact types in different graves. In this, women and men were numerically equal in both upper and lower halves of the distribution, suggesting gender equality in status (Whelan 1995:58).

One important and potentially fruitful way to study kinship is through burials. The social implications of proximity in cemeteries have been teased out in several ways. Ian Hodder explores some of the possibilities of interpreting the communal tombs of the European Neolithic. "European earlier Neolithic societies are usually assumed to be kin-based, especially in areas where burial is in communal tombs. It seems reasonable to argue that kinship and reproduction defined social roles at this time and that women therefore played central roles expressed through female symbolism" (1991a:12). He further suggests, "The tombs of the SOM culture in the Paris basin contain large numbers of human bones and the settlement data suggest that these represent kinship rather than residence units. The megalithic tombs of northwestern Europe generally provide independent evidence about the importance of kinship and communal labor (as seen in the construction of the monumental tombs)" (Hodder 1991a:14). While these do not explicitly engender these societies, further research may be able to do so.

Artifacts
Combined with other data, such as from text, grave goods, depictions, or the direct historical approach, gendered artifacts may seem to be the best approach. However, caution as usual must be applied. Susan Kent (1995) has observed that even the most gendered of artifacts can be used in

unexpected ways—for example, a woman stirring the cooking pot with her husband's spear.

J. M. Kenoyer finds interesting patterns in Harappan cemeteries. While both men and women were buried with hidden beads, other kinds of pendants, made from black or green stone, are found only in burials of adult women. These special pendants may have marked a social subset of married women. Bangles of various materials also seem to have had some important meaning for women. "Glass bangles came to be used in specific ritual and social contexts as non-verbal symbols of status, marriage, or widowhood" (1995). Thus, attention to the details of ornaments, rather than merely counting them, opens up interesting possibilities for gender studies.

Linda Donley-Reid provides some ethnoarchaeological descriptions that may be relevant to the Harappan case. In studying Swahili society, she found that porcelain, incised pottery, and beads are objects that can be used to protect women against evil outside influences. Similarly, these artifacts can protect *men against women,* as women in Swahili society are perceived to be polluting to men. Both the domicile itself and the inhabitants can be protected in this way. Imported porcelain plates are not merely good luck charms, they are used to absorb evil eye, which otherwise would harm people, bringing sickness and death. Latrines are particularly dangerous places, often protected with a porcelain plate. Even broken plates are valuable, since it is their evil-absorbing properties that caused them to break. Potsherds therefore make effective charms. Thus, plates should not necessarily always be interpreted in an archaeological context as food servers, nor their presence used as indicative of a place where food was eaten!

Glass beads have protective advantages, too, and can prevent evil spirits from attacking women and children. Blue beads and coral beads are best for this purpose. Red beads, worn next to the skin for their medicinal value, are reminiscent of the discovery of hidden bands in the Harappan cemetery. Unlike the Harappan case, however, Swahili men never wear beads, though women and children wear them regardless of class.

Decorated pots are associated with women in Swahili society. Pottery with incised lines, and even earthenware containers, are also believed to absorb evil influences. However, they can also transmit pollution, and since women are polluting, pottery as women's products can be dangerous to men.

Brass pots are safer for those at risk, such as the risk of pollution, but iron is the best of all because it actually wards off evil spirits. Food can be used to rid oneself of pollution, especially if shared with the spirits (Donley-Reid 1990). Clearly, much can be learned about gender relationships from the distribution of these artifacts in Swahili sites.

Other uses of artifacts that can be attributed to women are legion. It is valuable to know that particular types of clothing may be worn differentially according to age and/or gender. Imperishable objects such as buttons or pins can represent the whole of the attire, in many cases. Anne Stalsberg has used the presence of women's objects from Scandinavia, found in Viking graves in Russia, to suggest that families, and not just men, were part of the eastward Viking expansion of the 9th to 11th centuries (1987). If other evidence substantiates the presence of Viking women, it will require rethinking of the historical narrative. There are important implications for women as settlers and colonists, and this topic could be usefully expanded with additional archaeological evidence.

Spatial Arrangements and Households
The organization of space may be gendered or not. Spatial organization within a household may depend on notions of gendered space (Kent 1997), or artifacts may be distributed according to gendered activities. Ethnoarchaeological observations show that what turns up in the archaeological record may not represent activity areas, but rather storage areas.

Another fruitful avenue for the understanding of prehistoric kinship roles is through household architecture. Ruth Tringham, as she began to insert people into prehistoric domestic architecture, found some likely scenarios that can be further refined with archaeological data (1991). People with faces have been turned into actors and agents in archaeologically visible change. Alterations over the life of a building or structure can be particularly telling. For example, Tringham compared houses at various Neolithic sites in eastern Europe. At Opovo they were less well made and occupied for shorter durations, had fewer storage facilities, and contained more wild animal bones. Room functions were simpler than other sites of the same time period. Most houses had no internal divisions, and no formal food preparation areas. This suggests that the entire site functioned differently from other contemporaneous Neolithic sites.

Furthermore, the demise of houses may also reveal aspects of gendered space. Some houses were abandoned and later disintegrated, while others appear to have been deliberately burned with very hot fires. Someone took the time to fill pits and wells with rubbish and debris from the burned houses, level the area, and build again, suggesting deliberate renewal as well as intentional burning. Abandoned houses were renewed in various ways. Opovo was built on a natural mound in a marsh, which possibly restricted the area on which to build, so the mound grew higher, rather than spreading out. Still, differences could be noted between rebuilding on the same floor, building beside the previous house, or constructing a building on higher ground (Tringham 1991). These variations may have gender implications.

Linda Donley-Reid's work on Swahili houses demonstrates that the way domestic space is structured in the present can also be found in excavating houses of the past, providing that the archaeologist is alert to the clues, as she demonstrates with her own work at Lamu, Kenya. Based on her ethnohistoric work, she has been able to identify features of house floors that otherwise would have been elusive and that had previously passed unnoticed. For example, the innermost room of the house is the site of women's rituals related to birth and death. Stillborn infants may be buried in this location, along with placentas, accompanied by iron nails to ward off evil. The pits with iron nails might otherwise be uninterpretable. Women also dig trenches in the floor to dispose of the water that has been used in washing a corpse before burial, trenches that can be detected upon excavation and that may be overlooked if their significance is not known. The way people create their own interior environment both structures their lives and reflects the social structure; this too can be discovered by careful excavation (Donley 1982, 1987; Donley-Reid 1990).

Patricia O'Brien excavated a burial mound and earth lodge at the C. C. Witt site in Kansas and was able to infer domestic activities from the location of remains within the lodge. Most of these were women's activities—grinding corn, processing hide and cutting meat, sewing, and basket-making. However, there is also evidence of making arrowshafts in the lodge; presumably men's work areas are also present. O'Brien (1995) explains the association of various artifacts with men and women based on ethnohistoric work, and looks at a specific site with its distributional data, not overgeneralizing it, but rather examining the details of this site.

Attention to households is not new in archaeology, nor is the idea that space might be gendered. Kent Flannery and Marcus Winter (1969) gave more attention to the economic activities implied by the debris on floors of prehistoric villages in Oaxaca, Mexico, than to gender implications, though they did note the separation of artifacts that often are associated with men and women into the left side for the men and the right side for women's activities. A more explicitly gendered study might be able to tease further strands of information out of the fabric of these distributions.

Richard Wilk and William Rathje focus on households, without giving much attention to gender. However, they do note that larger households may have more flexibility for child care arrangements (Wilk and Rathje 1982). It would be interesting to see whether, following this clue, some traces might be left in house floors that indicate how toddlers were restrained from the hearth—or from falling over the edge of the precipice, as in the cliff dwellings of Mesa Verde.

Ian Hodder (1991b) uses domestic architecture in quite a different way to interpret societies of the early and middle Neolithic in southeastern Europe and southwestern Asia. Houses are elaborate in terms of interior divisions, and highly decorated. Thus, the importance of the household is underscored. One wonders whether this can apply equally to the decorated houses of India and Africa.

Conclusions

The most effective ways to find gender in the past are to use several lines of evidence together. Tight arguments are needed to gender the past convincingly, and the use of various kinds of analogies always requires specific justification as to how they are applicable in a particular archaeological site or culture.

CHAPTER FOUR
IN THE BEGINNING
Archaeology, Gender, and Origins

Our search for origins reveals a faith in ultimate and essential truths.
—Michelle Rosaldo (1980:393)

The categories that we are to look for . . . have already been defined. . . .
Origins research tends to make decontextualized phenomena seem inevitable.
—Margaret Conkey (1991:114)

Rudyard Kipling's *Just So Stories*, purporting to explain the beginnings of many features of our world, from the alphabet to the elephant's trunk, are captivating. They satisfy an urge to know (or guess) how familiar things began. Unlike some of Kipling's tales, however, our archaeological origin stories are human-centered, and they are taken seriously because they have the imprimatur of science, implying that they are accurate and well researched. Thus, what our origin stories imply or state about gender can lend a specious air of antiquity, permanency, and unchangeability to present gender arrangements, inserting them into the past with the appearance of perfect plausibility.

Research into the origins of human cultures has been one of the mainstays of anthropology. Just as Darwin began with the physical variation in plants and animals in the time of his historical present as a problem that needed explaining with reference to events in the past, so cultural anthropologists from Darwin's time to today have attempted to explain the evolution of everything from society itself (Spencer 1895) and monotheistic religion (Tylor 1865) to Victorian gender relationships (Bachofen 1861, Maine 1861), to kinship terminology (Morgan 1877), by means of reference to how each began. The assumption was rife that everything evolved, thus it was necessary to find primitive versions of contemporary institutions and to postulate them as similar to earlier entities. Past structures were simple and undifferentiated, and at the beginning either human society was a noble paradise or life was "poor, nasty, brutish and short" (Hobbes 1642), with decided emphasis on the last—but in either case the past was expected to provide a reflection of important facets of humanity. Leslie White, who retired in 1969, used to tell his classes that evolution was believed in the 19th century to have culminated in the Victorian gentleman, and any other cultural arrangements were lower on the evolutionary scale. European nationalities, in fact, were each attempting to demonstrate that the males of their nationality had the biggest human brains, and therefore were the most intelligent (Gould 1981:73–112).

It can be argued that there are only two purposes for origins research— either to show that we humans are what we are because of how we began and nothing can change us, or to demonstrate that we civilized folk have come very far from such primitive beginnings and deserve to be the lords over all creation. Whatever the purpose, as Marcia-Anne Dobres indicates, the underlying assumption in origins research is that "current situations are directly connected to a common beginning, and that if we can 'know' this past we can explain the present" (1988:32). Nearly every group of people has an origin myth. Since origins are so important, and are taken so seriously, it behooves us to try to get them right, as far as possible.

Origin stories, whether those of relatively isolated cultures or our own, can be viewed as texts. Misia Landau, in an extended discussion of hominid origins research, is interested in the way these stories about the past are told. Although the events and characters are rearranged in different scenarios, she finds they are only permutations of a hero-centered myth. "Paleoan-thropologists have told the same story over and over" (1991:178). The hero myth is basically a male myth; it is no wonder that it is the story of the ascent of "man." Donna Haraway similarly presses this case, finding all the social sciences "story-laden" (1983:79), whether discussing origins or other topics. But origins in particular capture the public imagination, and the lure of origins is magnified when presented as a story.

Origins research, however, has a fatal flaw: it essentializes whatever "origin" it is seeking, and it assumes the existence of this characteristic, institution, or structure from the present backward into some distant past, where the essence of what now exists can be faintly detected. It is thus "presentist" (or present-ist) (Conkey with Williams 1991), and as such it is particularly susceptible to the attribution of present characteristics to very different pasts. For example, seeking the origin of the division of labor by gender reifies the division of labor itself, and forces us to assign tasks by gender into the dim past. It requires us to expect the division of labor by gender to have kept the same recognizable form for thousands or perhaps millions of years, depending on when the "origin" is expected to have begun. Seeking the origin of the family, or of gender hierarchy, works the same way. Contemporary gender relationships are often inserted into the past in this way, and can easily escape detection, since the scenario is so familiar. The subliminal message is that gender relationships are immutably fixed, and nothing can change them.

Origins and Evolution

Origins spawn an interest in evolutionary stages. But the evolutionary schemes of Tylor and Morgan proved too crude to stand up to the detailed ethnography that began in the early 20th century (Boas 1909, Lowie 1915). For a time, evolution went out of style in American anthropology, and grand evolutionary schemes were seen as illusory. Single "traits" might still be followed in a diffusionist way, with an unspoken understanding that these "traits" had some constant essence that could be recognized in all times and places. Physical traits, such as hair texture or skin color, were equally essentialized. Some evolutionary schemes have been shown to be embarrassingly racist, as well as sexist (Gould 1981). Women's supposedly smaller brains (not factored, of course, for differences in body size) were a handicap that females could not overcome. On the basis of skull measurements, Gustave Le Bon in 1895 concluded that, "In the most intelligent races, as among the Parisians, there are a large number of women whose brains are closer in size to those of gorillas than to the most developed male brains" (quoted in Gould 1981:105). It isn't hard to guess that Le Bon was a male Parisian, defending the efforts of men of his class to oppress women.

A need for "science" and the big picture brought cultural evolution back to anthropology. It was perhaps inevitable, with the pace of technological change in the 20th century, that the "capture of energy" would be offered as the clue to understanding human sociocultural evolution (White 1959). White's version of evolution presupposes worldwide change along similar lines in all cultures, though not at the same rate or at the same time; this was scorned by the Boas school as "unilinear evolution." A growing interest in ecology brought evolution back to the center of anthropology by comparing cultures at similar "levels of development" in similar environments. The ecology school did not suppose that only a single track could be followed from simple to complex, but instead proposed "multilinear evolution" as a more nuanced way of looking at changes in the past, in the guise of comparing ecological adaptations (Steward 1955).

Technological change has always been archaeology's stock in trade, and archaeology necessarily has to come to grips with the past, requiring attention to diachronic change. Changes in stone tool technology were perceived as progressing from crude bashing of rock against rock to create a flake with a sharp edge, to preparing cores for the same purpose, to creating composite tools. Stone tools were followed by metals, bronze, and then iron, creating successive "Ages" (Thomsen 1836) during which "Man" became more adept at manipulating *his* environment. This technological age system became the basic organizing principle of archaeology, which continuously told or implied the grand story, not just of change through time, but also of increasing human control over the environment through the use of artifacts. At the same time, the increasing power of some humans over others came about through political control. Archaeology was thus ready to spring onto the bandwagon when Leslie White (1959) and others (Service 1966) made evolutionary thinking respectable again. Technology and environment were the key concepts through which evolution was reinvigorated in archaeology.

Thus was reborn an interest in how things began, divided into several stages. The beginnings of various subsistence strategies were of interest: the origins of hunting in early hominids and the origins of agriculture in the post-Pleistocene period. Political forms came in for scrutiny, too, especially "chiefdoms" and the origin of the state. On a less universal scale, the origins of art had a siren call, though the discoveries of the astounding cave paintings of France and Spain, with their realistic animals, made arguments about simple beginnings more complicated. In this process, reified categories were created—hunting, families, agriculture, chiefdoms, art—about which grand origin questions could be posed.

Archaeologists believed they had the tools and data to answer these evolutionary questions, and no sooner had Elman Service (1962) divided the evolutionary trajectory into bands, tribes, chiefdoms, and states, than archaeologists were describing their sites in these terms. This evolutionary scheme put the emphasis on the forms of political integration in any society, rather than on its subsistence base, its social organization, or its ideology. These "systems" were seen to be systematically interrelated, however, so that if one knew the level of political organization, other parts of the culture could be inferred (Flannery 1982). Although this paradigm seemed to be exceedingly fruitful at first, eventually it tended to become a "pigeonholing" operation: the question became, "Is my site a tribe or a chiefdom, a chiefdom or a state?" Comparison to trait lists was expected to answer the question. Furthermore, as more and more attention was paid to the characteristics of bands, tribes, chiefdoms, and states, the less firm the distinctions became. The edges were fuzzy, the categories blurred. The category of "bands" proved to be so loose that various band types had little in common except simplicity of subsistence base, and the "patrilocal band" proposed by Steward (1955) dissolved with reference to actual forager societies. Morton Fried suggested that tribes were not an evolutionary stage, but rather a creation of the western, colonizing world, in which the demand to "take me to your leader" *produced* a leader (Fried 1975). The whole question of states and their formation proved to be slippery, too, especially when nonurban states were considered. When the prehistory of the whole world, and not just that of southwest Asia and Europe, was factored in, the categories were found to be less and less useful.

But this particular origins question performed a practical function for archaeology, in addition to being a paradigmatic framework around which to organize research questions. The evolutionary trajectory provided a "scientific" paradigm, with the emphasis on science necessary to qualify for funds from the National Science Foundation (Trigger 1986, Kehoe 1995). The public, too, could relate to this simple scheme, and could easily understand what archaeologists were doing when they found the beginnings of something. As Margaret Conkey astutely notes, "Origins research makes archaeology relevant" (1991:106).

Evolution Constructed as Male

In the meantime, others had entered the origins sweepstakes. A spate of books on origins by nonanthropologists became best-sellers in the 1960s. Desmond Morris in *The Naked Ape* (1967) purported to explain human sexuality with reference to animal behavior, while Robert Ardrey in *African Genesis* (1963) used the fossil record of hominid forms, as well as particular interpretations of those discoveries, to insist that "man's" aggression was innate (both human and male were intended). In a later book on the same theme, Ardrey rejected the mounting evidence of the importance of vegetal food for forager societies, together with the fact that in human groups it is women who collect most of the calories and the bulk of the food. Instead, Ardrey insisted, "The mother, her young and the next generation depended almost totally on the proficiency of the adult males in her society" (1976:90). With a two-million-year-old scenario, he made the "testoster-one-made-me-do-it" argument seem reasonable, in a culture that found this plausible.

Just when the Women's Movement was gaining momentum, a conference on "Man the Hunter" in 1966 made explicit the androcentric bias of origins research at that time. The standard spiel was that the term "man" included women, which spawned the joke, "anthropology is the study of man, embracing woman." But the conference publication made it crystal clear that this was not the case, and in fact women were often not "embraced" by the term, and instead were shut out by it. Sherwood Washburn and C. S. Lancaster insisted that maleness and humanity are the same thing:

> It is significant that the title of this symposium is Man the Hunter for, in contrast to carnivores, human hunting, *if done by males*, is based on a division of labor and is a social and technical adaptation quite different from that of other mammals. Human hunting is made possible by tools, but it is far more than a technique or even a variety of techniques. It is a way of life, and the success of this adaptation (in its total social, technical, and psychological dimensions) has dominated the course of human evo-lution for hundreds of thousands of years. In a very real sense our intellect, interests, emotions, and basic social life—all are evolutionary products of the success of the hunting adaptation. (1968:293, emphasis added)

This paean to manhood set and kept the tone of the whole meeting, including the discussions. William Laughlin similarly rhapsodized on the benefits of hunting for the evolution of humanity:

> Hunting is the master behavior pattern of the human species. It is the organizing activity which integrated the morphological, physiological, genetic, and intellectual aspect of the individual human organism and of the population who comprise our single species. Hunting is a way of life, not simply a "subsistence technique," which importantly involves commitments, correlates, and consequences spanning the entire biobehavioral continuance of the individual and of the entire species of which he is a member. (1968:304)

Emphasis on male behavior is insistent, but one could still, at a stretch, suppose that women had some evolutionary impact on the species. On the contrary, Carleton Coon demonstrated that in his opinion, women and children are not really human. He declared that "[h]unting . . . separates the men from the boys. It is highly stimulating and distinctly human" (1976:69). In retrospect, it seems breathtaking that such blatant sexism could so much as be spoken and *published* as academic treatises. But in the field of anthropology it was considered "highly stimulating," even a breakthrough.

Man-the-Hunter was a tempting target for academic feminists, especially physical and cultural anthropologists, to attack, with a focus on Woman-the-Gatherer (e.g. Linton 1971, Zihlman 1978, Dahlberg 1981). Attention to these publications was less than that given to Man-the-Hunter, though ultimately the critique was effective within the discipline. Unfortunately, the genre of "male aggression" books continued to sell well and titillate the public. These volumes had provocative titles, such as *The Inevitability of Patriarchy* (Goldberg 1974) which purported to show that men are naturally dominant over women, or *Men in Groups* (Tiger and Fox 1969), a treatise based on the odd assumption that only men know how to form groups. As the debate grew, the emphasis on males by the hunting school was unsubtle:

> One of the most important effects of hunting was to widen the gap between males and females as far as behavior was concerned . . . when we recall that the brain doubled in size during the initial hunting period . . . we will see that the selective factors that went into this change

must have been rigorous indeed. The early primate pattern of bonding became the new and phenomenally significant pattern of cooperative hunting. (Tiger and Fox 1969:20)

Women, if anything, were a bit of a drag on the human species, since they needed to evolve a wider pelvic opening to give birth to bigger-brained (male?) babies.

Women's Responses

The first reaction from awakening feminists was a "women too!" response. Women did *too* have an input into evolution (Zihlman 1978); gathering *was* "women's work," but it was as important as hunting (Dahlberg 1981); some women *did* hunt (Estioko-Griffin and Griffin 1981); speech *may* have evolved for the communication of mothers with babies, not hunters (Morgan 1972). The first gods were *goddesses* (Stone 1976); women were the *rulers* before they were the ruled (Davis 1971). These and other efforts were largely rejected by many archaeologists—as not provable, not scientific, and, in some cases, embarrassing in their lack of grounding in archaeological evidence.

But feminists who reacted to male origin myths had asked some important questions. If men were hunting and creating culture, where were *women*, and what were they doing? Shivering naked in the cave with the children? It didn't make ethnographic sense. From these seeds the Woman-the-Gatherer model developed further, along with its corollary, Woman-the-Inventor-of-Agriculture. As it became clear that gathering plant food contributed vastly more than hunting to the diet in most human groups, the emphasis on hunting began to decrease, though even today it has not disappeared.

Unfortunately the Woman-the-Gatherer scenario was just as essentialist in its own way, and just as blind to differences in cultures and societies as was the androcentric model. The absolute division of labor by sex was taken for granted, argued on the basis of women as child-rearers (e.g. Brown 1970, 1975). Women were mothers, so they simply had to do the mothering—as mothering is defined in the present. As Gerda Lerner expressed it, "[M]y point here is the *necessity* which created the initial division of labor by which women do the mothering" (1986:40). Although this argument seemed persuasive to many women at the time it was written, it too has been demonstrated to be untenable and essentialist.

These unacceptably reductionist formulations began to be critiqued by feminists, sometimes with equally reductionist results. One important "origin" for feminists was the origin of "women's oppression," perceived to be universal in both the present and the recent past. When some feminists argued that women were not everywhere subjugated (e.g. Leacock 1978, Rosaldo 1980), the time frame of women's oppression shifted, transmuted into a popular feminist view that all societies had evolved from egalitarian beginnings. Again, Lerner summarizes this point of view: "There are a few facts of which we can be certain on the basis of archaeological evidence. Sometime during the agricultural revolution relatively egalitarian societies with a sexual division of labor based on biological necessity gave way to more highly structured societies in which both private property and the exchange of women based on incest taboos and exogamy were common" (1986:53).

Eleanor Leacock's arguments were not evolutionary; she did not demand that all societies follow any particular trajectory. She was more interested in understanding the changes caused by western contact. She wrote, "[T]he historical dimension [of the origins of women's oppression] requires that the myth of the 'ethnographic present' be totally eradicated, and that anthropologists deal fully with the fact that the structure of gender relations among the people they study does not follow from pre-capitalist production relations as such, but from the ways in which these have been affected by particular histories of colonization" (1983:263). She did not believe that equality was inevitable in precapitalist societies, but rather that equal treatment depended on equal contributions to production: "The egalitarian relations that obtained in most foraging and many horticultural societies around the world at the time of European expansion rested on the fact that all mature individuals participated directly in the full process of production" (1983:266).

Michelle Rosaldo, a pioneer of feminist anthropology, originally focused on the roots of women's oppression (1974), though she later revised her views about the universality of that oppression. "To look for origins is, in the end, to think that what we are today is something other than the product of our history and our present social world, and, more particularly, that our gender systems are primordial, transhistorical and essentially unchanging

73

in their roots" (1980:20). If the search for origins is not always a pernicious way of bolstering present practices, it is still a useless one. Matt Cartmill debunked the whole notion:

> People who study human origins sometimes claim that their investigations will shed new light on human culture and so help us to understand ourselves and predict the future. But this is wishful thinking. A thing is what it is, no matter how it got to be that way; and human appetites and impulses are what they are, no matter where or what we came from. Knowing their history adds nothing. If it were proved tomorrow that people evolved from cottontails instead of apes, we would still prefer bananas to clover as an ingredient in pie. (1983:65, quoted in Landau 1991)

The process of pursuing origins research as a path to success in archaeology has also been critiqued, pointing out the career-enhancing effect of the successful claim to "ownership" of the origin of anything by the person (usually male) who establishes the claim most effectively. Martin Wobst and Arthur Keene perceived origins research as having the shape of a cone, in which the controller of the point of the cone has the "political economy" of the academic game well in hand. The archaeologist with the earliest site of a given kind becomes the researcher who must be cited, the basic authority on the subject, the person in control of the knowledge on this topic. This is even more effective than quoting circles, because even those outside the circle have no choice but to refer back to the controller of the point of knowledge, who has become the gatekeeper (Wobst and Keene 1983). Margaret Conkey, appropriating this powerful (in several meanings) metaphor, remarks that,

> It is not surprising that those subjects that are at the points—early "man," tools, fire, agriculture, the family, the state—are fertile grounds for territorial and competitive practice. . . . The successful competitor in the territoriality of origins research can have wide-spread impact upon the public and can be attributed with superhuman powers. (1991:113)

A number of recent papers have analyzed the bias of origins research (Conkey with Williams 1991, Dobres 1988, Lloyd 1993), which has often been exposed as both racist and sexist. These topics deserve even closer scrutiny. Categories of particular interest to gender studies include primate research applied to models of human evolution, Paleolithic art, origins of the state, and the evolution of gender hierarchies.

Primate Research: Our Own Reflection

Nonhuman primates—monkeys and apes in particular—have been used as stand-ins for early hominids, to speculate about the origins of human culture. Both in the laboratory and in the wild, nonhuman primates have been used to explain "human nature" and to speculate about the origins of human culture. Since apes are our nearest phylogenetic relatives, and by definition don't have culture, the assumption is made that through them and other nonhuman primates, we can perceive a precultural human condition, or understand what human beings would have been like on the verge of becoming human. From the very beginning, primate research had a sexist agenda. Early work in the Yerkes primate laboratory has been exposed as androcentric both in the language used to describe chimpanzee behavior as well as the assumptions behind the ascription of "dominance" to the males and of soliciting sex to the females, and in the very emphasis on dominance itself. Josie, the chimpanzee so charmingly "interviewed" by Ruth Herschberger, explains,

> When Jack takes over the food chute, the report calls it his "natural dominance." When *I* do, it's "privilege"—conferred by him. If you humans could get enough perspective on your language, you'd find it as much fun as a zoo. While I'm up there lording it over the food chute, the investigator writes down "the male temporarily defers to her and allows her to act as if dominant over him." Can't I get any satisfaction out of life that isn't allowed to me by some male chimp? Damn it! (1940:11)

Observing primates in the wild was heralded as an advance that would improve the validity of these studies. While it is true that new and previously unimagined troop structures were observed, they were described in language more appropriate to human groups than nonhuman primates—the anthropomorphizing was vivid. Baboon behavior became the model for hominids, with ranking among males from alpha to omega (if there were enough of them in a troop) and "dominant" males lording it over "harems" (implying subservience, lassitude, and sexual servitude) of females. The lesser males were reduced to being "sentinels" for the troop (e.g. DeVore and Washburn

1963). These caricatures of human life made easy targets for feminists. Susan Sperling, in an article delightfully entitled "Baboons with Briefcases vs. Langurs in Lipstick," begins by reminding us that "studies of monkeys and apes have never been just about monkeys and apes. . . . In the Western imagination, primates are now central to the iconography of the human past, including the meanings of sexual divisions in human societies" (1991:204).

Primates are in contention in the constructionist versus essentialist debate in social science, and right in the thick of it is sociobiology, which assumes that behavioral patterns are programmed in the genes and can be explained by reproductive success. "Recent critiques in evolutionary theory challenge reductionist-adaptionist models that collapse variation into theories of male and female reproductive strategies" (Sperling 1991:225). However, the reproductive success of dominant males is not established (Fedigan 1986), and some evidence exists that the "friendly" male primates may in fact sire more offspring (Wright 1993). Even among chimpanzees, the alpha male doesn't always win the gene wars. In the Gombe Reserve, Tanzania, a middle-ranking male, Evered, "turned his attention elsewhere and became quite popular with the females; he was sought after as a consort. Goodall estimates that a large proportion of chimpanzees born in the last ten years at Gombe were probably sired by Evered" (Zihlman 1991:8).

The very use of living primates as models of human evolution needs to be questioned. Sperling takes women primatologists and sociobiologists to task as well as men holding those titles: "The new female primate is dressed for success and lives in a troop that resembles the modern corporation: now everyone gets to eat power lunches on the savannah" (1991:218). Patricia Wright also critiques the simplistic use of primate data for modeling early hominid behavior. She perceives the writing of the present into the past as "corporation type" males whose origins had to be found; their roots were discovered in primate history. The problem, she believes, was a limited data base. "The simple fact that evolutionary pressures act on both males and females was ignored. . . ." In spite of the traditional emphasis on males, "females play an important role in structuring primate societies" (1993:127–128). In studying lemurs and other primate troops, she found not just one pattern but many variations of female "dominance." One of her observations of great interest to mothers of small children in our own society concerned the division of infant care, which in some primate groups is a largely male occupation. A scenario of hominid evolution based on male care of infants would look quite different from baboon "harems." Perhaps it would throw a different light on human child care. It is interesting to note Wright's observation that male care of infants is not associated with female "dominance." The emphasis on dominance itself is perhaps a last vestige of androcentric thinking in standard primatology. What other important relationships might be missed, one wonders, while "dominance" is being studied?

Another feature that Wright shows to be unrelated to dominance is relative size, especially when expressed as sexual dimorphism, markedly different sizes of males and females. Wright's studies show that bigger is not necessarily better, nor more dominant. In fact, she found that "no simple selective pressure emerges that explains the dominance of one sex over the other in any society" (1993:140). It is also suggestive for human origins that while subsistence pursuits have no division of labor—it's every primate for, well, herself!—yet "gender hierarchies with both males and females higher in the society or equal have been documented." Wright found that females could be dominant in several ways: vocalizing, leading, or arriving first at the food trees. Wright concludes that "the data . . . should convince us that the evolution of primate behavior has no simple explanation" (1993:138).

However, the story of the meat-eating male chimpanzee, and by extension the early male hominid, who "provisions" females (another androcentric concept) for the sake of leaving his genes in the future gene pool, appears to have won the hearts of too many males to be allowed to die. One version has females as agents in this transaction: they barter sex for food (shades of Josie!) and protection for their young (Fisher 1982). The title of Helen Fisher's book detailing this story tells it all: *The Sex Contract*. Here we have a just-so story about the origins of the "oldest profession."

A slightly different version of Male-as-Meat-Provider has recently appeared in the central journal of American anthropology, *American Anthropologist* (Stanford 1996). The author acknowledges that most observed meat eaten by chimpanzees in the wild has been acquired by scavenging rather than by hunting. However, Craig Stanford proposes that the chimpanzees he reports really do hunt. To do this he must define hunting, and the process reveals the not-so-latent hero story: these chimps cooperated in dangerous activities, and furthermore shared food. New data are said to include the amount of meat eaten by chimps plus the fact that it is mostly males who do the eating. He alleges that acquisition of the meat is done cooperatively in "dangerous activities" and "intentionally" by males. The danger is clearly part of the myth, for the assertion that it is dangerous is not backed up with any set of data. Are these small monkeys more likely to do any damage to the chimpanzees than would the fruit that is the major source of food? Meat is still only a small part of the diet of these chimpanzees. Mammal food is consumed in only 1 to 3 percent of the time spent feeding. Furthermore, Stanford ignores female protein acquisition, having defined as not-hunting such activities as termiting, as well as provisioning themselves with other insects and even small animals—behaviors well documented in female chimps (Zihlman 1993). Stanford fails to account for the female hunting of larger animals, which he admits occurs, but "rarely"—for only male hunting demands explanation, since in this scenario it is *their* genes for hunting that are needed to expand the gene pool. Females need only passively accept male's genes.

Stanford asserts that "[m]ost kills are by . . . males hunting in groups," yet his own description of these events does not suggest that the groups were deliberately "hunting" until they came across a tree containing colobus monkeys. "Hunts of red colobus frequently involve planning of execution; typically the hunters, in the course of plant food foraging, encounter a tree holding colobus and scan the tree crown for desired victims" (1996:98). How, one wonders, is this different from scanning a fruit tree for fruit? The only obvious difference is that the monkeys are mobile. He has not made the case for hunting, though he uses loaded words, such as *predators* and *prey*. Both males and females kill "prey" animals. Are they any more "prey" than the fruit, or does simply being animal rather than vegetable make them prey? In the latter case, termites and grubs are also "prey."

Although the reader is not told exactly how the group cooperates in the hunt, assertions of intentionality abound, such as "planning of execution" and "decision-making element"—even though one chimp's impulse to chase the monkeys might simply trigger another to chase them too, like fish in a feeding frenzy. Another possibility is that a chimp won't attempt to catch the mobile "prey" without another chimp to head it off. This kind of "cooperation" may be in the eye of the beholder. How would it look different if this behavior were simply prompted by each chimp's merely trying to catch a monkey? Stanford acknowledges this problem: "It often appears to observers that Gombe hunters are pursuing selfish individual hunts simultaneously" (1996:100) and his own description suggests to me that those observers are correct. But in a way it is irrelevant, for there is no indication that meat eating is an ancient chimpanzee behavior. It has been suggested that meat eating among the chimpanzees could be an effect of restriction of resources, caused by encroaching human groups (Sperling 1991:223), though this critique is not addressed.

Adrienne Zihlman (1993) and Zihlman and Nancy Tanner (1978) have shown that the anthropomorphizing of nonhuman primates has a barely concealed androcentric agenda, and indeed Craig Stanford's conclusions bear this out. He finds similar patterns between Pliocene hominids and chimpanzees, notably that "the capture, possession, and control of meat were used by males for their own political and reproductive benefits" (1996:108). His conclusions go *far* beyond his evidence. The assumption that hunting confers an advantage on males in mate selection underlies the rationalization of the chimpanzee behavior as "hunting," though no evidence is presented to support this. It has been observed that females get meat only if they are present at the kill. Presumably they helped kill the animals (the chimps are involved in "cooperative" hunting) and are simply entitled to their share, rather than having it conferred on them (for sexual favors or anything else). Furthermore, if it is usually estrous females who are feeding with the males, perhaps they are accompanying the males for sex in the first place, and not for meat. Linda Fedigan (1986:58) notes Zihlman's attempts to include all available data in her gathering model, rather than limiting it to fossils or primates, "and yet her interpretation of early hominid life has received no more attention from the paleoanthropologists than other less 'data-based' models."

Stanford has presented the same tired old arguments, and he may well have the causality backward. "That captors do in fact enjoy advanced mating success . . . has not yet been tested against copulation data surrounding meat-eating episodes" (1996:101). But he goes on to draw the standard sociobiological conclusions nevertheless. He further speculates: "The implication of this behavior [stealing meat by the alpha male] is that meat sharing and the mating behavior associated with it [he mentioned earlier that this is not tested, yet here it becomes a fact] fall within the arena of dominance and add more ways in which dominance among male chimpanzees may be exerted" (1996:106). The behavior described seems more like that which Barbara Bender has called "opportunistic sharing" (1987:86) than activities on which a whole school of hunting enthusiasts would want to rest their case.

The scholarly debate engaged in by Stanford in this article is in fact not with feminists or the Woman-the-Gatherer model, but instead with Lewis Binford and the scavenging model; Stanford does not engage the feminist critique of the hunting hypothesis at all, even after a quarter of a century of circulation of these ideas.

Margaret Conkey notes that underneath these generalizations lies the "fundamental and unquestioned assumption—and object—of knowledge—that there is a gender-based division of labor (man-the-hunter/woman-the-gatherer) in early hominid life (some 2 million years ago!), a specific division of labor that is then taken as an *essential* feature of human social life" (1991:127). It also assumes that the division of labor is absolute—an untenable position.

As Donna Haraway reminds us, the studies of nonhuman primates not only reflect but also *construct* our social reality. "The biosocial sciences have not simply been sexist mirrors of our own social world. They have also been tools in the reproduction of that world, both in supplying legitimating ideologies and in enhancing material power" (1983:127). She suggests a remedy: "[O]ne of the first steps has been to switch the focus from primates as models of human beings to a deeper look at the animals themselves— how they live and relate to their environments in ways that may have little to do with us" (p. 137).

Much sociobiology is based on primate studies, and uses assumptions about genes to generate statements about the human past. Sociobiology tends to be extremely reductionist in its gendered scenarios. Val Woodward suggests that the gene is only a metaphor, and that the scenarios are "guessing-game relationships between genes and phenotypes" rather than any kind of science (1994:48–49). For example, she quotes Gould and Gould: "What aspects of the hunting our male ancestors must have perfected would select for a more dichotomous brain, in which spatial and analytical functions are kept separate? What requirements of the gathering our female forebearers [sic] practiced might favor a more integrated mind? . . ." It is easy to see how these questions are "presentist." Thus primate stories, like Kipling's *Just So Stories,* are often "just-so" stories of the human past, intended to prove that present gender arrangements are inevitable.

"Early Man" Studies, and the Absence of "Early Woman"

One of the most androcentric fields of archaeological study is stone tools, the older the better. Joan Gero (1993) uses the view of science as constructed, to deconstruct the androcentrism of Paleoindian studies, often still called "Early Man" research—in spite of multiple objections. This is an origin story because the projectile points are constructed as a "First"—they are evidence of the First Americans. "Early Man" is jealously guarded territory. Few women have engaged in the archaeology of America's earliest inhabitants (Gero 1993:32) though a notable exception was Marie Wormington (1957). Gero demonstrates that Paleoindian studies analyze various practices, including technological, literary, and social ones, that maintain the boundaries and preserve the exclusivity of the territory.

In terms of technology, bifacial stone tools glossed as "projectile points" are all-important, and, to judge from most of the publications, the hunting of big game seems to be the only occupation of these early occupants of the Americas. The fluted point, presumed dispatcher of "big game" animals, defines the Paleoindian. Besides its association with large hunted animals, the fluted point is also admired because of the technical difficulty of its manufacture. Several men have devoted a considerable fraction of their research time to learning how to replicate these stone objects.

It is mostly males who replicate and experimentally use these artifacts, especially points. "It is fascinating—or embarrassing—to observe the very fine line between male replicative science and macho-drama; shooting arrows into newly killed and (very importantly!) still warm boar strung up in wooden frames . . . illustrates a particularly lurid kind of research design in which only males participate"(Gero 1993:37).

Gero notes that little interest has been shown in defining regional or temporal differences of the Clovis "hunters." "The constructed universality of the Paleo-phenomenon, despite the lack of a fine-grained chronology, provided the classic origin story for all American peoples that the almost exclusively male archaeologists could study everywhere in the country . . . Paleo-man is an earliest common denominator, a base-line of American technological prowess and ecological efficiency" (1993:35). Several sites in South America suggest that there are problems with this time line, and they show the difficulty with the homogeneous view of "Early Man" in the Americas. But earlier and different sites are consistently debunked by establishment males, as are the excavators scorned, perhaps a bit more viciously if they happen to be women. The list of possible pre-Clovis sites in South America is in fact quite impressive, though most of them have been challenged, on various grounds (Roosevelt et al. 1996).

Not only are vegetal food sources ignored, but meat is the focus of inquiry only when it is bleeding—freshly killed or butchered. Preparation and cooking of meat, or utilization of the nonfood parts of the animals, tend to be neglected (Gifford-Gonzalez 1993). One wonders if it is uninteresting because it is "women's work" to cook food, tan hides, and make clothing. Heroes hunt, they do not cook, though after the hunt they may sit around the campfire telling tall tales.

Patterns of exclusion in professional networks keep the presence of both women archaeologists and Paleoindian women to a minimum, especially in publications. In both lithic studies and faunal analysis the work women are believed to do is marginalized. Noting the difference between Paleoindian archaeology, where few women are permitted, and historic archaeology with half of its practitioners women, Joan Gero asks, "Why are women allowed to play in the shallow pits of the past but not to penetrate the more limited resources of early time?" (1993:38). This is actually a "hierarchy of labor," not a division of labor, in which those in the hierarchy with the power and prestige to enforce it are at the "point of origin" that controls the topic.

Gendering the European Paleolithic

"Cave Man" is a notion in popular culture that has had several manifestations. Among them are Alley Oop, Fred Flintstone, and many Gary Larson "Far Side" cartoons. The cave man carries a large club and drags cave women around by the hair. How does it happen that this brute also produced cave art? It is necessary to shift gears and admire the artistic skill of Cave Man, while preserving his qualities as hunting hero and leader of the tribe (or at least the family).

Paleolithic art was gendered from the beginning by the French researchers who first reported it, who assumed without question that it was made by males, for male purposes. They were particularly captivated by the female figurines, though the imposing animals painted on cave walls and ceilings also fired their imaginations. Several explanations for this explosion of painted images have been championed. Some experts have seen them as art for art's sake, others as hunting magic, still others as fertility magic (Bahn and Vertut 1988). That it was either just art, or just doodlings, seems equally unlikely. The notion that the paintings were created for "hunting magic" is the commonest explanation in the vast literature on the painted caves, repeated as if it were a magical incantation by most text books. Paul Bahn has shown in detail the fallacy of most interpretations of hunting associated with the cave art. Assertions that animals are depicted as wounded, or bleeding, or full of projectiles, turn out to have other possible explanations, given the most free-ranging interpretation.

The underlying gender assumption is that *men and only men* were the hunters, as well as the artists. When some smallish heel prints, small enough to be clearly not those of adult men, were found in the back of several caves, the impressions were described as resulting from a dance—one in which boys were being initiated. This clearly assumes that only males were permitted in the deep recesses of the cave (because it is hunting magic, and women aren't allowed, or because prehistoric women were afraid of the dark . . . or of mice . . . or of spiders), though the smaller feet could just as well have belonged to females and represented girls or women dancing at their *own* ceremonies at the back of the cave. Artists' reconstructions in the Time-Life series *The Emergence of Man* [sic] make these assumptions visible, with a bearded man doing the painting in one illustration, and only men and boys present at a ceremony in another. The caption of the latter illustration is revealing: "In a cave's deepest recess, elders supervise an initiation rite that confers the privileges and duties of adulthood on six boys. An essential part of the ceremony is the frightening passage through dark tunnels to reach the sacred painted chamber" (Prideaux 1973:32–33). One wants to inquire if the passage was so frightening that women and girls were excluded by sheer terror. It presents a picture of rather timid Upper Paleolithic women, who must have had to confront rather larger and more real terrors, such as cave bears and snakes.

As for fertility magic, much of what has been described as depictions of copulation and birth in animals is "wishful thinking" (Bahn and Vertut 1988:160). André Leroi-Gourhan has suggested that the paintings are permeated with references to sex (1967:144–148), and vulvas are seen everywhere (1967:123). These are still more fantasies of human sexuality.

The point is not that art has never been correctly gendered, but rather that explanations of the Upper Paleolithic art have been mindlessly gendered, according to Victorian norms and ideals. It is time to ask new questions rather than assert old answers. In actuality, an impartial gendering of Paleolithic art has yet to be done. Barbara Bender notes the "increasing exclusiveness of cave art" (1987:91). More and more kinds of artifacts are highly decorated, which she suggests may reflect a differential access to social knowledge. She argues that it might be women who are excluded, though she offers only possible hunting rituals as a reason for this guess, which seems to be circular reasoning. Nevertheless, this kind of reasoning will move us farther than merely engendering the cave art with present prejudices.

Conclusions

Origins narratives are typical *Just So* stories. The holders of various androcentric versions of origins are unwilling to let them go in spite of the evidence to the contrary, because they fit so satisfyingly into their world view.

To return to Martin Wobst and Arthur Keene, origins research provides us with an explanation for the success of sweeping evolutionary schemes in all branches of anthropology. "Origins research is so pervasive today, and has been so pervasive in our discipline, because of its superb fit with the political economy within and beyond the niche which archaeologists occupy" (1983:83). The origins game is clearly one of power and prestige, in which gender plays an enormous role.

CHAPTER FIVE

GENDER AND
THE DIVISION OF LABOR

It is assumed in American middle-class culture that childrearing is a full-time occupation, with young children thought to be best cared for at home by their mothers . . . These attitudes are generally assumed to obtain in all societies. It is clear, however, that childbearing and rearing are not the defining features of women's lives universally.
—Susan Carol Rogers (1978:135)

The female [hominid] had to accept her role as a kind of prison warden, jailed as much as her troublesome offspring by the infant's slow-growing brain.
—Robert Ardrey (1976:82)

What work women and men do as a consequence of their gender roles in various societies, and how particular tasks may be gendered or not, are often treated as if they were straightforward, even obvious. In fact these are vexing and difficult topics. Cultural anthropology has been as much a hindrance as a help, with its universalizing tendencies regarding women's roles and activities as mothers, and with men's roles and activities, though more varied, nevertheless stereotyped. Thus ethnographic analogies, if they are not used with extreme care, may lead down blind alleys.

Two linked assumptions have prevented archaeologists from perceiving gendered work in prehistoric sites. The first is that the category "women" means mothers and that all women are limited to their mothering role, therefore their work must be compatible with child care, that is to say, safe

Presumption #1
women's work vs. men's work

for children and easily interruptible (Brown 1970, 1975). Women's work, runs the argument, tends to be repetitive and dull, the same the world over, and studying it would not be productive or interesting (e.g. Posposil 1963). Out of sheer disdain for women's work, the male establishment has concentrated on what they imagine men do (everything that is active, heroic, and fun), and as a result women's work may be either overlooked in the archaeological record or attributed to men.

Presumption #2

The second assumption is even more pernicious—that the division of labor is absolute: if men do it, women can't, or don't, or are prohibited from doing it, and vice versa. G. P. Murdock, creator of the Human Relations Area Files, places this division of labor in the beginning of humanness, in hunting and gathering societies, and asserts that it is biologically determined (1949:7). Furthermore, according to Murdock, all hunter-gatherers are believed to be alike: "There is a strikingly uniform division of labor in hunter-gatherer societies. The women gather, the men hunt" (1968:335). This is a perfect example of gender polarization. All tasks are perceived as divided into men's work and women's work. Women replace the toilet-paper roll and men take out the garbage. It is not surprising that with such authoritative statements, this division of labor is easily projected onto archaeological sites. An example of a recent overgeneralization about Korean Neolithic sites reads, "on the whole, pottery vessels were stored in the inner recesses of the dwelling where the females performed their functions, while implements for outdoor use were left near the entrance, the living space occupied by male members of the household" (Li 1992:10–12). This is simply inaccurate regarding the placement of the pots on most excavated dwelling floors (Li is a historian, not an archaeologist), and "inner recesses" are not very far inside in houses that cover only 12 to 35 square feet. Yet this glib statement passes as a proper description of gender roles in the Korean Neolithic, and I have heard it repeated as gospel on more than one occasion.

Middle-class post–industrial revolution concepts seem to be unconsciously at work here—the men go out of the house to their work (hunting or trading or preparing the fields, for example) while women stay at home by the hearth, caring for the children. Of course, societies in which women spend all their time at home are rare, and endless counter-examples could be cited in the past as well as the present (Boserup 1970, Rogers 1978,

Leacock 1978, Oakley 1974). But the myth persists, with amazing perti- nacity. Thus, proclaiming excavated artifacts as related to male or female tasks is believed to solve the whole problem of discovering gender in archaeology, even on the occasion when a problem is perceived. Attributing the jobs to a gender is accomplished; there is nothing further that is deemed important about gendered work.

Gendered work is often explained by motherhood, though this logic is questionable. Not every woman becomes a mother, and tending children is not necessarily limited to females, nor is infant care the exclusive task of the biological mother. Even women who *do* give birth and care for their own children are not tied to child care throughout their adult lives. The division of labor based on child care as a misleading and even pernicious concept will be revisited after examining some archaeological examples of women at work.

Ethnographic details confirm that women make significant contribu- tions to the world's work in the present, but because the kind of work women do is frequently not *paid* labor in capitalist societies, it is often discounted and may not even be seen as work. This was highlighted for me when, in the middle 1970s, I was asked to give a public lecture for Colorado Women's History Week on "Women's Work in Other Cultures," as the token anthropologist/archaeologist in a series of lectures on women's work in history. As I set about to outline the kinds of work that women do around the world, documented by as many ethnographies as I could digest, I discovered that few tasks can be named that women *don't* do, in one society or another. The often-quoted ditty "Man may work from sun to sun, but woman's work is never done" appears to be a world-wide phenomenon, possibly excepting leisured classes, where some of women's (and men's) activities may not be productive labor, although that could be argued.

It is critical to understand that the bulk of the maintenance work in many societies is done by women. The preparation of food and the clean-up afterward; the construction and maintenance of clothing; the care of children, the sick, and the elderly; even the construction of dwellings and their repair and cleaning—all are construed as women's work in many societies. In addition, women do much of the subsistence work. In forager societies, women gather most of the plant food eaten by the group and often much of the smaller animal food such as shellfish, as well as helping in the collection of animals hunted communally, for example rabbits. In horticultural and agricultural societies women plant, weed, and harvest crops. But because the western definition of work is attached to participating in the paid labor force, daily maintenance does not count as work when calculating Gross Domestic Product, unless a salary is attached. Thus, when a woman in American culture is asked, "Do you work?" this is understood to mean "Do you earn a salary?" and all her labor directed to children and family, her attention to food and crafts and cleanliness, is thereby disparaged and declared not real work. The work women do around the world becomes invisible, or at best unimportant (Nielsen 1990:8).

paid vs. maintenance work

In middle-class western cultures, women's work is often presented as "only" supportive, not creative work. But women also create. Most women in preindustrial societies make their own tools to fashion the objects they need, and many products made by women are highly decorated whether the artifacts are pottery or baskets or cloth or houses or ornaments. In the hands of collectors these become prized possessions, yet their makers are rarely esteemed as artists.

artists

This common attitude toward women's work as uncreative is often applied to prehistory, resulting in the invisibility or trivializing of the work women do, no matter how important it may have been to the society being studied. Women's work is also often assumed to be dull, and to have low prestige value, because this is the case in the West. Women were believed not to have any "technology," only craft skills, because technology meant tools and tools meant males (McGaw 1996). New studies of "women's work" by women are beginning to draw out many facets of women's technologies in basketry, pottery, clothing, and even stone tool-making. Aspects of women's products can reveal facets of social structure as well, and demonstrate the possibility of throwing light on gender in the past.

technology

Engendering work in the past takes women's work as seriously as men's work, and allows a more complex sense of how various kinds of work interdigitate, as well as the way work assignments may shift depending on circumstances.

Observations are dependent on expectations (Nelson and Kehoe 1990). A particularly telling (although ungendered) example is discussed by James Schoenwetter (1990), in which he follows the divergent logic of two kinds of evidence as they lead to different archaeological conclusions about the same site. Schoenwetter details the ways conclusions about the site of Guila Naquitz in Mexico are different depending on whether palynological or archaeological evidence is given preference. The same kind of binocular vision needs to be applied to gendered prehistoric work. "Powers of observation" are sharpened and narrowed by hypotheses and by attention to newly relevant data. Although is it possible to recognize entirely new phenomena, the more subtle aspects of women's work are easy to overlook under the present dominant paradigm with its emphasis on stone tool-making, hunting, and heavy butchering as not only exclusively male activities but also the most important research topics. It is necessary to bear in mind that "observation is a dialectic between expectation and recognition" (Kehoe 1990a:23) and not "the facts" clamoring to be discovered and understood.

James Benedict excavated a site in the Colorado mountains that he identified as a location where women performed their work. The activities implied by the artifacts recovered were quite varied. It is worth quoting the last two sentences of the abstract in full, to see gender stereotyping at work (which may be accurate in a given case, even though it is still a stereotype).

> Throughout its history the site is thought to have served as a women's work area—a pleasant slope, not far from camp, where plant or animal foods were bulk processed using grinding tools and large ovens, bones were broken for marrow and to make single hide-working implements, skins were tanned, clothing was sewn, and other domestic tasks were performed. No evidence was found of activities traditionally attributed to males, such as hunting, initial butchering, or weapons manufacture and repair. (1993:1)

Benedict suggests that this is a site where men's work is invisible. But note that, although the activities are called "domestic tasks," they were in fact performed outside, although "not far from camp." Women are perceived as constrained to stay near camp, although the camp itself is believed to have been moved fairly frequently. Women, who presumably have ranged through the entire territory, are nonetheless conceptualized as tethered to the home base, like domesticated animals.

The Womankind Museum (a short-lived anthropological museum at the University of Denver devoted to women around the world, which I created in 1983 but was unable to sustain), in its sole exhibit, examined questions of women's domestic labor: creative work that occurs inside the house. The exhibit, called "Working Within Walls, the Products of Women's Labor," took place in 1984. Because of financial constraints the exhibit contained only items from the anthropological collections at the University of Denver. As we[1] considered which objects to include in the exhibit, few artifacts in the collections had to be ruled out, as made outside the home or probably made by men. While most of the objects exhibited were collected from living societies, a few archaeological artifacts, especially baskets and pots, were so visually interesting they clamored to be included. This was an "aha!" experience for me, revealing the archaeological implications of an emphasis on women's work. Other work by women archaeologists in museums and elsewhere leads to similar conclusions about the visual and artistic importance of women's artifacts, as well as their contribution to the economic system. Contrast this perspective with the assessment of G. P. Murdock, who disparages these artifacts, "when these societies [hunter-gatherers] fish, the men manage the more complex techniques; while the women do basketry, fishing, gather shellfish, etc." (1968:335). The nature of "more complex techniques" is left unspecified, but it is clear that basketry, among other things women do, is not complex in his view.

Taking it upon themselves to look more closely at technologies from a number of standpoints, several archaeologists have examined various facets of women's work in different contexts, and their publications demonstrate the variety of women's economic contributions both within and between cultures. Results of these studies are at the least encouraging, and sometimes even revolutionary in increasing the power of archaeological interpretations.

Early critiques of archaeology noted the emphasis on (presumed) men's work—such as hunting and stone tool-making, as in *Man the Toolmaker* (Oakley 1959) and *Man the Hunter* (Lee and DeVore 1968)—but it was often said that was because stone and bone were the main artifacts left, while

---

1. The exhibit was created by Jenny Younger and me, with the help of Helen Pustmueller and, in an early stage, Jill Newmark.

women's artifacts and the results of their collecting were perishable. The problem of "finding" women was considered to be too great. Women's work was declared to be invisible in the archaeological record, since it was assumed that women made only perishable artifacts and collected perishable plants. On closer inspection, this is not the problem at all (Kornfeld and Francis 1991). It stems instead from the underlying western assumption about what work is, and the notion that *work as so defined is gendered male.*

In the following sections of this chapter, both critiques of the ways gender has been applied to work in the past and substantive engendering of specific sites are discussed. Topics include tool-makers, gatherers, farmers, potters, and weavers.

Tool-Makers: The Critique

Stone tools have been a major preoccupation of the prehistoric archaeologist. In fact, "considerations of activities other than tool-making [in the Pleistocene] tended to become a minor, semi-disrespectable adjunct to the interpretation of selected artifacts" (Isaac 1968:253–254). This is a startling admission from a researcher who was in the thick of Pleistocene archaeology. Stone tools above all are regarded as a masculine invention, and stone knapping is presumed to be a male occupation, even when no gender attribution is made. It is the tacit norm, against which women's nonknapping activities are measured, created by the androcentric lens that sees what men do as normal. Among archaeologists, it is men who learn how to replicate stone tools, who are interested in the details of the technology, as Joan Gero (1991a) so forcefully calls to our attention. When tool-making is the topic, it is almost always exclusively stone tools that are under consideration, especially patterned tools and those that require preparation of a core for their manufacture.

Indeed, tools for collecting and transporting are not seen as tools at all, but as "containers," clearly a kind of Freudian allocation of such things to women, not-too-subtly representing wombs and referencing women as mothers. This has even been transformed in popular culture as symbols representing men and women, for instance *The Chalice and the Blade* (Eisler 1976), the chalice being the container representing women and the blade (both tool and weapon) standing for men. This kind of reductionist thinking about men's and women's tools and products is no doubt seductive, but it makes the particularities of gendered prehistoric life not only elusive but irrelevant. Using this reductionist perspective, it will not be possible to discern the real women who used real knives, as women do today, to chop their cabbage and mince their meat, or for many other kinds of "daily" tasks. The notion that men don't use containers is odd, too; what about creels for fishing gear, tool boxes, golf bags? Didn't prehistoric men need quivers for their arrows, bags for food provisions, a container for bright bits of stone that might be chipped later, as they went about their heroic hunting tasks? Consider the "Ice Man" who was found with his normally perishable containers intact (Spindler 1994). A female buried in Australia, with good preservation, similarly demonstrates that women also needed both tools and containers (Ellender 1993). The dichotomies produced by our language and our categories tend to obfuscate what could be learned about the prehistoric past, thus preventing us from encountering the variety left by the actual users of the tools.

Joan Gero has elaborated this theme in two publications, one on stone tool production in general (1991a) and one specifically addressing Paleoindian research (1993), which has already been discussed. As she demonstrates with well-chosen examples, the assumption that men are makers of all stone tools is inherent in most treatments of tool-making. "Man the Tool-Maker" cannot be "Woman the Tool-Maker," although making tools has been one of the characteristics used to define "man" as opposed to animals—at least, until it was discovered that chimpanzees made tools for termiting, and female chimps at that.

Woman-the-Maker-of-Stone-Tools in ethnographic reports and in archaeology was not so difficult to detect when the effort was made. For example, when ethnographies and ethnohistorical accounts of aboriginal Australia were consulted, women as tool-makers and tool users were ubiquitous in all environments, and in all regions of Australia (Bird 1993), as well as the Andaman Islands (Gorman 1995). The question of what counts as "hunting" comes into play here (Wadley 1997) just as it did in primate studies. Women in aboriginal Australia used "weapons," specially valorized and often highly decorated objects, the purpose of which was killing animals and sometimes people. The evidence amassed by Caroline Bird shows that in aboriginal Australia, women frequently killed small animals for food, and sometimes hunted larger animals such as kangaroos; in addition, they were important participants in communal hunts. Bird demonstrates that women making and using stone and wooden tools are neither an aberration nor a regional or isolated phenomenon. In several Australian locations, women made wooden tools such as digging sticks and fighting sticks for their own use. Some women made wooden bowls, while others finished bowls roughed out by men by grinding them with rough stone. The wood-working tools, often hatchets, were made of stone, as were the knives used for various tasks such as cutting meat and severing a newborn infant's umbilical cord. Women used stone hatchets for collecting food such as honey, grubs, and small animals. They also gathered adhesive materials, and in some cases stone and wood for making tools. Women fashioned their own ritual objects for ceremonies. Women were even observed helping to manufacture spears. These events were not recorded as unusual, or in any way surprising, but simply as activities women had been seen doing.

As we have noted, the tools that have been most highly valorized in archaeology are weapons. These include objects from stone spear tips of Paleolithic Europe to bronze and iron swords of Korea and Japan. Bifaces identified as projectile points are first and foremost, supposedly used for warfare and hunting tasks believed to be carried out only by men. These artifacts are admired for the skill needed for production, the adaptation to their presumed purposes, and often for their esthetic qualities as well. Other shapes of stone tools are given the names of objects that might be in a contemporary tool box: "knife," "hammer," "axe," "graver," implying functions from the shapes of the tools.

In standard archaeological reports these pieces of worked stone are sorted by their patterned shapes, now labeled tools, enumerated in tables by their functional names, and illustrated, often with both drawings and photographs. At one time pieces of stone not perceived as patterned tools were not even collected, although it is present practice to collect everything whether it is considered "diagnostic" or not. After patterned artifacts have been located, sorted, categorized, and counted, the leftovers are "amorphous" flakes with evidence of wear, but without pattern and of unknown specific use. These stones fall into a category generally called "utilized flakes," and characteristically little else is done with them. Use/wear analysis on such flakes shows that they may have had a number of functions, like prehistoric Swiss Army knives, but they are surely tools (Gero 1991a:165).

Joan Gero argues that women in prehistory must have been tool-makers, for they would have needed sharp flakes to carry out a number of their tasks, and it seems unreasonable to suppose that they would have waited for a man to produce them, like a 1950s girl waiting for her date to open the car door.

The archaeologists' preference for specific shapes, for retouched and preferably bifaces and symmetrical tools rather than amorphous flakes, reflects a concern with typology, more often for the purpose of differentiating sites, as in the French Paleolithic (e.g. Bordes 1968), but sometimes, as Joan Gero (1993) demonstrates for the Paleoindian artifacts known as Clovis points, the typology is instead used for the purpose of showing that over a wide area and time span the sites are all the same! In either case, flakes are deemed to have no value in typological studies, though other information may be gleaned from them. This is one of the many instances in which a gendered prehistory changes the focus of research by calling standardized categories into question and requiring attention to previously unnoticed details.

Focusing on tools in the Upper Paleolithic of sites in France, Alice Kehoe (1990a) suggests that "points," which are construed as masculine by the simple expedient of drawing them with their tips up, have been privileged over "lines," often constructed and used by women. Cordage from Upper Paleolithic sites has rarely been recognized, and the small amounts that were actually found are not used to create the prehistoric "story." Kehoe's analysis emphasizes the fact that the concept of "projectile point" is not value-free. Points have been valorized beyond their usefulness to known groups of people with similar technology, in similar climates and environments. In ethnographic settings like that of the late Upper Paleolithic, objects made with "lines," or cordage—for example traps, nets, and snares—are more important in the acquisition of animal food than the points with which the animal may finally be killed. The adventure story, in short, has become more important than accuracy. Kehoe (1990a) suggests that an emphasis on "Men-Brutes of the Forest" (William Douglas, cited in Kehoe [1992b:7]), is the basis for the neglect of nets and snares. A stress on male = active = hunting (also see the analysis of plant domestication by Watson and Kennedy, on page 101) results in blanking out other less heroic (dangerous and independent) means of acquiring meat. Traps are silently declared to be uninteresting, like the women who probably made them and who perhaps collected the ensnared animals.

Joanna Casey (1997), on yet another continent, uses what she calls basic tools (also known as expedient or informal tools, or utilized flakes) to discuss gender in the Kintampo Complex, a West African Late Stone Age archaeological complex that included pottery. Casey argues that basic tools are just as useful as formal tools. If this is so, what purpose may there be for more elaborate tools? She thus problematizes the production of formal stone tools. Her conclusion is that projectile points are likely to be lost in hunting territory that may be used by other groups. Thus, they can be found and the style identified, as a kind of "calling card" of their presence in that location. She suggests that women's tools taken on long distance travel may be similarly encoded, but perishable so that they are not available to use as a comparison.

In these various ways, Gero, Bird, and Casey use the prism of gender to make women more visible as both makers and users of stone tools, even as Kehoe demonstrates the importance of cordage in the same pursuits.

Strategies for Bringing Women's Tool-Making to Light

Women's work has been "found" in the archaeological record in a number of ways. An appeal to universals is the least satisfying of these. Even if certain tasks are always the responsibility of some woman or group of women (and this needs to be demonstrated in particular cases), other women may be exempt from these tasks. Ethnographic analogy can be productive if used with care, but an appeal to tendencies reported in the Human Relations Area Files is unconvincing when simply applied to an archaeological site. The best cases of analogy are made using the direct historical approach—employing ethnographically known beliefs or activities to interpret archaeological sites of descendants of the people described ethnogeographically.

Using the Direct Historical Approach (arguing for a continuity from ethnographic reports of the Pawnee to remains in the same region in Late Prehistoric times), Patricia O'Brien (1990) concludes that women produced some of the stone tools at the Holidome site near Manhattan, Kansas, dated to the 13th century. Pawnee Indians maintained many of the cultural patterns, such as earth lodges, that are found in excavated sites. The association of Pawnee practices with the site appears to be quite robust.

The site was a salvage excavation, where a midden concentration was found with a post hole not quite in the center. Associated artifacts indicated that this was a work area, a place where activities such as gardening, storing produce, processing and drying meat, and cleaning and preparing hides occurred. These were women's tasks in Pawnee society, and thus, O'Brien argues, a woman's work area. Chert-knapping implements were found in the same location. O'Brien argues that since everything else in this location is associated with women, it seems likely that these women made and sharpened their own stone tools, as well as used them in their work.

In the site of Huaricoto, in Peru, it was possible to note change through time in the expedient tools, the category usually called utilized flakes (Gero 1991a). To accomplish her goal of engendering the tools, Joan Gero accepts minimalist definitions of how women make and use stone tools, going on to examine the kinds of stone often disregarded by other archaeologists. If it is believed that women did not go far away to get stone, Gero will look only at locally available raw material and consider only expedient flakes, that is, pieces of sharp stone that could have been the by-product of other stone-knapping activities, or that were simply struck from a larger piece of stone without further retouching. She proposes to find women's stone tools by looking at habitation areas where women's work presumably occurs. Her argument of association is similar to that of O'Brien's.

Given these assumptions, Gero examined the utilized flakes and found that they tended to be made with local raw material. In the later periods at the site, there was less retouching, but a great increase in the number of flake tools. If these are agreed to be women's tools, it is interesting to note that they are found not only in association with domestic architecture, but also in the temple areas, suggesting women's work in sacred precincts, although there is a broader range of stone tools in the village. This is a giant step forward in considering women as makers and users of stone tools in the archaeological record.

Awls are another pointed implement, frequently accepted as evidence for basketry, and mostly attributed to women. Awls rarely receive the kind of attention accorded to projectile points (Kehoe 1991). Other bone tools that may indicate women's work include polished bone spatulate implements similar to those used elsewhere to make nets, bags, mats, and snowshoes. While they may not tell "heroic" stories, they do indicate that overlooking supposed women's implements results in an incomplete understanding of the past.

Janet Spector (1991, 1994) focuses on a single awl to create a possible "story" of the woman who made it, decorated it, used it, and lost it, resulting in its appearance in the archaeological context of a trash pile. Spector demonstrates by this device the multiple layers of meaning embodied in a single artifact and the potential richness of the archaeological record. Earlier, Spector (1983) created the notion of task differentiation, a variant of which is the goal of Marcia-Anne Dobres.

Dobres's attempt to engender prehistoric tools focused on bone and antler technologies during the Late Magdalenian period in France. She makes no assumption about which gender performed which task, but she does assume that gender played a role and that "social identities are expressed through the making and remaking of artifacts" (1995b:111). Magdalenian bone and antler tools, like stone tools, are usually studied as formal types, and thus are analyzed as entities out of context. Dobres *reverses* these procedures, examining the tools in sections, and considering the context carefully. The assumption that men and women had "active roles in creating, making, and giving meaning to the objects" requires a much closer scrutiny of the artifacts within their setting, and of their variation both within sites and from one site to another. Considering prehistoric technology as "the embodiment of social rules," Dobres compares not just whole tools, but also sections of bone tools, finding striking differences between assemblages in different sites. When examining them with this level of detail, she found no common patterns between sites. The mix of artifacts tended to vary between sites. Some sites had much more evidence of repair than others, and even the technologies for making the barbs on harpoons were not shared. At the site of La Vache, where many more harpoons were repaired than elsewhere, a unique hafting technique was also used. Mas d'Azil was unusual in containing more preforms and blanks than the average site. "These different social and material contexts imply different kinds of face-to-face interaction and it is reasonable to hypothesize that the organization and dynamic quality of interpersonal relations of production were not necessarily the same at these two sites." Dobres postulates that social positions were negotiated in three ways, "1) through the control and display of technical know-how and skill, 2) through differential access to raw material resources (not so much the bone or antler but more likely the retouched stone tools with which they were modified) and/or 3) through differential access to the finished products themselves" (1995b:40).

The flexibility implied by this variation is interpreted as "the embodiment of a general flexibility of social conduct situated to the specific settings in which people found themselves . . . [they may have had] equal access to material power and social power, such that everyone had the *opportunity* to develop and express influence and skill in and through their technological acts. . . . Technological skill and access to resources were most likely 'negotiable,' rather than rigidly fixed or ascribed by virtue of gender, age, or other social affiliation" (Dobres 1995b:41).

Gathering and Hunting: The Critique

In her classic paper, *Woman the Gatherer: Male Bias in Anthropology*, Sally Linton (1971) first critiqued the Man-the-Hunter model, suggesting that perhaps women as gatherers also had an impact on the evolution of human capabilities, with the increased intelligence needed to raise the more dependent infants. This was followed by a new interest in women in hunter-gatherer societies, much of which focused on subsistence. These new studies established that women contribute a large proportion of the food in most foraging societies (e.g. Lee 1979), that there are many known societies in which women hunt with men or even alone (e.g. Estioko-Griffin and Griffin 1981), and that women do not usually suffer from status lower than men in these societies (e.g. Leacock 1978).

Lyn Wadley (1997) argues for the presence of women meat providers in African prehistory. Her use of the term "meat provider" is better than "hunter" because it sheds all the baggage of implied masculinity and the implications of the hero's quest. Wadley marshals a great deal of ethnographic accounts of many kinds of hunting in which women participate. These include snaring small game, driving larger game into nets and pit traps, and scavenging game killed by lions. Women among the Ju/'hoansi of southwest Africa (formerly called !Kung) do not hunt with bow and arrow or spears, though they contribute to meat provisioning in other ways. Wadley shows that gender relationships among these groups contain considerable variety. Differences in animal procurement are evident in African prehistory, especially as post-Pleistocene changes affected the size of the animals usually hunted. In the Holocene, the distribution of bones around several hearths suggests game-sharing. The number and placement of sites also suggests hunting changes. There are smaller groups, though larger numbers of groups, especially visible in cave and rock shelter sites. While none of this specifically engenders the hunting from these camps, further research may do so now that the question has been raised.

The problem of unearthing gathering activities in an archaeological context, however, seemed to be intractible (Thomas 1983). Not only are the remains of vegetal food more perishable than those of animal food, but also many of the artifacts women use for gathering are made of highly perishable material—wooden digging sticks, for example, and containers made of leather, basketry, cloth, or wood, to transport the gathered food back to the base camp. But finding the artifacts (though traces of them may, in fact, be discoverable) is not the only avenue to recovering women's work. Examining tool technology has been shown in the previous section to contribute to that goal. Other archaeological approaches to gathering consumables focus on stone artifacts such as milling stones and weights for digging sticks, which are no more perishable than projectile points and are less likely to be pocketed by passing collectors in the present.

Strategies for Engendering Hunting and Gathering

Synnøve Vinsrygg (1987) uses a chain of evidence, especially the combination of rock art and artifact distribution, to identify cross-shaped stones as digging stick weights in Bronze Age Sweden. These objects, made of heavy polished stone with a central hole through which a pole or handle could pass, had previously been identified as the business end of war clubs. Depictions of women on rock painting using a digging stick with a cross-shaped weight provide primary evidence for her alternative explanation. Vinsrygg then considers ethnographic parallels, and finds that weighted digging sticks are indeed used in several societies. Finally, she notes that the distribution of "potential plants that might require digging sticks" correlates with the distribution of these artifacts. A sound case has been made for a reassignment of these items to subsistence rather than to war. Surely interpretations of other factors in these sites would shift with this new interpretation of the weights.

In California archaeology, equipment for grinding plant foods is found in two forms—milling stones made of a slab of rock and a grinder, and "bed-rock mortars" consisting of holes ground into boulders too large to move. The former type of grinding apparatus is known to be earlier, and because of their ubiquity, the time period is known as the "Milling Stone Horizon." Living sites of this culture tend to be very similar, in terms of percentages of different kinds of artifacts, which suggests that gender organization was "much less circumscribed" (McGuire and Hildebrandt 1994:41). There is little evidence of hunting at the living sites or in burials, though by contrast milling equipment is found at all sites and in 93.6 percent of all burials. These burials without gender markers suggest a "lack of [gender] polarity" in the division of labor.

Kelly McGuire and W. R. Hildebrandt buttress their argument with ethnographic examples that include groups of California Indians possibly descended from those who left the archaeological cultures, thus calling on the direct historical approach. They found that among the Cahuilla, both women and men gathered pine nuts and acorns, though women were the primary processors of nuts. In contrast, men and boys harvested and cooked agave. Shellfish collecting was engaged in by both women and men, and rabbit-hunting was communal, utilizing everyone in the group. In this allocation of tasks, many could be performed by either sex, and neither men nor women were exclusively associated with either plants or animals. The lack of gender polarity is thus seen to have time depth.

Change in burial artifacts occurred coincident with a shift to bedrock mortars (Jackson 1991). Increased numbers of points and bifaces in male burials suggest a new and more stringent division of labor. Additionally, fewer men were accompanied in death by milling equipment. In spite of this tendency, the various categories of artifacts are still mixed in many burials, suggesting that an absolute division of labor by gender had not taken hold.

Collecting shellfish is another type of labor known ethnographically to be often done by women, and is a common example of women providing protein for themselves, their children, and other members of the group. Although the ability to demonstrate that any specific shellmound was the result of women's labor is improbable, burials may provide corroborating evidence. Cheryl Claassen (1991) studied the Shell Mound Archaic, which began some eight thousand years ago in the North American southeast.

Immense heaps of shells indicate the enormous amount of activity in this endeavor. In the accompanying burials, more women than men had been treated with red ocher at death, and objects that appear to be ceremonial equipment were more often found with women. Claassen infers that women are central to the society, with the rich or burial goods perhaps referring to their subsistence contributions. She has thus combined ethnographic analogy with burials to add gender to her sites.

Woman-the-Gatherer, whether of shellfish, nuts, or other food, has become an accepted fact in anthropology, and archaeology has largely followed suit. What about female farmers?

Farmers: The Critique

Women are frequently the gatherers of plants for food, as well as plants for medicine, clothing, cord, containers, and other purposes. Surely even before plant domestication occurred, close attention to plants made women aware of plant characteristics, including their preferred locations, seasonality, and growth habits. In spite of this, the domestication of food plants is often implicitly or explicitly attributed to men rather than women, or (oddly) to no one at all.

Patty Jo Watson and Mary Kennedy (1991) discuss this tendency in the context of the dichotomy that is stressed when the notion that men hunt animals, which is seen as active, is contrasted with women gathering plants, equated with the passive. This of course fits well with a present culture in which women are still believed to be (or wished to be) passive. Therefore, Watson and Kennedy argue, cultural innovation cannot be attributed to women. They take as their example the domestication of plants in Eastern (U.S.) Woodlands. In this region it was not the familiar American food crops of maize, beans, and squash that were first domesticated, but gourds, sunflowers, chenopods, and amaranths. These "weed" crops appear in Late Archaic sites. They consist of wild forms at first, but the seeds become larger through time and are thought to have become domesticated, because larger seeds are an important indication of domestication. These plants would have been collected in the wild by women, according to standard gender attribution, but by sleight of hand plant domestication is attributed either to men or to no one.

In one version, the plants are said to have domesticated themselves, as in the theory of the dump heap, where plants that grow well in soils rich in nitrogen, provided by human waste near human habitation, would have sprouted and flourished (Anderson 1956, Sauer 1952). Even V. Gordon Childe, who supposed that women might have been the domesticators of plants, disparages this work: "Probably at first cultivation was an incidental activity of the women while *their lords* were engaged in the *really serious business* of the chase" (Childe 1951:71, emphasis added). The only example of gender being attributed to the innovators is to men, in the form of presumed male shamans, who might have needed gourds for rattles to use in their ceremonies. Watson and Kennedy suggest that the underlying reason for the failure to perceive women as innovators is the association of women with the passive—they couldn't have been innovators, for that reason. It is also interesting that the shamans in question are presumed to be male, since there are many ethnographic examples of societies in which the shaman may be male or female, and in the case of Korea (e.g. Kendall 1985), as well as other places, they are almost all women. There is no a priori reason to gender the shaman as male, even if domestication for the sake of gourd seeds is a supportable hypothesis.

It is quite clear ethnographically that women in small-scale food-producing societies do a great deal of the productive work, as well as most or all of the maintenance, cleaning, repairing, child care, and food production. While it appears to be quite common for men to prepare agricultural fields, women frequently do much or all of the planting, weeding, and harvesting of plants, as well as processing and storing them after the harvest. Thus, in particular cases agricultural tools may be argued to have belonged to women. Preparation of food is also frequently women's work, and archaeologically women can be made visible by examining the artifacts used in food preparation, especially their disposition, distribution within the site, and changes through time. When women are the owners of the land, they may also be in charge of food storage, so that facilities for food storage can also be an avenue to gender in archaeology.

On the other hand, Pamela Crabtree examines the evidence for a division of labor in the Natufian culture of southwest Asia, some ten to twelve millennia ago, and concludes that there is little reason to suppose that such existed. She suggests that plant and animal domestication may have led to a more rigid division of labor by gender, because the different requirements for scheduling created a shift to farming (1991).

It has recently become possible to study bones from burials to learn whether there are dietary differences between men and women, and to infer differential access by sex to various types of food (e.g. Hastorf 1991, Cohen and Bennett 1993, Bumsted et al. 1990). In addition, bone morphology can be used to learn whether the work was assigned to a particular gender. An interesting study by Patricia Bridges (1989) demonstrates changes in male and female diaphyseal bone structure between burial populations in the Archaic when people were foragers (before 1000 B.C.) and in the Mississippian period (A.D. 1200–1500) in the southeastern United States, by which time farming was well established. She found changes in the bones of both sexes, but more marked changes in women, lending strength to the hypothesis that women were the main farmers.

Ethnographic analogies indicate that where women have some economic independence, there is spatially discrete storage (Hastorf 1991:134–135). This is related to the fact that in many cultures the land, and by extension the food produced from the fields, belongs to women. These are often dual-descent or matrilineal societies. Still, more archaeological work focused on gender and farming is urgently needed.

Food Preparation: The Critique

Processing that which is gathered, whether from the wild or cultivation, into edible food that humans can digest, may be labor intensive and often requires several steps. Another kind of food preparation is the butchering of meat, often believed to be men's work, suggesting that our ancestors butchered the mastodon like Dad carving the Thanksgiving turkey. Diane Gifford-Gonzalez shows that there is a research bias in analyzing stones and bones in favor of primary butchering tools, construed as men's work, to the detriment of "culinary processing" most likely to have been done by women (1993:181). She points to a number of gaps in traditional analyses of bone, which can be traced to this preference for primary butchering over food preparation. Foremost among the overlooked potential studies, she notes, is the effect of cooking on bone. A good deal could be learned about food preparation and diet with this approach. She suggests that knowing whether bone cut-marks were made before or after cooking would help to understand the process of preparation for cooking, the method of cooking, and the way meat was served. Furthermore, even processing at the kill site is affected by the intended means of cooking. Different sorts of cooking methods depend on whether pots or pits are used, or skewers over the fire (roasts versus stews, for example). This lack of interest in meat preparation is clearly gender bias operating. It favors hunting, and slaughter (presumed male activities) over skilled culinary meat-cutting (alleged to be women's work).

Food Preparation: Archaeological Examples

Elizabeth Brumfiel (1991) describes a more complex allocation of labor, in which Aztec women spent much time, up to eight hours each day, grinding maize and making tortillas, but were still expected to perform other productive labor. The technology for grinding the maize was present before the plant was domesticated, demonstrating the close association between the plant itself and methods to process it. Grinding stones are very common in the High Plains Archaic, for example. In the Aztec territory of Mexico, the ground meal was used in various ways. Archaeologically, small griddles on which tortillas were cooked, and large pots for stews, are evidence of two ways corn meal was made edible. The whole process of food preparation is grueling (the word itself is interesting—having to do with the making of porridge? And we also speak of "grinding labor"). The dried maize must be boiled with water and lime, then drained and rinsed, and pulverized on the grinding stone. To prepare the flour as tortillas, the woman must make balls of dough and pat them into thin rounds, which are then cooked on a griddle.

Sauces are made in stone or ceramic mortars, while stews are cooked in earthware pots. Tamales are particularly laborious to prepare for they have to be assembled, wrapped in corn husks, and steamed. Perhaps because of their labor-intensive nature, they are a food of the nobility, which common-ers have time to make only for ceremonial occasions. It might be noted parenthetically that "holidays," especially for women, are times of intensi-fied work, rather than a rest from their labors! Brumfiel suggests that relative frequencies of griddles and pots in different sites can reveal cooking strate-gies. She emphasizes the way cooking methods indicate the proportion of wet and dry food in the diet. Wet foods, that is foods cooked in pots, are preferable today in Mexico and presumably also were preferred among the Aztecs, but they are not portable. Artifacts to cook wet or dry food take on additional interpretive significance in this context. At two archaeological sites, Xaltocan and Xico, near Mexico City, "the ratio of pots to griddles decreases dramatically from Early to Late Aztec times," while at Xuehotla the proportion remains the same. Variations in women's labor, as it changed in two contemporaneous villages but remained the same in another, thus become visible and meaningful. The switch to portable dry foods cooked on the griddle suggests other changes, very likely a labor force that needed to carry food, because the location of the work was too distant to allow workers to return home for the midday meal (Brumfiel 1991:241). Brumfiel relates this whole complex of changing artifact frequencies to the public labor extracted by the Aztec elite. Both corveè labor (labor required of peasants on behalf of the state) and cloth products were required. Men performed the corveè labor, but cloth production and corn grinding were both time-consuming occupations allocated to women. Women were associated with cloth and food production, though the archaeological distribution of artifacts demonstrates varying amounts and kinds of work at different sites, allowing for a more nuanced understanding of women's activities. If women were required to produce more cloth, they might make fewer tortillas, or if they needed to raise additional crops, they might weave and spin less.

Another example of the careful study of food and food technology in archaeological sites is provided by a study of dietary changes in Peru, carried out by Christine Hastorf (1991:132). Her site is in the Upper Mantaro Valley, where historic continuity exists between the present inhabitants, known as Sausa, and the archaeological cultures called Wanka I, Wanka II, and Wanka III. Among the Sausa, maize is highly regarded, especially when consumed in the form of a kind of beer at rituals. Potatoes are also important in the diet, though they are not ritually valued in the same way as maize. During the transition from pre-Inca to Inca times, this group became incorporated into the expanding state, changing a number of characteristics that can be observed with archaeological evidence. For example, dietary evidence from the burials demonstrates that the distribution of certain types of food became more restricted in Inca times—to the disadvantage of women. The isotopic values of sexed burials show no difference in male and female dietary intake in Wanka II. Bone chemistry is interpreted to show that both sexes primarily ate quinoa and tubers, with lesser amounts of maize. The diets of both sexes also included some meat, which must have been mostly llama, judging from the number of llama bones left in the sites. However, differences between men and women do appear in Wanka III times, especially in the consumption of maize. It is interesting that both men and women consumed relatively more maize than either did earlier, but "50 percent of the male diets are significantly enriched in maize beyond the female diets" (Hastorf 1991:150). Not only did half the men have diets richer in maize, but they also ate more meat. Presumably, only some men could be ritual participants, accounting for differential consumption of llama meat and maize beer at festivals. It also suggests incipient class stratification, since not all men had access to increased meat and maize.

Potters: The Critique

The construction, decoration, and functions of pottery have been studied in various ways. Although women are frequently the potters, especially when the potting is done without a potter's wheel, nothing about the making of pots should be inherently gendered (Rice 1981:437). Women and men can do all the tasks required to produce a finished pot, and many examples of men and women working together are known ethnographically (Stahl and Cruz 1997). Rita Wright (1991) suggests that, to engender prehistoric potting, a broader definition of a potter is needed, as is a better understanding of the process of making pottery. In common parlance, the person who forms the pots is "the potter," but many other tasks are involved in making pots. Necessary production sequences, such as obtaining the clay, processing it, forming pots, decorating pots, firing them, and so forth, need not all be done by the same person, but all have contributed to the final product. In some instances the allocation of these tasks may reflect a gendered division of labor.

Strategies to Engender Pottery Production

Whether potting is a full-time or part-time activity, together with the gender of the potters, are characteristics that can lead to an under-standing of the allocation of other duties by gender, as well. Kenneth Sassaman considers the distributions of ceramics in Woodland cultural patterns, in order to explore the social nature of production. "How the work of several individuals is divided, articulated, and coordinated exemplifies [the joining of tools and laborers]" (1992:71). For example, pottery was introduced in the context of shell-fishing. Both are attributable to women's labor, and because of that he suggests that they are mutually exclusive seasonal activities. This insight helps clarify the distribution of work in the whole society.

In the Harappan culture and its antecedents in northwestern South Asia, pottery apparently developed indigenously, from unfired clay products to low-fired, straw-tempered vessels, to finer vessels with surface treatments such as burnished slip. Since the development of pottery technology parallels that of bread-making, they both may well be women's products. Furthermore, even after the invention of the potter's wheel, production was associated with households at the site of Mehrgarh, suggesting that women continued as the potters. At Harappa specialized pottery production areas have been speculated to belong to kin groups, and there is no reason to suppose that women were not among the production team (Wright 1991).

The question of whether the potter's wheel, and/or state-level society, was responsible for the shift of pottery production from women to men is taken up by several authors. Prudence Rice (1991) accepts that this shift occurred, and suggests that it must relate to reasons other than strength, since women are known to habitually perform many more-strenuous activities. She provocatively suggests that the ways that workshops versus home production have been understood are ethnocentric, and perhaps an emphasis on specialization automatically skews the discussion toward males.

Another approach to pottery focuses on the utility of pottery containers, especially for cooking or storage, and the resulting changes in the cultures that make and use them. The invention of cooking pots permitted an important change in food habits. Rita Wright notes that some foods cannot be consumed at all without cooking, and other foods taste better when exposed to heat (1991:204–206). Although there are multiple methods of cooking that do not require waterproof containers, including on sticks over a fire or in earth ovens, foods can be cooked in pots at higher temperatures for a sustained period, thus increasing the variety of ingestible plants and more thoroughly extracting nutrients from meat and bone. Foods in pots can also be prepared and left to simmer, allowing the cook to pursue other activities while the food is cooking, as well as melding the flavors. Furthermore, only with container cooking can food be made mushy enough to feed infants to supplement milk and to feed elderly members of society whose teeth are failing them.

Ceramic containers may have uses other than cooking, such as preserving and storing, especially liquid foods, and those that require preservation and storage in liquids such as brine or vinegar. Preservation of vegetables, in particular, to sustain a population through cold or dry seasons, would have been particularly important. For example, two methods of preserving cabbage, sauerkraut in central Europe and kimchi in the Korean peninsula, would have been impossible without impermeable containers. Alcoholic beverages are also dependent on vessels that could hold liquids (Braidwood 1953, Hastorf 1991). What differences did such brewing make in Neolithic societies, and were they gendered differences?

In another approach to gender through pottery, Ann Stahl and Maria Cruz (1997) use both ethnographic analogy and the direct historical approach to examine shifts in craft production in response to the market economy in Ghana in the 19th and 20th centuries. They note that both individual choices and specific historic events influence the distribution of pots. The archaeological sites under investigation are of two kinds, designated as Early Malaka and Late Malaka. Early Malaka dates to the early 19th century and Late Malaka to the early 20th century. Sites of both are near current villages. Early Malaka was abandoned suddenly, suggesting warfare, known to have been endemic in this region during the times the sites were occupied. Increased homogeneity in ceramic assemblages is notable.

Neutron activation of both pottery from sites and clay sources shows that pots in the Early Malaka were being obtained from west of the hills, but in Late Malaka there is a shift to sources east of the hills. Change from a geographically restricted to a dispersed pattern is traced to unstable political conditions. Warfare, and especially the practice of enslaving, may have kept women from traveling to the source of pot manufacture. The burden of transport shifted from the consumer to the producer.

Spinners, Weavers, and Tailors

Textiles are an example of ordinarily perishable artifacts that often (but not always) are the result of women's work. Fragments and even whole textiles may survive in unusual conditions, such as the aridity of burials in the Peruvian desert, the wetness of Danish bogs, a few Chinese tombs, or the frozen tombs of Siberia, but under ordinary temperate or tropical conditions cloth does not survive long. In spite of their perishability, there are other ways that textiles can be "visible" archaeologically. Textiles are sometimes depicted, painted on walls or as clothing on figurines, as in the Neolithic of Turkey, Crete, and Eastern Europe. Tools or parts of tools for spinning and weaving may also survive. Thus, where sought, the manufacture of cloth and clothing may have left recognizable traces. Textiles are almost always attributed to women, though men weave in a number of societies—for example, in West Africa and in Hopi villages.

As we have seen, as early as the Upper Paleolithic in France, bone needles with eyes had been invented, implying sewing. Awls for basketry and cord for nets and traps have already been noted (Kehoe 1990a, 1991). These tools imply fairly advanced skills. Figurines at the Siberian sites of Malta and Buret appear to be clothed in trousers and fur cloaks with hoods, another indication of tailoring by Upper Paleolithic people. Both leather and fur clothing were probably needed to survive the cold winters. Possible traces of summer clothing also exist. Elizabeth Barber (1994) notes the depiction of a possible string skirt on an Upper Paleolithic figurine from Lespuges, and suggests a kinship through time with much later string skirts preserved in Danish bogs. While the markings on this figurine might be interpreted in other ways, it is an interesting potential connection.

Mary Parsons's (1972) statistical analysis of spindle whorls in the Valley of Mexico demonstrated the presence of two distinct sizes of spindle whorl, each with a different range of sizes for the central perforations, implying two sizes of spindles. Two kinds of thread were thus being spun, and two kinds of materials, cotton and maguey fibers, used for cloth (1972). Cloth for everyday wear was made from leaves of the maguey cactus, a readily available local resource. The spinner can create fine as well as coarse maguey thread. Cotton was always finely spun, and required only a lightly weighted spindle. Elizabeth Brumfiel (1991) applies the numbers and sizes of spindle whorls at various sites to understanding the varieties of the work of Aztec women. It is not necessary to demonstrate archaeologically that women were the weavers, since the codices, written by Spanish scribes shortly after the Conquest, show women weaving, even as other documents describe women as skilled weavers. Women were also cooks, as noted above, and these two activities were both labor intensive. In addition, where market conditions were appropriate, women might also work in the fields, salt and dry fish, and prepare maguey cactus. However, the proportion of time that women spent at each activity varied from site to site, as Elizabeth Brumfiel carefully demonstrates with the relative numbers of artifacts at sites in the Valley of Mexico.

Brumfiel's analysis is particularly interesting because variation between sites is found in spite of the fact that the entire valley became more populous. Population growth was based on the household economy, for which women's work was essential. As noted in the section on cooking, women's workloads increased greatly under the Aztec tribute system. In addition to producing cloth for family consumption, women were required to weave cotton mantles that could be used as currency in periodic markets. Brumfiel used the frequency of spindle whorls in archaeological sites to gauge the intensity of cloth production, and found "[n]otable differences in the frequencies of spindle whorls between sites" (1991:232). Without repeating Brumfiel's elegant argument, it is sufficient to note that she concludes that the more agricultural production, the less cloth, and vice versa. For example, the site of Xico, in the chinampa zone, had relatively few spindle whorls, but at Huexotla, with rainfall agriculture, much cloth was produced. A plausible explanation for the inverse relationship of intensive agriculture and cloth production is that these represented alternate employments for women's labor. Spindle whorls are fewer at both sites under the Aztecs. At another site, Xaltocan, maguey whorls (the larger ones) decline in numbers, but cotton whorls stay the same. Brumfiel suggests that "the less intensive production of cloth was made possible by increasing participation in market exchange" (p. 234). Families still needed to be clothed, but cloth was available in markets, perhaps in exchange for agricultural products. Other activities attributable to women varied from site to site as well. At Huexotla, high frequencies of artifacts were noted for collection of maguey sap, and at Xico and Xaltocan, high frequencies of fabric-marked pottery, associated with production of salt, used in the preservation and transport of dried fish. Thus variations in women's work can be observed from site to site, allowing a much more detailed and nuanced picture of the activities of ordinary people than is usually teased from archaeological materials.

Conclusions

The division of labor by gender is rarely absolute. Overlaps of work activities between women and men have been noted in several of the cited studies. Just as it is foolish to suppose that women could not or did not make and use stone implements, it is unwarranted to insist that no men participated in potting, weaving, cooking, child care, and so forth, for we know that some did so, even when it was designated women's work. Which person performs which tasks may be a matter of talent, training, and convenience as often as constructed by gender considerations. Furthermore, cautions should be heeded about assigning specific tools to men or women without evidence (Bruhns 1991, Crabtree 1991). To suppose that hunting and gathering are so different that the diets of men and women will create separate ecological niches (Jochim 1988) seems rather extreme, but the division of labor, however strict or lax, *does* need to be considered although it must not be assumed.

The gendering of workplaces is also difficult, and it must be borne in mind that gendered work is not necessarily sex-segregated work. Men and women could have performed different work in the same locations, either inside or outside. Or they might have shared tasks, on some occasions both doing the same thing (like married couples today who might "job-share"), perhaps harvesting crops or hunting rabbits with nets, at other times working together at different parts of the same project.

Asking gendered questions about work in the prehistoric past often is the impetus to ask new questions and to seek another level of detail. Gendered archaeology brings attention to facets of sites that have previously been neglected, and organizes archaeological material in novel ways. Thus, even the economy, technology, and the subsistence base—areas that have been intensively studied by archaeologists working under other paradigms—can be enhanced through a study of gender.

CHAPTER SIX
FAMILIES AND HOUSEHOLDS

It must be emphasized that many topics of interest to anthropologists and primatologists are in general not amenable to archaeological investigation. Kinship systems and marriage arrangements . . . can scarcely be considered in relation to the archaeological evidence for the Pleistocene.
—Glynn Isaac (1968:254)

With few exceptions, twentieth century anthropology has treated women as at best peripheral members of society and at worst as nonexistent. Males continued to be viewed as the only social actors.
—Susan Carol Rogers (1978: 126)

It seems likely that most households in the past held both sexes and a range of ages, yet "household archaeology" rarely attends to this fact. It is as mothers, daughters, sisters, and wives that women have featured most prominently in ethnography, yet these roles are virtually unnoticed, unresearched, and unmentioned in archaeological accounts. Why is this so? All women are daughters, and as such have some rights in a kin group or family. Only in a few societies, such as prerevolutionary China, have daughters been so completely given to the husband's kin group that they are not accorded permanent membership in the natal group. The birth of a daughter may be a *Small Happiness* in modern China, as in Karma Hinton's film by that name, but it is still a happiness. Sisterhood, a woman's place as an adult in a kinship group, seems likely to have been a common experience, and groups of siblings have played important roles in various societies (Sacks 1979). Motherhood is the one role for women that we can guarantee was necessary for at least some women at all times and in all places, for the continuation of the group. And even if "marriages" did not exist in the same way in all societies, something like wifehood—a sexual and perhaps economic partnership with one or several men—must have been a likely role for most women.

It is noteworthy that these roles that must have occurred in some form, and that are so prominent in sociocultural anthropology, have been virtually neglected in archaeology. In fact, because there are few archaeological examples to discuss, it was tempting to simply omit this chapter altogether. But the subject is important because arguments about matriarchies are based on past societies, which ought to be the province of archaeologists. A new return to "Social Archaeology" needs to be gendered to provide balanced accounts of past societies. Perhaps this chapter will stimulate others to ponder the problem of researching prehistoric kinship. It may be feminist resistance to these apparently subordinate roles (because made so in our society) that has made them less interesting to seek in the archaeological record. Or perhaps it is because they have been proclaimed to be out of reach with archaeological evidence, or other factors may be at play. After all, men's roles within families and households have been similarly ignored.

Although kinship roles have been considered difficult to research in prehistoric societies, there are sites for which documentary evidence may apply, or images may be available, painted on pottery or carved in stone, that can serve as guides to the society's gender arrangement. For late prehistoric groups, known continuity with living or historical cultures, which might have testable social arrangements, can be adduced, using the direct historical approach. Even in societies with none of these avenues into social structure and social organization, some theoretical issues can be tackled, which begin to open a space for understanding prehistoric kinship systems. Still, much remains to be done. This chapter is thus more about possibilities than results, and more about directions for future research than examples of recent work.

Matriarchy, Matrilineality, and Matrilocality

Matriarchy is a system in which women systematically rule, matrilineality is a system in which membership in the clan is traced through the female line, and matrilocality is a system in which a woman stays in her family's house at marriage and her husband moves in with her. These have been discussed in various ways with reference to the archaeological record. Matrilocality as a way of structuring households has been studied by means of pottery decoration. The societal position of adult women when the primary kin groupings includes siblings (a matrilineal society) is said to lend higher status to women than societies where women's status is more dependent on the marriage bond. Matriarchies are often declared not to exist. None of these structures is easily made visible in the archaeological record. To find them, it will be necessary to work out the material correlates in particular instances.

In the feminist literature of the 1970s, the matriarchy question was primary, as was the decline of women's status in "patriarchy" (e.g. Rohrlich-Leavitt 1976, Rapp 1977). The universality of women's decline under patriarchy was assumed; the questions posed were how men acquired control and whether women acquiesced in their own subjugation. The archaeological evidence of various sites in Turkey, especially Çatal Hüyük, seemed to fortify the inference of a prior matriarchy (Barstow 1978). Clearly a "matriarchy," if one existed, would be unlikely to grow out of familial social arrangements with a strong patrilineal base. But the antecedents of Çatal Hüyük, or other societies where women's importance is alleged to be visible in the proliferation of "goddess" figures, have not been the focus of any investigations that emphasize kinship.

Matrilineality/matriarchy is a topic that has deep roots in Victorian social anthropology. The underlying attitudes about women that were encoded in the debate have been discussed and assessed by several writers (Coward 1983, Fee 1974). These analyses suggest that, although the question of whether matriarchy or patriarchy was earlier in social evolution was fiercely fought among (male) anthropologists, the issue was ultimately not whether matriarchies, or their milder cousins matrilineal societies, preceded patriarchies; but rather how best to describe the achievement of male Victorians in oppressing women. The underlying assumption of *both* schemes was the superiority of patriarchy. Those favoring the prior existence of matriarchies, of course, thought that societies with women in power were obviously lower on the evolutionary scale, while those insisting on patriarchal precedence simply considered matriarchy laughable, indeed impossible (e.g. Maine 1861). The latter is close to the present position of cultural anthropology. As Elizabeth Fee paraphrases John Lubbock, one of the

John Lubbock

archaeological founding fathers, in *The Origin of Civilization and the Primitive Condition of Man* (1870), he thought that "the patriarchal family was not *natural*, but the proud product of millennia of development. The system whereby males ruled their families was *better* than natural (i.e. primitive, i.e. savage, i.e. disgusting); it was *civilized*" (Fee 1974:94, emphasis in original).

The question of whether women ever had rights in men, in the same way that men are alleged to have rights in women in many societies, seems to have been answered in the negative for the most part. That is, a matriarchy as a kind of inverse patriarchy is declared improbable. But there are staunch defenders of equality and gender complementarily in ethnological contexts (e.g. Leacock 1975, 1978, 1993), and the notion that men dominate women in all societies (e.g. Rosaldo and Lamphere 1974) was later modified by feminist ethnography and more nuanced theoretical approaches (Rosaldo 1980).

One reason that these topics have been neglected in archaeology is perhaps that the anthropological formulations are thoroughly steeped in androcentrism, and even misogyny. The study of kinship has been pursued from a thoroughly male point of view. Emile Durkheim, in discussing the division of labor by sex, explains that women were once the same as men in size and intelligence, but now (in 1864) they had become physically weaker and their brains were smaller due to the benefits of civilization. He supposed that "the farther we look into the past, the smaller becomes the difference between men and women. The woman of past days was not at all the weak creature she has become with the progress of morality" (1893:57).

In this intellectual climate, it is understandable that male scholars would not consider women as part of the social order. It was Claude Lévi-Strauss who made it clear that women and children are not part of the society, complaining that the "whole village" disappeared in boats, leaving him with the women and children (quoted in Wylie 1991a:38). Therefore it is not surprising that Lévi-Strauss was adamant about describing marriage as the exchange of women. "In human society, it is the men who exchange the women, and not vice versa" (Lévi-Strauss 1963:47). He muses further that "apparently there is something in the nature of males which precludes the realization of an exchange of males between groups of females. It is always the male who exercises authority, and this also applies in matrilineal societies practising uxorilocal marriage" (1969:298).

This is because men are "naturally" dominant (as we have seen satirized by Josie the chimpanzee). In fact it is remarkable that, even when it comes to kinship, presumably not in the domain of primates, primate studies are used to bolster images of male dominance. It is worth quoting Robin Fox on this topic:

> There is a good deal of the primate heritage that is relevant to any study of human society: dominance and hierarchy, territoriality, group cooperation, consort and mating behaviour, ritualization, etc. But the "facts of life" with which man has had to come to terms in the process of adaptation, and which are immediately relevant to the study of kinship and marriage, can perhaps be reduced to four basic "principles":
> Principle 1. The women have the children
> Principle 2. The men impregnate the women
> Principle 3. The men usually exercise control
> Principle 4. Primary kin do not mate with each other. (1967:31)

Note that men exercising control sneaks in as an uncontested part of the syllogism.

Even in the matriarchal fantasies of Victorian social anthropology, women were not discussed as active agents. Males were always perceived to be in control, even in matrilineages, which brought us the "puzzle" of the mother's brother—why a man would favor his sister's children over his own, especially when it came to the disposal of "his" goods (Malinowski 1922). Fox implies that it could be worse. While one of the basic principles of society is that "men exercise control," he sees this as a silver lining because otherwise "an Amazonian solution would serve. In this *sinister vs. natural* the women would hold the property and the power, men would be of no account and would be used for breeding purposes only. Such a sinister practice exists only in the imagination" (Fox 1967:113). The reverse, of course, is not sinister, but "natural."

This attitude may explain the failure of "social archaeology" even to notice gender as a process in human life. Colin Renfrew, in *Approaches to Social Archaeology*, considers only social arrangements between men; women in his scheme of things are utterly invisible. For example, he asks, "does the great quantity of artefacts found in association with a skeleton in a particularly 'rich' burial indicate that the deceased was a *man* of wealth or of social prominence, or perhaps a sacrificial victim interred with particular ceremony?" (1984:4, emphasis added). Women not only are distinctly not active agents in this kind of social archaeology, they are missing entirely. Even when the household became the focus of study, women were mysteriously absent, as indeed were men and children. The only people were "faceless blobs" (Tringham 1991).

Processual archaeology had as one of its tenets that all facets of cultures, including their social and ideological dimensions, could be studied with archaeological data (Binford 1962). That this goal was not achieved reflects the fact that archaeologists have firmly maintained the standard anthropological attitude toward women, carrying all the baggage of cultural anthropology, including their lenses of androcentrism, into their analyses. Processualists began a more detailed examination of archaeological discoveries, but were unable to take the topic as far as some recent gender studies have done, precisely because of their gender assumptions.

Kin Organization: Stylistic Analyses

Pottery, with its varied decorative techniques and patterns, was the focus of several early studies by processual archaeologists. The variations could be imagined as reflecting social organization, especially matrilineality, or better yet the shift to patrilineality. Pottery was known to have been made by women in most Native American groups, therefore its manufacture could be associated with women in the Americas, to seek patterning that would reflect the social structure. Coincidentally, matrilineality was also observed among many Native American groups, and archaeological cultures that were presumably ancestral to these groups could be studied with reference to their matrilineal organization. Ways to observe the occasional shift within one group from matrilineality to patrilineality were sought in archaeological contexts, for various reasons. The twin assumptions that all women were potters, and that styles of pottery decoration reflected the teaching or example of elder women potters to their younger female relatives, were critical in these arguments. Thus the studies appear to focus on gender relationships, though in fact they concentrate on stylistic elements of pots and their statistical manipulation, rather than on *people*.

In the budding processual archaeology of the 1960s, several studies focused on the decoration of pots. Archaeologists examined the distribution of stylistic patterns to enable them to interpret the social system (e.g. Deetz 1965, 1968; Longacre 1966, 1968; Whallon 1968; Hill 1968). These studies might have been pathbreaking by perceiving women as actors in pottery production, as well as in educating the next generation with both technology and the passing down of tradition. Unfortunately, the research methods suppressed any such emphasis and women ceased to be agents, their place being taken by the pots themselves, or more often just the rim sherds.

One of these early studies considered designs on ceramics at the Medicine Crow site, intended to elicit changes in stylistic patterning through time, in order to illustrate a shift from matrilocal to patrilocal marriage patterns (Deetz 1965). This pioneering study has been critiqued on several grounds. The statistics James Deetz used were faulted as not demonstrating the associations they were intended to show (Whallon 1968), and Deetz's own criticism delimited the perils of attempting to ascertain descent with archaeological data, also suggesting that these exercises could lead to "sterile methodological virtuosity" (Deetz 1968:48). Christi Mitchell (1992) notes that "Deetz's sources do not include women in the count of village inhabitants," which reflects the attitude toward women demonstrated by ethnographers, such as that exhibited by Lévi-Strauss.

In William Longacre's study of the Carter Ranch site, though it is entitled "Some Aspects of Prehistoric Society in East-Central Arizona," no people at all appear in the chapter until an explanation of the statistics relates artifact frequencies to location. Longacre begins with the environment, then describes the pueblo itself, and proceeds to the statistical manipulations. Associations of ceremonial artifacts with weaving tools, and of chopping tools with arrow-shaft manufacturing tools, were used to suggest "a fairly strong division of labor and functionally specific male and female activity areas at the site," though no specific place is interpreted as a female work area (1968:97). But the main intent was a test of postmarital residence rules, with the locations of painted pottery design elements in rooms, kivas, burials, and trash. Again, design elements and rules take precedence over people as agents.

James Hill examined activities in various categories of rooms in Broken K Pueblo, but his delineated activities are strangely ungendered. The extensive use of the passive voice makes this result appear to be deliberate, but, whether it is deliberate or not, it is certainly true that gendered activities were not the point of his paper, and it is possibly the case that the gender of the actors was taken for granted (1968).

Women do not appear at all in Robert Whallon's study of the prehistoric social organization of Upper New York, except with a brief mention of their production of the pots that form the unit of analysis (1968). William Engelbrecht, using similar data, took a different tack. He begins in the usual manner, stating that among the Iroquois, women were the potters in historical times and must have been potters in prehistory as well. Through a statistical analysis of the rim sherds, he shows that similarity of designs increased through time. This is a test of his hypothesis that women had more contact with other villages after the League of the Iroquois was formed. He concludes that there was more interaction between tribes at that time, and suggests that it occurred not because of warfare but instead because of increased trade. The model, based on historic records, assumes that women actively engaged in such trade. Thus archaeology was used to confirm and extend the historic record (Engelbrecht 1974). This study actually does pay attention to women as active agents, and shows that it was possible to do so using the tenets of the time. But none of these studies was motivated by an interest either in women per se or in gender. Perhaps new studies of this kind can be used to extend an understanding of kinship in particular societies.

Work that attempted to delimit tribal groups with the use of stylistic attributes of pottery has not been applied to gender studies as far as I can discover, yet it seems to be a potentially fruitful direction to pursue. For example, I used pottery attributes to search for tribal boundaries in the Korean Neolithic, without ever giving the slightest thought to the possible agency of women as potters (Nelson 1987). However, this model, like the papers discussed above, assumes that decorative patterns and techniques are taught to daughters by mothers, or at least to female kin within a matrilineage, or matrilocal living arrangements. The focus on boundaries extends the analysis of pottery beyond specific villages to the entire group. If pottery decorations (or other stylistic characteristics) can be used to indicate tribal boundaries, can these tribes, clans, or other groups be assumed to be matrilineages? Are there ways to test this possibility with ethnoarchaeological studies? Can other lines of evidence be teased out of the archaeological record?

In societies where Marxism was the dominant ideology, matrilineal societies were treated in a doctrinaire fashion in archaeology, whether in the Soviet Union (Soffer 1983), China (Pearson 1981, 1988; Zhang 1985) or any of the satellites. It was simply "known" that matrilineal societies were earlier than patrilineal ones, so the interpretation was *pro forma*, rather than argued. Chinese sites are particularly rich in detail, and may reasonably be used to understand gender in China, although the full potential has not yet been tapped.

The site of Banpo, a Yangshao site near the Yellow River in China, in the 5th millennium B.C. is predictably and classically interpreted as a matrilineal society. The site brochure calls it a "typical matriarchal clan community" in which the people "lived in a society where there were no classes and thus no exploitation of man by man [sic], and led a primitive communist life in which the people worked together and divided among themselves what they had gained" (pamphlet from Banpo with neither author nor date indicated, obtained in 1985). The site is large and divided into three areas, one for housing and one for ceramic production, as well as a large cemetery (Chang 1986). There is no internal division within the houses, but a larger-than-average building was excavated, which is interpreted as a communal center. The cemetery contains graves with multiple burials grouped in various combinations of ages and sexes. Possibilities for extending the analysis of this society abound, but are often not considered necessary in China because the early Neolithic is determined a priori to be matrilineal.

It is clear that the interpretation of the burials figures heavily into the assignment of the early Neolithic in China to the "matriarchal clan communes" in which "land, houses and livestock belonged to the whole clan." But, "as agriculture and animal husbandry developed, beginning about four to five thousand years ago, men began to replace women in the leading role in production and daily life and the clan commune became a patriarchal one with kinship determined by blood relationship with the father" (Chiao 1978:52). Thus the next putative stage in evolution is used to interpret the archaeological record.

The site of Majiayao in Gansu, around 3000 B.C., with a cemetery of more than a thousand burials, is among the sites used to demonstrate the "transition from the matriarchal to the patriarchal clan society." A "social division of labor" is said to be evident in the graves, because men and women had different types of burial goods. Men were buried accompanied by stone tools, while women's graves contained pots as well as spinning and weaving implements. Unfortunately, we do not know whether or not this is an absolute distinction, or whether burials were sexed by their grave goods rather than their skeletons. But the distribution of grave goods is said to demonstrate that "men had assumed the dominant position in farm and handicraft production and women engaged mainly in household work like spinning and weaving" (Anonymous 1977:22). The logic that calls men's creativity "handicraft production" while disparaging pottery, cloth, and clothing production as "household work" is a typical example of reading present gender attitudes into the past. These graves also have considerable differences in size and richness of grave goods. One example contains 90 artifacts, and several burials are accompanied by very little. Burials interpreted as human sacrifices comprised additional burials in the larger graves. These were mostly women, buried flexed on their sides, some of them appearing to have been tied up, according to the report. Clearly there are gender issues and several lines of evidence to explore.

Zhang Zhong-pei (1985) examines social structure in a cemetery at Yuanjunmiao, a large Neolithic site in central China. The cemetery was divided into two sections. Many graves contained multiple interments, which Zhang refers to as collective tombs. He uses the standard Chinese terminology of clans and tribes to interpret the site. Furthermore, he suggests that the relative equality of the grave goods reflects an egalitarian society, in spite of rather striking and quite interesting variations among the burials. For example, one grave containing the bodies of two girls has an extraordinary number of bone beads, and another contains 25 pieces of pottery. These are interpreted as reflecting differences in family wealth. "The mother who was wealthy and high in social status enabled her daughters to attain benefits through inheritance" (Zhang 1985:31). There is no way to know which grave might be the mother's, or whether the girls were sisters, to confirm or refute this assertion. Two other burials, interpreted as girls on the basis of their "adult" grave goods, are used as evidence that girls had higher status than boys, a case of circular reasoning. Zhang refers to Morgan's description of a "tribal clan" cemetery in which people were buried in rows by clan affiliation, and points out similar characteristics of the Yuanjunmiao site, which was divided into two sections, which might represent moieties. Collective burials often include both sexes and a spread of all ages, which does bolster his interpretation.

The discovery of a burial in Leizi with shell laid out in the form of a tiger on one side of the skeleton and a dragon on the other was interpreted as the grave of "a very powerful person," since both tigers and dragons imply power in historic China. "Since the remains were male, this has led to speculation that the matrilineal, rather egalitarian cultures of the neolithic period may have given way to a more stratified society in China a thousand or more years earlier than had been previously thought" (Da 1988:48). Again, a gendered prehistory needs to be argued more thoroughly. What did the *other* graves look like, and who was buried in them?

The site of Xinle in Shenyang, Liaoning Province, China, is also instructive in this regard. In the original excavation, two houses were excavated, one larger than the other. On the floor of the larger house, a partially decayed wooden stick was found, with an elaborate carving of a stylized bird. It appeared to have no practical use, and was interpreted as a wand of authority. By this association, the larger house was therefore assumed to be that of the woman chief. A colorful mural covering an entire wall in the museum dedicated to the site tells this "story" far better than words. A young woman, with bare breasts to demonstrate that these people were not "civilized", stands flourishing the wooden baton, while all around her other young bare-breasted women frolic and dance. This is quite a joyful rendition of a matriarchy (Nelson 1991a).

These examples could be multiplied with practically every Neolithic site in China. Richard Pearson critiques this manner of interpreting sites, concluding that "relative power of males and females, matriliny, patriliny, and rules of inheritance . . . cannot be established from burial data" (1988:39). This seems to me to be too pessimistic a conclusion, although it is true that in the Chinese examples there is no attempt to establish these, nor any felt need to do so. Pearson suggests that it may be possible to find "ritual and social groupings," though he does not address the question of engendering the archaeological record more accurately, through biological sexing.

Still, it is possible to identify lineages archaeologically in rare circumstances. An example of a matrilineal society in which women potters enjoyed wealth and prestige is provided from Khok Phanom Di, a mound in Thailand (Higham and Thosarat 1994, Higham and Bannanurag 1990). This mound contained both houses and a burial ground, but it is the cemetery that is of particular interest at the site. The total mound, all of which is artificial, is seven meters high, having accumulated over a period of 500 years, by C_{14} dating.

Beneath the top layer, six meters of deposit contain burials in clusters. Vertically between the burial clusters, shell midden and other trash was found, marked off definitively as though there had been wooden barricades around each cluster throughout its use span. The average life expectancy of the population was low: only 28 years, and very few persons in the cemetery had lived beyond age 35. Genetic studies of the skeletons allowed them to be identified as family lineages. In addition, the skeletons show the practice of tooth removal, but different teeth were extracted for different families, further suggesting that people buried in these clusters were related, and of successive generations.

The fortunes of any particular family group can be followed by the rise and fall of the number of artifacts buried with successive women in the same burial plot. The rich burial of a woman, whose status as a potter was clear from the clay cylinders and burnishing pebbles surrounding her, suggested to the excavators that producing fine pottery for trade conferred high status in that society. In addition to some of the tools of her trade, this woman was accompanied by 10 ornate pottery vessels. Her burial goods also included some 120,000 shell beads; 2 shell disks, 1 on each shoulder; 950 large I-shaped beads on her chest; a headdress; and a bangle on her left wrist made of exotic shell. This array of worldly goods was considered to be a result of her own achievements, but an infant, presumably her daughter, was similarly buried with rich equipment, demonstrating family riches.

An interesting feature of these clusters was that they could be divided into poor families and rich families at any particular time, but through time a lineage was not constant in its means. The excavators conclude that "esteem and status had to be attained through personal achievement" (Higham and Thosarat 1994:64). Since the shells were not local, they suggest that pots were traded for exotic shells. This was refreshingly interpreted as a "Big Woman" system: "At Kok Phanom Di, we find that the later generations were dominated numerically, and in terms of wealth, by women" (Higham and Thosarat 1994:55). Women were potters, whose increasing status is reflected in the fact that they began to have more burial equipment than men during the 12th generation of the cemetery. This system was stable, lasting another three hundred years, but by the 20th generation, the sea retreated from the site, making it no longer habitable, and the site was abandoned.

Motherhood

Beginning with "plausibility arguments" is one avenue that takes us partway into the prehistoric past. Kathleen Bolen leads into a discussion of prehistoric mothering by considering the variations in ethnographic examples. This is refreshing because archaeologists have been far too ready to accept motherhood as unvarying behavior and as having the same meaning in all cultures. Susan Carol Rogers reminds us that the American preoccupation with women's full-time roles as mothers is not a cultural universal (1978:135). Kathleen Bolen examines this notion in more detail. "Cross cultural and ethnographic research demonstrate tremendous variety in what mothers do, what it means to be a mother, what expectations are placed upon mothers, what maternal behavior entails, and who actually mothers" (1992:49). "Mothering" activities, Bolen points out, can be undertaken by anyone in the society—including adult males, the elderly, and older children. It is parenthetically interesting to note that we cannot call this behavior when practiced by males "fathering," for that has quite a different meaning! Child care is not restricted to females in most societies, let alone restricted to the natural mother. Indeed, as we have seen, males do much of the infant care in a few primate societies (Wright 1993). Therefore it is not unreasonable to expect male "mothering" in some prehistoric societies, and we should be alert for potential evidence for this phenomenon.

Furthermore, the notion that women are always burdened with infants and small children to tend can be "stood on its head": some argue that "the spacing and rearing of children must be accommodated to the requirements of women's subsistence roles, and not the other way around" (Friedl 1975, Nerlove 1974 [quoted in Tiffany 1979:9]). Judith Brown cites a study of reindeer herders by Bogoras (1904) to demonstrate that it is the subsistence activities that determine the child care, and not the reverse. Brown inter- prets this report as showing that "the population is divided into child- watching and non-child-watching members" (1975:40). Salvatore Cucchiari (1981) has made a similar argument in imagining an early ungendered group of humans. He assumes there could have been a genderless "nurturing ideology" without the assignment of nurturing to women. However, he assumes, contrary to much ethnographic evidence, that the gender system is "universally bipolar and . . . the two categories are universally stratified" (1981:41), making his theoretical argument less compelling. The archae- ological component of his argument, placing the "gender revolution" in the Upper Paleolithic, is quite dependent on André Leroi-Gourhan's (1967) assignment of gender to "signs" on cave walls, a rather imaginative flight of fancy based on Freudian "universals."

Other aspects of women's wombs are likely to have left traces in the archaeological record, and may be recognized when this is seen as an important consideration. Birthing huts and menstrual huts, like latrines, are rarely recognized in prehistoric archaeology; these structures, however, could be important for understanding female rituals surrounding fertility and may be identified by soil analysis when the possibility is considered.

Patricia Rice suggested that the Upper Paleolithic female figurines may represent several stages of womanhood, and could have been used to teach girls about the female life cycle. Figurines were coded as juvenile, reproduc- tive age, and old, as well as whether or not they appeared to be pregnant. A high degree of agreement among the coders as to which category each figurine belonged to confirmed that variability in age is likely to be repre- sented by the figures (1981).

Other possibilities include the engraved bones of the Upper Paleolithic, which Alexander Marshack (1972) has studied microscopically. Rows of markings on decorated bones were made in groups that he thought repre- sented phases of the moon. Another interpretation, which might fit the facts even better, since the precision of the 29.5 day lunar cycle is not required, is that they are menstrual calendars. Perhaps Upper Paleolithic women were cognizant of the cause of conception, and had some inkling about the process and duration of pregnancy. This possibility has not been explored, perhaps because it is an uncomfortable topic for men. Gloria

Steinem (1980), tongue in cheek, suggests that if men could menstruate the process would be glorified.

Daughters and Sisterhood

Daughters appear in the written record, but in archaeology it is very rare to have a situation, such as that at Khok Phanom Di discussed above, in which actual genetic relationships can be inferred. However, in protohistory, when some written documents are available, the archaeological record can enrich the documentary evidence to reveal facets of inheritance by daughters. High-status burials, being by definition richer than others from the same group, contain more variety and may include heirlooms that imply descent, or even inscriptions that specify familial relationships. When the sex of the interred can be determined directly from the skeleton, even more secure inferences can be made.

Inheritance in noble families is the most common avenue to such inferences, and examples in which daughters inherit high status are well known. This pattern is particularly common in succession to kingship, for royalty may descend through the female line either exclusively or bilaterally—ancient Egypt, ancient Hawaii, Yamato (Japan), and the Silla Kingdom in Korea, for some examples. It is the husband of the king's daughter (or perhaps more accurately and appropriately the queen's daughter) who is eligible to become king in many of these societies. The right to rule inheres in the women, even though the male is the nominal ruler (at least according to western historiography). It is worth considering whether an earlier matrilineal system is being hidden and transformed by later documents. The more important figure may have been the queen, succeeded by her daughter (Nelson 1991b, 1993). Co-rulership is another possibility, which was practiced in Japan (Piggott n.d.).

Karen Sacks has emphasized sisterhood in her study of African kingdoms (1979). She suggests that when women are part of a kinship group, as sisters, they retain higher status than when they are merely wives.

Wifehood

The transition from chiefdoms to states was famously seen as the "world historical defeat of the female sex," and private property was fingered as the culprit (Engels 1881). Since men became the holders of property that they naturally would want to pass on to their sons, so the story runs, it was necessary to ensure that offspring (sons!) were sired by the husband. Thus, virginity of brides and fidelity (and fertility) of wives became important. But men could not constantly accompany their wives, so virginity and fidelity could only be ensured if women were secluded, veiled, locked up with chastity belts, genitally mutilated (as in some "civilized" countries even today), or legally "owned" by men. Women themselves became property, to be "exchanged" by men.

Another explanation for the ownership of women by men is militarism—women were a reward for victorious soldiers, or could be captured in war, and women were in danger of being raped by a victorious and pillaging army (see Harris 1993). There is no doubt that rape in warfare was a potent weapon against women, as has been documented from Bosnia to the Korean "comfort women" enslaved by Japanese troops. However, since there were societies in which women could be warriors, this is not satisfactory as a universal answer, though it may well apply in particular instances.

Nonarchaeologists, using archaeological and other evidence, considered the classical shift from kinship to territory as the definition and organizing principle of the creation of states. The way this shift disadvantaged women was the subject of their scrutiny. Two influential books, Gerda Lerner's *The Creation of Patriarchy* (1986) and *Beyond Power* by Marilyn French (1985), tackled this problem, but each considers mostly southwest Asia and Europe, and neither has the benefit of sophisticated archaeological background and analysis. One flaw in both arguments is that not all states are organized by territory alone; examples of kin-organized states are known, especially ones in which membership in the kin group continues to be of primary importance in assigning a place in the social structure (Sacks 1979). In the context of this chapter it is important to note that class may override gender as a dividing principle of society. Early Silla society in Korea was divided into endogamous "Bone Ranks," for example, in which only the Holy Bone could rule and nobles were drawn from the ranks of the True Bone. Sumptuary laws kept members of each Bone Rank from rising above their station, with prescribed clothing, housing, horse equipment, and so forth for both men and women of each rank. However, women seem to be entirely equal to men at each rank (Nelson 1991b, 1993). The need to study kinship is summed up by Irene Silverblatt, based on her study of Inca society: "We do not do justice to the diversity of women's experiences by generalizing that all (or even most) gender ideologies produced in state contexts colluded in downgrading kin spheres, reifying women as child-bearers, and belittling females because of their link to kin group reproduction" (1988:442).

Conclusions

Social structure and social organization are elusive in archaeological contexts, but assertions about these topics are made nevertheless. It seems that a responsible archaeologist would make the recovering of gender relationships an explicit goal, and would use all available powers to delineate specific social structures.

CHAPTER SEVEN
THE LARGER COMMUNITY

An emphasis on topics like leadership, power, warfare, exchange of women, rights of inheritance, and notions of property—to name a few—can all be cited as issues of special interest to males in particular historic contexts and sociopolitical structures.
—Margaret Conkey and Janet Spector (1984:4)

To talk of women's status is to think about a social world in ultimately dichotomous terms, wherein "woman" is universally opposed to "man" in the same ways in all contexts.
—Alison Wylie (1992a:55)

In many archaeological contexts, ranking and/or class stratification can be inferred from a number of indications such as relative sizes of dwellings, sumptuary goods, and burials with varying amounts and quality of grave goods. But how can women's roles (or men's roles) in the public sphere be identified? The tendency has been to gender leaders as male without explanation or argument. Is there a way out of the trap that simply genders leadership as male, and homemaking as female, reflecting our own gender ideology? Where did this public/private dichotomy come from? Is it built into the human genetic makeup, or hormones, as a few die-hard androcentrists still insist? Archaeological evidence shows the constructedness of leadership, and denies that it is universally male.

One of the early debates in feminist cultural anthropology concerned whether most cultures have been divided into domestic spheres and public spheres, gendered female and male respectively. While at one time this division seemed to describe all societies (Rosaldo 1974:23–25), on closer examination of the ethnographic realities, feminists in cultural anthropology realized that the very formulation of public versus private spheres was an example of the androcentric lens through which we had all been trained to see the world (Rosaldo 1980). This understanding freed feminist archaeologists to perceive what existed all along: women in many past cultures acting publicly, with earned prestige or legitimate power.

One definition of activities in the public domain is "control over people, resources, and property" (Linnekin 1990:56). A question to begin with is whether "control" is the key concept in the public sphere. It is important to consider whether influence is as pertinent as control (or is another form of control). What public roles have been available to women and men in different cultures? Are they roles of control or influence?

Whether as rulers, traders, healers, or even warriors, women's contributions to society often had a public aspect, separate from or in addition to a domestic one. Finding and documenting ethnohistoric examples of women with public roles opens further possibilities for seeking evidence of women, and of gendered relationships, in archaeological contexts. It has often been the case that women occupying such positions were considered exceptions, women taking on roles "properly" gendered male, and therefore of no particular interest. In Chinese historiography, women in public roles, especially rulers and (worst of all) empresses, were cited as examples of misrule, of society gone wrong. The same attitude can be perceived toward women who take on public roles in our own society. Thus there is a purpose to the disapproval of public women, sending women back to their "place." The insistence that it is biologically unreasonable for women to have public roles is simply an attempt (often successful) to oppress women and to deter them from the public sphere.

In fact, archaeological and ethnohistoric data fail to uphold the idea that women have never played public roles. In various prehistoric and protohistoric societies, more and more public roles are being discovered that could have been filled by women as women. Publicly visible women might have included such roles as religious practitioners, healers, and traders, as well as chiefs and rulers, even despots and tyrants. Furthermore, we know from ethnographic sources that an individual woman might fill more than one of these roles in a particular society, and several or all public roles might be open to women, depending on an assortment of factors. Categories other than gender may structure how gendered roles and meanings are articulated.

A severe impediment to recognizing women in public roles in archaeology is the double standard that has frequently been applied in interpreting sites. A male in a rich burial is interpreted as a leader, or at least a man of wealth (Renfrew 1984:3), while a woman's burial, just as rich or richer, is seen as the leader's wife, a woman dependent on a male for her status. Independently wealthy women, and women who achieve on their own, seem to be an uncomfortable concept for some men, even when the female achievers lived in the distant past, and far away.

Howard Winters, describing burials at Indian Knoll, notes that women's graves contained imported marine shell, while men's did not. But Winters has an explanation that will uphold the superiority and dominance of males: "Of course, such an exclusion does not mean that males played no role in the control of the resource, since the public display of the ornaments often may be linked to females, the procurement and distribution to males, who apparently receive their satisfactions from the control of wealth, with females serving as the observable symbols of that wealth—a procedure not without parallels in contemporary American society" (1968:205). With the final twist, Winters has turned his speculation into a fact that can be *compared with* the present, effectively concealing the fact that it is *derived from* the present in the first place. And note that what is seen to be important is *control*, a particularly masculine concern in our culture.

Another example of different interpretations for the same phenomenon depending on whether it is related to men or women is found with regard to Harappan statues, in the aptly titled "Emergence of Man" series published by Time-Life. The "disproportionate number of statues of women in the ruins of Moenjo-Daro's houses lead archaeologists to believe the inhabitants venerated a female deity—perhaps a mother goddess" (Hamblin 1973:128). The author goes on to note that the figures were "endowed with a figure exaggerated beyond reality," implying both sexuality and the male viewer, which seems incompatible with the previous speculation that they are representations of goddesses. In contrast to the goddess-as-sex-object, a statue of a nude male torso is found under the rubric "Figures of Authority." The text tells us that, "[a]lthough male figures rarely appear among sculptures dug up at Moenjo-Daro and Harappa, the few that do all seem to represent men of importance...there is a common theme...regality and godliness" (Hamblin 1973:133). Pictured beside this text is a broken statue of a stiff-postured standing male wearing nothing at all, not even any jewelry. Naked men are regal and *godly*, while partly dressed women are intended for men's gaze. It is important to note the different treatment by sex, and the snicker of sexuality applied differentially to female figures, while respect is accorded male figures, even if they are buck naked.

Allowing women a place in public sometimes is associated with a lack of complexity, or specifically with a lack of warfare. But societies in which women play a public role are not just simple or peaceful ones. On closer inspection, even some societies considered highly male and warlike can include women in public roles. An interesting example is the Aztec, those fierce Mexican warriors who so astonished Cortez and his Spaniards by ripping out the living hearts of prisoners, as sacrifices to their gods. Sharisse and Geoffrey McCafferty have shown that women in Aztec society were not excluded from trade, warfare, or the priesthood, all roles in the public sphere. "In our analysis of documents from early Colonial Mexico, we have found numerous examples of powerful women, either in these same occupations, or else in analogous tasks" (1988b:48). Women's economic activities were important to Aztec society (see also Brumfiel 1991); perhaps it should not be surprising that public roles were available to women as well as to men.

The ancient Hawaiians, who practiced human sacrifice on a much smaller scale, had a number of public roles for women, including military leaders and priests, as described from ethnohistoric documents by Joyce Linnekin (1990). Archaeologists should be wary of labeling all public roles as male, even in the most apparently warlike societies.

Another important debate of feminist anthropology relating to the public/private dichotomy centers on whether a change to state-level society was responsible for a reduction in women's status or autonomy (Rohrlich-Leavitt 1976, Rapp 1977, Sacks 1979). Through the mid-1970s, universal domination of women by men was the standard anthropological stance (Rosaldo and Lamphere 1974:3). Sherry Ortner (1981) claimed to have found cross-cultural substantiation for this situation, and posited that women's still-lower status in states was related to the need for purity in women to carry on men's patrilines. The topic of women as a cause of disunity among men was thus reintroduced from the origins theme. Eleanor Lea-cock, however, questioned the data on which this generalization was based, and demonstrated that many North American Indian cultures, which are treated as if they were pristine by the use of the "ethnographic present," had in fact changed significantly with the impact of European settlements. In particular the demand for pelts in the fur trade upset the previous gender balance by placing an inordinate emphasis on trapping fur animals (1981). These ethnographic considerations indicate that women's public roles in various societies should *always* be a question. With appropriate attention to details, archaeology may be uniquely able to research these topics. Rita Wright (1996:86) notes that women in periods preceding Ur III in Meso-potamia were both wives of rulers and priestesses who owned their own seals and had "control over some economic activities and . . . possessed significant authority."

Although archaeology is in a position to correct historical distortions in the data, with reference to actual sites, nothing will be accomplished if explanations begin with generalizations that obscure past gender relations and obliterate women altogether (see Hayden 1992 for an example of this principle in action). To engender public roles with data instead of assumptions, historically specific examples of women in social systems are needed to provide a sense of the full range of human possibilities. This procedure produces a more textured sense of the past, with many kinds of possibilities for women and men, varying from one society to another, but rarely confining women completely to the household.

Ethnohistorians have led the way in this endeavor. Viana Muller (1985) questioned the universality of the requirement of virginity for women at marriage in state-level societies, using data from northwest Europe. Irene Silverblatt studied women in the Inca state, and found considerable variation in women's positions and roles that had been overlooked: "Andean structures of gender parallelism ensured that women, independently from men and through a line of women, inherited access to political and religious office" (1991:147). Joyce Linnekin (1990) similarly examined the roles of sacred queens in Hawaii, and once again found that the details added up to something other than the sweeping picture of male dominance that had been presented. Some specific public roles that women may have held there include traders, healers, warriors, and both religious and political leaders.

Traders

In spite of the rhetoric that would confine all women to within a few miles of their domicile, if not within house walls, ethnographic examples of women as long-distance traders are not rare, and are especially well reported in East Africa (see Gifford-Gonzalez 1997). Ethnographic examples of this kind can be compared with the Aztecs, where both men and women could be *pochteca*, long-distance traders (McCafferty and McCafferty 1988b). Women traders among the Aztecs are illustrated in the pictorial codices. Exactly how to detect women traders in the archaeological record is not yet clear, but allowing for the possibility is a beginning. Burials of women associated with trade goods might actually represent women traders. The role of women as traders has not been completely neglected. William Engelbrecht posited women traders among the Iroquois to account for changing heterogeneity of designs on pottery. Iroquois women were recorded as long-distance traders, though the changes in pottery ornamentation had been interpreted in other ways (1974). This shows that when the possibility of women as long-distance traders is allowed, evidence that could lead to such an interpretation is less likely to be overlooked.

Healers

"Medicine men" or "medicine women" are not commonly identified in archaeological sites, though we can infer they must have been often present. Many societies are known to have had women healers. In Korea, the *mudang*, almost exclusively women, are healers even in the present, called on to improve health and fortune of individual clients or to restore harmony to a village, as may be required, by "trancing" and driving out mischievous spirits. It is likely that, with sufficient thought about relevant archaeological traces, activities of *mudang* of the past, who must surely have existed, could be detected in Korean sites.

The usual problem with ascription of shamanism to women is that if women are posited as shamans, strong proof is demanded, while if any activity is gendered male, not even a bridging argument is required. Recall, for example, those mythical male shamans who were said to have domesticated gourds in eastern North America so that they would have rattles to use in curing (Watson and Kennedy 1991). This attitude toward women

shamans in the [
are the norm. M
ancient histories, :
to A.D. 668), whei
documents refer to
shamans performin
conveniently ignore
equipment in Korea
from the proto–Thre(
because objects with r
today use similar bror.
have belonged to a ma.

Women's roles as h
edge of plants, and by (
with many millennia of
which traces of women a
Preclassic and Aztec in C
in the Old World.

This is
mainly women" (1980:88). in arch
(whether women *or* men) in arch
from Korea) is based on mate
ent on images, iconograp
ing such roles are nee
recognized. App
one region to

Religi

Pr

...in
...u include the Middle
...exico and the Minoan Crete and Sumer

Some of the "Pretty Lady" figurines of the Mesoamerican Formative suggest curing ceremonies (Guillén 1988). Among the Aztecs, we read that, "Priestesses of Tlazoteotl and Toci were also skilled physicians and herbalists," implying that these occupations could have been real roles of real women (McCafferty and McCafferty 1988b). The excavated areas of Minoan Crete include murals in which women are depicted in active and public roles, including processions (Evans 1930), and excavations in Thera have unearthed additional Minoan wall paintings that depict women in public roles (Doumas 1983). Figurines up to 34 cm high of well-dressed women holding snakes in their hands, or on their arms and entwined around their heads and bodies, surely depict important women. Although the statuettes are more often described as "Goddesses," they might be better interpreted as healers—given the fact that snakes had a role in medicine in later Greece. The entwined snakes that now define the medical profession were on the staff brandished by the patron of healers in Greece.

Regarding Sumer, Ruby Rohrlich relates, "The oldest medical tablet found so far dates back to the last quarter of the third millennium B.C., when Gula was goddess of healing and medicine, and doctors were probably still

a rather sparse roll call of healers
...eology, and none of it (except the hoard
...al culture alone. These examples are depend-
...y, and the written record. New ways of identify-
...ded so that prehistoric healers (of either sex) can be
...opriate archaeological evidence will naturally vary from
...nother, but nevertheless it is likely to be found if it is sought.

...ous Leaders

...ests and prophets were other public roles open to women in various
societies. These too are difficult roles to deduce with purely material
evidence, and even when priests/priestesses can indeed be inferred, it is
often impossible to infer the sex (or the gender) of the officiant. Women
with prominent religious roles are known from Mesopotamia, among the
Celtic and Germanic peoples, in North American Indian groups, and in
many parts of Siberia and Asia, for a few examples.

Again, much of the evidence is historic or ethnohistoric, but still it has
implications for archaeological inquiry, especially in the questions asked and
the models used for interpretation. In the Sumerian world, "females might
hold high positions in the temple hierarchy. Particularly at Ur, they seem to
have been the major administrators.... Under certain conditions they
appear to have had extremely high status" (Zagarell 1986:417).

Viana Muller reminds us that "Tacitus reported that [Germanic]
women were held in great esteem as prophetesses and were consulted before
important clan decisions were made" (1985:95). Women as the voice of
oracles are common in the ancient world. They are known in ancient
Greece, especially at Delphi and outside Rome, for example.

A shaman/leader of Japan, of the polity of Yamatai in the 3rd century
A.D., is documented in the *Wei Zhi*, an early Chinese history. She is referred
to as "Queen Himiko." Himiko is said to have lived in a walled compound
surrounded by watchtowers within, but separated from her city. It is
intriguing that a site answering this description has been excavated in the
Early Yayoi period in Kyushu. While there are dating problems with
the convergence of the site and this historic reference, the site of Yoshinogari contains an inner area surrounded by a wall, with large postholes that
could have supported watchtowers. Besides, it is an extraordinarily rich site,

with 350 pit houses and 2,350 graves containing some two thousand burial urns in its huge cemetery. Each end of the site has an unusually large mound with a central burial and subsidiary burials. In the northern mound, the central urn contains a magnificent sword and a necklace of long, tubular blue beads (Hudson and Barnes 1991). It is not likely that Queen Himiko herself lived at Yoshinogari; the date of the site is much too early, but Yoshinogari has been popularly assigned to this queen while the archaeological establishment spurns this designation. It is amusing that the site, open to the public as a historical park, has a gift shop that sells sweatshirts, coffee mugs, and other souvenirs with Himiko's "portrait," using some of the finds from the site to depict the jewelry and headdress of this unofficial queen.

The tradition of shaman-queens may have been widespread in Japan—a proposition that requires archaeological testing—but it may be distantly reflected in the *yuta* (female shamans) of Okinawa and the "princesses" of Shinto shrines in Japan that have lasted into the present, as well as the *mudangs* of Korea.

Many women priests and shamans are recorded in the ethnology of North American Indian groups (Leacock 1978), and "participation in the priesthood was probably the greatest source of female power in pre-Columbian society." Priestesses for both male and female deities wielded great social power by officiating at the different rites of passage in the life cycle (Brown 1983:50). Royal women participated in Classic Maya public rituals, as seen on a great variety of contemporary stelae and monuments (Joyce 1992). In many of the Siberian cultures, from which the word *shaman* was derived, women could be shamans, according to ethnographic accounts.

Warriors and Athletes

The "woman warrior" may seem to belong more to myths recalling fierce, one-breasted Amazon fighters than to reality. But while women in battle may seem to be more of an anomaly than some of the other public roles women have held, some unexpected finds, such as a group of *female* soldiers in Qin Shihuangdi's famous pottery army (Anonymous 1993:64), should give us pause. While the woman warrior in China is a feature of myth and story (e.g. Kingston 1975), it is extremely unexpected to find a whole troop of women soldiers produced in pottery—especially at a time in Chinese history when the government was consolidating its rule with particularly draconian measures, and emphasizing the putting of women in their place (Duyvendak 1928). Whether the pottery army reflects a real detachment of women soldiers is unknown, but no one has doubted that the rest of the pottery army represents real people. For example, a leading authority in China declares that "the pottery figures are true images of personnel of the Qin army" (Qian 1981c:82).

Jeannine Davis-Kimball has excavated mound tombs of the Saurama-tian culture on the Eurasian steppe about 600–400 B.C. These graves often contain a woman with substantial weapons, including iron swords and arrowheads. Some of these were mounted warriors as shown by a bow-legged girl who must have spent many hours on horseback. Males and children were buried as well, though women's graves were richer than men's. Women can be divided into three classes. The largest group of 28 burials was characterized by spindle whorls, mirrors, and beads; these were considered to be ordinary women. Five burials, containing "clay or stone altars, bone spoons, bronze mirrors, and seashells" (Davis-Kimball 1997:47), were interpreted as priestesses. Several females had the trappings of warriors: iron swords or daggers with whetstones for sharpening them, as well as projectile points.

Celtic women could be leaders of armies as well as rank-and-file warriors (Muller 1985:95). The famous Boadicea (or Boudica), who led an army against the Romans in Britain on behalf of her ill-treated daughters, comes to mind immediately. Antonia Fraser provides other historic examples of queens who led armies in various times and places in the past (Fraser 1989).

Women warriors in other cultures, however, may not always perform the same functions, or have the same meaning. It is documented in Dahomey that the king had an all-female army, who were supposedly his wives but in fact were like eunuchs—not allowed sexual expression and forbidden to bear children (Muller 1985). This is thought to have prevented the formation of alternative groups of kin who might ultimately mount a challenge to the government.

Thus, while the fact of "amazons" (in the generic sense) may be established in various places, each instance needs to be examined on its own merits. On the other hand, to suppose that indications of warfare are "inconsistent with a society dominated and run by women" (Hayden

1992:38) is to overgeneralize the data, and furthermore to essentialize women. The association of women with peacefulness should have been shattered by Margaret Thatcher, Britain's "Iron Lady" prime minister. Why shouldn't *some* women be warlike?

Women can be competitive athletes, in the past as well as the present. At least one of the Central Mexican "Pretty Ladies" is arrayed as a ball player, and women polo players are painted riding horses on tomb walls of Tang China. Minoan bull dancers include girls, and women of Sparta were portrayed as athletes on mosaic floors.

Leaders: Big Women, Chiefs, and Queens

Authority has been so successfully gendered male in our own culture that leaders are presumed to be men without any argument, whether archae-ological or ethnographic. Sharon Tiffany notes the difficulty: "Both formal and informal political roles of women remain unexplored in the anthropo-logical literature" (1979:434). How much more is this true in the archae-ological context! A typical discussion of leadership in the archaeological record is the following: "A major common factor in the development of leaders is the cultivation and retention of a group of followers. As the scope of a leader's power in decision-making is a function of the deference and respect of *his* followers, an aspiring leader usually implements a series of strategies that strengthen and extend *his* sociopolitical ties on a local and regional level" (Lightfoot and Feinman 1982:66, emphasis added).

In fact, the concept of chiefdom seems to presuppose men-in-charge, and the descriptions of "Big Man" societies, generalized to all of prehistory (although they are only described in Melanesia), serve to suppress *any* possibility of women leaders at *any* stage. Critiques of this sort of reduc-tionism are met with a self-righteous insistence that generalizing is the only scientific way to understand prehistory (Hayden 1992:33–34). On the contrary, the use of generalities is often a way to obscure "exceptions" to whatever has been set up as "the role of women."

The notion of the "Big Man" derives from Melanesia, where in some regions power is negotiated by ambitious men who compete for status by giving feasts and acquiring loyal followers for warfare. In the classic descrip-tions of these jockeyings for status, the cycle has to be maintained by feasting, and the foods for the feast, both vegetable foods and pigs, are the result of women's labor (e.g. Rappaport 1967).

The Big Man model has not only exerted an appeal as a way to understand approaches to chiefdoms, but it also sometimes seems to achieve the status of an evolutionary stage. Brian Hayden (1990) adopts the idea of feasting or competition based on food resources for creating and consolidating power, as the motive for plant and animal domination. Prestige is thus initially based on access to extra food, and this access is used to explain why the earliest known domesticates in some areas are not food staples. Calling these seekers-after-power-and-prestige "accumulators," Hayden asserts that "aspiring accumulators can be expected to exert all their ingenuity to bribe, coerce, cajole, and con other members of the community into supporting competitive feasts and producing as many delicacies or other high-quality foods as possible for feasts" (1990:36). They do this because they have a "competitive nature" (p. 37), a description rather than an explanation—and a tautology at that. Although these activities are largely ungendered, the accumulators are implicitly gendered male, and the drudges who are conned are female.

Hayden's defense (1992) of his reading of gender roles into the early Holocene (1990) is not convincing. He completely ignores the literature that demonstrates androcentrism in ethnography, he assumes that the division of labor by sex is absolute, and he considers what is designated male to be normal. He also argues by assertion, for example, "[T]here is little general doubt that this patterning of gender behavior is the expression of a fundamental principle of organization of hunter/gatherer societies and even more complex traditional societies" (1992:35). Thus, in a single phrase, he dismisses the entire feminist critique in both sociocultural anthropology and archaeology. In Hayden's argument, it all boils down to genes or simple hormones, without any attention to the contrary evidence. He cites only studies that assert male/female brain differences, not the critiques of these studies.

The Big Man story is based on an androcentric viewpoint. Men are able to give the feasts and become Big Men because of a surplus of food. The fact that the surplus is created as a result of women's labor is ignored. A question that is rarely asked about the Big Man system, in which women supply the labor power, is why women cooperate with it (Arnold et al. 1988,

Nelson 1994). Women are usually seen not as participants, but only as pawns. Why marry an ambitious man if you just have to work harder? There is no coercive power in these societies. The fact of women's cooperation in the system suggests that an element is missing from the traditional explanation. Diane Gifford-Gonzalez (1997) notes that Gusii men in East Africa have to negotiate with their wives to get them to brew beer for feasts. More attention to such negotiations might provide a more balanced view of Big Men societies.

The Big Man model has been applied to the origins of stratification in several parts of the world. Gary Webster creates a model from the ethnographic literature, and then compares it with Europe before 2000 B.C. He suggests that "big houses" in the center of tells (artificial hills formed from human occupations) in Bulgaria represent prominent families, although others have considered them to be structures for the entire community. Thus he concludes that labor control is the source of emergent stratification, but, although he says it is "grounded in the ethnography of power relations" (1990:346), we never quite learn how that labor is co-opted in the first place. Webster also notes African kingdoms in which "a chief's status was highly correlated with the number of wives . . . he possessed." Note that wives are described as possessions, denying them any agency. More important, polygyny is not noted among the salient characteristics of such "middle-range hierarchical societies," so it is unclear how relevant the observation might be to Europe four thousand years ago.

The entrenched assumptions of the Big Man model are also inherent in an apparently nongendered paper on early pithouses in the Mogollon region of the American Southwest. Kent Lightfoot and Gary Feinman posit "suprahousehold sociopolitical organizations" at the shift to sedentism in this region, and suppose that "household heads" existed, of whom a few "increasingly monopolized administrative authority in a community by achieving high status, influence and political power" (1982:64). Their paper reads like an ethnographic description rather than an archaeological explanation. It does not emerge until page 66 that these household heads are gendered male. In this case the household heads solve "managerial problems" rather than harnessing women's labor to create the new status; apparently it is the ability to organize households that catapults these persons to power. An organization of village leaders is the next step in creating hierarchy, in their scenario.

Surplus production enters without fanfare. The new male leader merits deference and respect from his followers by "amassing a surplus" that he achieves by "increasing the production [of food] in both their own gardens and those of close relatives. . . ." The present Pueblo cultures are not explicitly referenced, though this would seem more sensible than bringing in Melanesian and African societies, since they are the most likely descendants of the Mogollon in the American Southwest. Among most Pueblo groups, the women owned both the gardens and the food produced in them. It would have been difficult for the "village leaders" to gain access to the women's "surplus." However, these leaders are said to have been augmenting the size of the immediate household. "Household size can be increased by attracting unattached people and by acquiring several wives" (p. 67). In Lightfoot and Feinman's analysis, no attempt is made to demonstrate polygyny, or to discriminate among various other possible reasons for differential house size. However, they speculate that these leaders increase their power by "participation in regional trade and ceremonial exchange systems." This is a thinly disguised version of the Big Man model. Rather than deriving from the archaeological evidence, the evidence is squeezed to fit the model. The archaeological facts could support several other "stories." If the genders in this scenario were reversed, it is impossible to imagine that this paper would have been published at all, let alone given the credibility of publication in *American Antiquity*.

Ian Hodder writes from an unselfconsciously male perspective in which he asserts a need to domesticate and control female sexuality (1987), a "need" that obviously pertains only to males. In another paper the same covertly masculine voice masquerades as humanity, with a hypothesis that "in small-scale lineage-based societies in which the major concern is to increase labor power, the control of women by men, and the negotiation of position by women will become the dominant feature of social relations . . ." (1983:61). "Control" of women, rather than securing their cooperation, is seen as a specifically masculine problem.

The Big Man model is strongly associated with feasting, and by implication drinking, which are masculine activities by the lights of beer-drinking archaeologists. But evidence of women at festivals can be found in archaeological contexts, consistent with ethnohistoric evidence. Joan Gero (1991a) begins with describing the site of Queyash Alto, Peru. The plaza area was deduced to be the scene of public feasting and festivals, because it contained sherds of drinking bowls likely to have been used for *chicha*, maize beer, as well as ladles for serving it and wide-mouthed jars to serve it from. The consumption of meat is also implied by ash and charcoal, found in pits with burned and unburned llama bone. Most of the stone tools associated with preparation of meat were found in this area as well. Another association with festivals is provided in the many fragments of panpipes. The merry-making can thus be heard as well as seen and tasted.

An important feature of the site, in Gero's analysis, is that the ceremonial area is on the flattened top of a steep hill, making access to it restricted. As a special location where particular ritual activities were carried out, it is important to note that this ceremonial area was not exclusively male. The presence of women is attested to by clothing fasteners made of copper, which are known to have been part of women's clothing, because such fasteners are depicted in drawings of Inca times. Women therefore had access to prestige items, implying again high status for some Queyash women, as well as their presence at festivals. Gero shows that "the traditional role that women play in food prepara-tion and food serving [was] fundamental to the negotiation and reaf-firmation of hierarchy and the subversion of kin relations to civic and state demands" (1992:16). Feasting was important in the transformation of gender roles, in being both symbolic and expressed in public. A gendered view of ceremonial activities shows that not all feasting fits comfortably into the Big Man model.

Additional evidence of women's status is found in the form of painted ceramic effigy jars, some of which depict women, with colorful and intricately woven clothing (Gero 1992). Other evidence points to the likelihood that women had important positions in Pre-Inca times. Female deities depicted widely in the Early Intermediate Period suggest that women had "opportunities to occupy positions of power," argu-ing that "women are more likely to be portrayed as godheads if it is socially conceivable that power can, or once did, emanate from a female form" (Gero 1992:22), an argument also made and elaborated by Peggy Sanday (1981) based on ethnographic data.

The most celebrated site of women's participation in the public sphere is Çatal Hüyük in Turkey. At this Neolithic site, women appeared to be powerful in a number of ways, as the site was interpreted by its original excavator (Mellaart 1962, 1963, 1965). For example, a statue of an obese woman, seated on a throne between two animals in a typically regal posture, seems to be the very embodiment of power. Indeed, this figure is sketched on the cover of *The Archaeology of Rank* (Wason 1994). Women were buried under large platforms, while men were interred in areas interpreted as of lesser prestige. Women often were buried with more substantial grave goods than men, and the 21 burials sprinkled with red pigment (ocher or cinnabar) were all or mostly women. James Mellaart interpreted rooms with wall frescoes as shrines, and the decorated walls as symbolizing women's power in the society (1962, 1963, 1965). In Çatal Hüyük, women were interpreted as having a "central role in agriculture" and as participants in long-distance trade.

One impediment to discussing women at this site is the overenthusiasm with which Mellaart's reports of this Neolithic site was received in some quarters. While it was heralded by historians, art historians, and goddess worshippers as an example of matriarchy, the site was treated with more reserve by most archaeologists. This is a key example of popular interest filling the void when archaeologists themselves fail to address questions of gender in a sustained and careful way. Paul Wason (1994) concluded that it was a ranked but not stratified society. Reopening the site will undoubtedly clarify many of the difficulties with site interpretations that have been noted. The site likely has a great deal to reveal about gender arrangements, as well as other topics important to understanding elaborate Neolithic sites, though the first reports have not tackled the gender issue with new data (Mellaart 1962, 1963, 1965). Linda Donley-Reid (1996) uses the breasts molded on vulture beaks to discuss the tension between comfort and dependency on the one hand and the wish for independence on the other, a theme also taken up by Gunnar and Randi Haaland (1995).

Another site with female iconography is Niuheliang in northeastern China (Nelson 1991a, 1996a, 1996c). Covering at least 80 square kilometers, this extensive site features high-status tombs, a lobed ceremonial building, and an earth pyramid (Guo 1995). Craft specialization can be inferred in what appears to be an incipient state based on a Neolithic economy (Nelson 1996a), with gender implications pointing toward female leadership (Nelson 1991b, 1993). The statuary and figurines depict women, in both large and small sizes. The iconography associated with the high-status burials is mostly associated with *yin,* the female principle in later China.

Bettina Arnold noted that an extremely rich burial of a young Celtic Iron-Age female, often referred to as the Princess of Vix, was reinterpreted as a transvestite warrior! The contradiction seen in the combination of women's jewelry and weapons in some graves was thus resolved in this rather odd way. Arnold suggests that the weapons may indicate rank instead of masculinity. Again, it seems that rich and powerful women are simply not acceptable, even in prehistory (Arnold 1991:95). However, textual evidence supports the high status of women in those societies. In Celtic and Germanic tribal peoples there is overwhelming evidence of women's high status both in archaeology and in documents. Celtic grave-goods of Great Britain and Ireland reveal that women were buried with more splendor and wealth of ornaments than were men. As we have already seen, Celtic women often held the royal rank that allowed their husbands to sit on the throne as king. Ruth Trocolli has uncovered many examples of women chiefs among the Indians of North America. For example, in the Timucua of Florida, women held positions of power and prestige in both political and religious settings and were deprived of their positions only with the arrival of the Spanish Conquest (Trocolli 1992). Similar arguments have been made for the Danish Neolithic (Damm 1991). Thus, when there are hierarchies of hierarchies, class may be more important than gender in assigning either work or rulership (Nelson 1993).

Rosemary Joyce demonstrates that depictions of women in the Classic Maya show men and women performing a number of tasks, including public ones. On large stelae, which are public images, women can be identified by their distinctive clothing, rather than by visible sex characteristics. Women on these public images are labeled as mother, rather than wife, and even when not depicted, the names of both parents of the ruler are found on stelae. The men and women form a complementary gender pair. These images thus construct gender as well as represent it (Joyce 1992). It can thus show how gender may articulate with other factors. In a later paper,

Joyce (1996) demonstrates the complementarity of gender roles as depicted on public monuments. David Freidel and Linda Schele (1997) similarly discuss women in the Classic Maya. They specifically note that the daughter of the king of a state of Tikal traveled through hostile territory to rally the forces of an allied king. This princess married a prince of the defeated kingdom and ruled it through her son, actually fighting wars to consolidate her power.

The concept of heterarchy (Crumley 1979; Ehrenreich, Crumley, and Levy 1995) may be particularly useful in understanding women's power. Heterarchy is a way to organize society so that "each element possesses the potential of being unranked (relative to other elements) or ranked in a number of different ways. . . ." This concept allows the separation of economic, political, and ideological control in various levels of society. Janet Levy (1995) uses the concept of heterarchy in Bronze Age (1500–500 B.C.) Denmark as an avenue for understanding gender relationships. She finds that buried deposits and hoards represent complexity, but may not be hierarchical. Equality and hierarchy are both present—equality in the villages, and hierarchy in hoards and burials. Thus gender meanings, too, are likely to have been negotiated, varying from egalitarian to hierarchical and back again. It is interesting to note that women were tallest in the Bronze Age among the Danish population, suggesting that their nutrition and health was equal to that of men. This society practiced both agriculture and the raising of cattle, sheep, and pigs. Crafts included textile production, woodworking, and metallurgy based on imported metals. Inhumation burials, in wooden coffins or structures, are found in the Early Bronze Age, whereas cremated remains in pottery urns are the modes of burial in the Late Bronze Age. Gender is marked by various artifacts, but both genders have metal and artifacts with ritual meanings. Differences are that ceremonial artifacts associated with women tended to be deposited in "watery places," whereas men are shown in rock carvings in processions in combat. Motifs are varied, and occur in many combinations. Thus gender meanings are present, and can be understood in context.

Conclusions

The awareness that women can hold various kinds of public positions is the beginning of "finding" gender in the political interpretations of archaeological sites. Further steps involve looking at public roles more in terms of negotiation and less in terms of dominance and raw power.

Power itself has many forms, and should not be seen as only involving the use or threat of force. Coercion by physical means is the least effective means of control. Ideology is probably the most effective, to be examined in the next chapter.

CHAPTER EIGHT

IDEOLOGY AND GENDER

Each culture must select a sex-role plan—that is, a template for the organization of sex-role expectations. . . . Such plans help men and women orient themselves as male and female to each other, to the world around them, and to the growing boys and girls whose behavior they must shape to a commonly accepted mold.

—Peggy Sanday (1981:3)

An article entitled "God: She's Alive and Well" in *Science News* in 1976 is accompanied by a photograph of the "Venus" of Willendorf, a small female figurine from the Upper Paleolithic. The figure is presented as a "mother goddess" and used to illustrate its similarity to mother-goddess worship in India, which is what the article is really about (Trotter 1976). Half a century earlier, E. B. Renaud, also referring to the Venus of Willendorf, proclaimed, "The first god was a goddess!" (Renaud 1929). Renaud then discussed some recent discoveries of female figurines in the American Southwest. These examples could be multiplied many times. What is it about that particular limestone statuette that makes it stand for all "goddesses" everywhere? How can we tell what it does (and doesn't) represent, when it seems to be more of an inkblot test for the viewer than an object through which we can learn more about Paleolithic peoples?

To begin with, it is important to recognize that there is not just one "mother goddess," as an eternal representation of the feminine. Just as women are different within and between cultures, the statues are diverse, not only from different times and places, but also in form, size, realism, and many other characteristics. Some of them probably had multiple meanings for the cultures in which they were made and used. To generalize about them through time and space is to deny their diversity, and by extension to deny diversity to women. Not all female figurines are the same, and even representations known to be goddesses differ widely. Furthermore, even the Upper Paleolithic examples are not all the same (Rice 1981, Nelson 1990), though there has been a tendency to overgeneralize the shapes. Leroi-Gourhan (1967: figure on p. 92) homogenizes a variety of shapes by the device of drawing circles over the breasts and triangles on the heads and feet. This form of generalizing ignores both context and fine differences, in the same way as the examples that open this chapter.

The area of gender and ideology is one of the most difficult in which to reach satisfactory conclusions with archaeological evidence, possibly because both gender and ideology are considered by many to be unreachable with archaeological evidence. Archaeologists as a whole have been highly suspicious of anything that smacks of "paleopsychology," though recent trends in cognitive archaeology are beginning to reverse this attitude. George Cowgill (1993) has suggested that to counter this rigidly materialist perspective we need Middle Range Theory of the mind: ways to test archaeological assertions with ethnoarchaeological or other actualistic studies.

In discussions of female statuettes, the disapprobation of excursions into ideology has not prevented archaeologists from making a great many assertions about ancient beliefs and practices. Certain figurines have been said to represent gods or goddesses, based on inscriptions, myths, or simply imagination. Monumental architecture may be designated as ceremonial structures without adequate argument. Various artifacts also have been readily interpreted as having "ritual" uses, because they do not appear to have any other obvious function. The standard archaeological joke that anything with an unidentifiable function is a "ceremonial object" can also be used to suggest the attitude of most archaeologists to spirituality and ceremony. It is a "left-over" category. If it isn't ecological, technological, economic, political, or social, it *must* be ideological. The public, on the other hand, is generally quite fascinated with just this aspect of archaeology, and is intrigued with tales spun from the flimsiest of evidence.

How, then, can archaeologists study ideology, especially religion, with any degree of certainty that we are approaching the beliefs of past cultures? Anthropologists generally find that the religion of a group reflects its culture. Marshall Sahlins explains this amusingly in terms of western history:

> When we were pastoral nomads, the Lord was our shepherd. We were His flock, and He made us to lie down in green pastures. When we were serfs and nobles, the Lord was our king. Sat regnant on the throne of heaven, His shepherd's crook now a jeweled scepter: monarch of feudal monarchs, even to a Prince of Evil, His own contentious baron. But we were mostly peasants, and our comfort and justice no longer lay in the green pastures but in the land. And we would have it. We would inherit the earth. Finally we are businessmen—and the Lord is our accountant. He keeps a ledger on us all, enters there our good deeds in black and debits our sins in red. The Lord useth double-entry bookkeeping; he writeth a man down in fine columns. And when the Great Businessman closes our accounts, to those who show a profit He shall pay eternal dividends; but for those who show a loss—well, the Devil take the hindmost. (1968:96)

Sahlins is demonstrating that the Judeo-Christian religion is made in the image of historical cultures—but does it follow that goddesses can be equated with female power, or that the more goddesses, the more power? What about the Virgin Mary? Her statues are ubiquitous where women have little power.

The fact that supernatural and transcendent beings in many cultures were represented as both male and female suggests to some feminists that the monotheistic male god of western religions has served to suppress women. Although the vast literature on women and spirituality may be set aside as not germane to archaeology, it is still necessary to ask how the ideology of the distant past can be approached, and what archaeologists might have to offer as solid ground for interpretation of female figures. Goddesses are not rare in ethnographically known cultures, and it seems that archaeologists are obligated to come to grips with representations of the supernatural.

Peggy Sanday (1981) has suggested that a belief in female deities is a "script" for women's lives, thus providing an opening for interpreting prehistoric female figurines that may represent goddesses. She shows, with a variety of examples, that the gender of a people's gods does indeed reflect their sex-role plan with consistency. Female figurines, which may or may not represent deities (and probably one explanation does not fit all), are found throughout many millennia and in many places. They have been a focus of much speculation, both by members of the archaeology profession and by outsiders.

Female Figurines

One of the most contentious areas regarding the archeological past is the interpretation of representations of women. They are found in many forms: painted, engraved, in bas reliefs, and in the round. Relatively realistic statuettes are found in the Upper Paleolithic, while some of the female figures from eastern Europe look barely human, often with distorted heads. Figurines from Jomon Japan are stiff and static but highly decorated and otherworldly in a variety of ways, while the "Pretty Ladies" from the Valley of Mexico wear various kinds of jewelry and clothing, and are portrayed performing a number of different activities. One of the problems with many interpretations of the female figures is that they attempt to make a single explanation cover a large variety of manifestations that have nothing in common other than the fact that they have breasts.

From the Upper Paleolithic to state-level societies, the most common interpretation of female figurines is that they are goddesses, most often "mother goddesses." It is not necessary for them to be stylized or other-worldly to attract this label; even realistic statues may be interpreted in this way. Furthermore, they do not have to be maternal (pregnant or associated with an infant) to be called "mother goddesses."

Other functions are sometimes suggested for various female figurines, in addition to their imputed status as mother goddesses. Occasionally they are considered to reflect male appreciation of the female form. They are also variously represented in popular culture as representative of matriarchies in which women ruled, as demonstrating peaceful societies, or as the natural propensity and right of women to worship female deities. While some of the statues are too stylized to represent real women, others might be interpreted in a variety of ways, and even stylized figurines are not necessarily representations of deities. A theory of ideology and its tangible expressions is urgently needed in order to be able to distinguish the use and intention of figurines on the basis of their characteristics and contexts.

Upper Paleolithic "Venus" Figurines

Among the earliest depictions of human beings, dating back to at least 30,000 years ago, are small statuettes of nude females, which are found across a broad belt in Europe from the Pyrenees in southern France to the Don River in Russia, with outliers as far away as Siberia. Almost 200 of these figurines have been discovered, ranging from explicit and realistic carvings to highly stylized and even dubiously human shapes (Delporte 1979). In addition, there are several bas reliefs, engravings on stone and bone, and a few cave wall depictions that have been interpreted as representing human females. Males and sexless figures are shown in two-dimensional media, though most of the known statuettes are female. Early *Homo sapiens* has thus left behind a good bit of evidence about her appearance.

It is the attitude toward these depictions of females, and the kinds of inferences that have been made from them, that are of interest to explore. Androcentric assumptions have obscured some very obvious and important features of this body of evidence. Ideas about the figurines can be grouped into three ways of perceiving them. The first is in terms of their use, role, or function in the societies that made them. The second deals with the underlying reality of body shapes that the figurines may represent, and the third with inferences that may be drawn about the societies that produced them.

When the first figurines were found in the late 19th century, it was their possible functions that captured the imaginations of their discoverers. One popular explanation was that they were used in fertility rites, and another that they represented an erotic ideal. Both of these interpretations focused on the fact that some of the figurines emphasize the torso, with sketchy extremities and few facial features (though there are many exceptions to this generalization). Both interpretations also assume that the figurines were made by and for the males in the society (see Nelson 1990 for a critique of this assumption).

A number of authors have considered various depictions in the round, carved or painted on cave walls, or carved into bone or antler, as having gendered meanings. André Leroi-Gourhan created an elaborate scheme, in which marks painted on the walls were interpreted as signs representing male (anything narrow or pointed) or female (anything wide). He further suggested that each kind of animal had a human gender referent, regardless of whether the animal itself was male or female (1967). This hypothesis is based on a number of assumptions about gender, and ultimately is untestable.

Depictions of Women Interpreted as Sex Objects

Elsewhere, the exclusive sexualizing of the female body is made manifest, as a male author philosophizes: "[W]e may deduce man's obsessive need for women who would bear him lots of children to offset the high mortality rate caused by the harsh living conditions" (Berenguer 1973:52). This mixes the erotic with the notion of fertility. The erotic fantasy model is extremely subjective, and seems to be idiosyncratic, but it is common enough that it has been satirized by Laurent (1968) in a cartoon. "Still unmarried?" asks a cave-man of the male carving the figurines and hiding one behind his back. From the point of view of the prudish and thoroughly clothed Europeans of the last hundred years, it was self-evident that nude female bodies must represent fertility and/or eroticism, without further discussion or justification.

Besides the sexual interpretations of the whole figurines, women's body parts are perceived in some very unlikely shapes. The "signs" that are interpreted as vulvas often look (to me, anyway) like molar teeth! Paul Bahn (1986) has debunked the notion that they have anything to do with women, fertility, or gender. The obsession that sees vulvas in unconvincing shapes has been thoroughly debunked as a "durable myth," though many male commentators are unwilling to relinquish this sexy mirage. Such interpretations have been based on wishful thinking, subjective selection of data, and unwarranted assumptions by modern scholars. There is very little evidence in the art to justify a belief in a prehistoric obsession with sexuality or fertility (Bahn and Vertut 1988).

Even more grotesque are some three-dimensional objects that have been described as "rods with breasts," and a tuning-fork-shaped object that is seen as a vulva with a rounded and perforated "head" and "legs" each ending in sharp points. These imaginative suggestions were taken seriously and are often cited as evidence of the "fertility religion" of the Upper Paleolithic. Some of the commentators have gone miles beyond the data: for example, "This statuette [the 'rod with breasts' from Dolni Vestonice] shows us that the artist has neglected all that did not interest *him*, stressing *his* sexual libido only where the breasts are concerned—a diluvial, plastic pornography" (Absalom 1949, emphasis added). Alice Kehoe has demonstrated that if one of the images of alleged breasts with rod-like "neck" from Dolni Vestonice, which has a hole for suspension, is hung on a string, it is not oriented at all like breasts. If it represents human body parts at all, it represents the scrotum with penis (Kehoe 1991). Noting that her observation about this object has been ignored, in a more recent note responding to a paper on representations of women, Alice Kehoe asks, "[A]re the gentlemen so fixated on female sex objects that their memories blank out any challenge to their objects of desire!" (1996). Margaret Conkey notes that "We have been operating with the long-standing implicit assumption that even in the Upper Paleolithic, women—or parts of them—were not only suitable but desirable as objects of depiction, as cultural commodities" (1991:121).

Several recent papers have concerned themselves with the shapes of the figurines from the point of view of the person or persons doing the looking. A creative approach suggests that the apparent exaggerations of body parts would result from a woman looking at herself, thus gendering the creator of the figures as female (McCoid and McDermott 1996), but this approach supposes that she had no other mature females to observe, which seems unlikely.

It is clear that an attitude toward women as sex objects has been read into the distant past. But it goes beyond even the pin-up mentality, with a mixing of the idea of the figurines as erotic with the notion of "fertility," which confuses sexuality with its (frequent) heterosexual result. Women are implicitly described as functional: their uses are to satisfy men's desires and to produce children. These twin attributes of women from a male point of view are then essentialized: "For them [Paleolithic men] as for us . . . the mother who gives and transmits life is also the woman who gives and shares pleasure: could the Paleolithic have been insensitive to this novel duality?" (Delporte 1979:308, my translation). Obviously, the "us" in the quotation is himself and other men, women are not considered relevant, and a woman reader of his book is not even envisaged.

Koenigswald (1972), however, considers the idea of fertility magic for human beings unreasonable, on the grounds that hunter-gatherer societies neither need nor value a high birth rate. This notion is based on the spacing of births several years apart among contemporary hunter-gatherers.

Emanuel Anati (1985) rejects the notion of fertility cults on other grounds. He points out that the cult activities are rarely demonstrated in these cases, and that even copulation scenes may nothing to do with ritual fertility.

Some commentators have seen the fertility of women as also applying to that of animals, and a wish for animal as well as human reproduction. Henri Delporte (1979), in reviewing all the then-known European figurines, as well as the literature regarding them, concludes that the female and animal art represents a kind of dualism, with the females demonstrating an identification with animals in the realm of reproduction, while showing opposition to them in terms of food. Both women and animals are thus part of "nature," and both are for the use of human males. In such musings, Delporte implies that the images were made by men for their own exclusive purposes.

But the makers of the statues, the users of them, and the reactions they invoke all need to be problematized rather than assumed. Although many examples of women artists in hunter-gatherer societies exist (see Fisher 1979), the male as artist continues to be presented in textbooks, and is especially prominent in illustrations (Nelson 1990, Hurcombe 1995). One book is even entitled *Prehistoric Man and His Art*, leaving no doubt as to whom the art was by and for. In the text of the book this assumption becomes more explicit: "How did the artist's vision, which reflected the ideal of his time, see her? For as with man, we can never know what she really looked like . . . so we have to make do with the version her companion, man, had of her" (Berenguer 1973:48).

Elsewhere, we read that, "Astre inferred from the similarity in style of all Paleolithic art that painting and engraving must have been a specialist activity of the sorcerers, passing *from father to son*" (Ucko and Rosenfeld 1973:135, emphasis added). Even if the concept of "sorcerers" as artists is correct, there is no reason these specialists could not have been women. There are plenty of ethnographic examples of women shamans to draw from.

Marcia-Anne Dobres (1992) observes that approaches to the figurines are studies of form without context. I suggest that this is possible because women themselves are decontextualized and universalized by most authors. When the context of the figurines is considered, less androcentric scenarios have been created. An elaborate argument by Franz Hancar (1940) based on the locations of figurines within the sites in eastern Europe, as well as artifact associations and ethnographic analogy, arrives at the conclusion that figurines were protective spirits of hunting to which offerings were made. Noting that the figurines were often found broken, he suggested that the figurines were deliberately destroyed as the people left a site, so that they would not give protection to another rival group. While this scenario is also somewhat fanciful (why wouldn't the people have taken them along, since they were small and portable?), it is an attempt to relate the figurines to their context, and is thus preferable to universalizing generalizations.

Several archaeologists have considered the figurines as depictions of real women, rather than as stylized goddesses. One of the early observations about the figurines was the fat deposition on the buttocks of a few of them, which was labeled steatopygia, a characteristic of some African populations. Both Luce Passemard (1938) and Evelyn Saccasyn Della Santa (1947) reviewed all the then-known figurines, and both came to the conclusion that they were not steatopygous. In a study I conducted, in which I measured photos of figurines from the front and side, I found that three of the figurines might be said to have steatopygia, but that it is not a common trait. Nevertheless, the Venus of Willendorf is used in a physical anthropology textbook to discuss steatopygia (Pfeiffer 1985), in spite of the fact that she has fat deposits on her hips but no fat at all behind her; her back is straight from shoulder to thigh.

As noted at the beginning of this chapter, the Willendorf figurine is far too often taken as the characteristic one, for she is not at all representative of the "average" figurine. In spite of the fact that this single statuette represents the greatest degree of adiposity of any that has been found, her attributes are often generalized to *all* the figurines. One writer has suggested that Upper Paleolithic women suffered from a condition called massive hypertrophy of the breasts (Harding 1986), and other gynecological diagnoses have been forthcoming from Jean-Pierre Duhard (1991). These are yet more examples of the male gaze on the female form.

The Willendorf figurine has also been alleged to be "heavily pregnant" (Ardrey 1976:167), though there is nothing in either her body shape or her stance to suggest that she is even slightly pregnant. My study found that the figurines divide statistically into fat, normal or slim, and steatopygous groups (Nelson n.d.). None are obviously pregnant, though some could be (my observation, but see also Anati 1985:5). It is difficult to distinguish between ordinary belly fat and the early or middle stages of pregnancy in a stone or bone statuette, though it seems that if the carver had intended to show a gravid female, she would have made it obvious, with a fully term fetus rather than a rounded abdomen such as can be seen on nearly all nonpregnant adult females who have given birth.

Thus, the Upper Paleolithic figurines have been taken to stand for Woman, both as sexual and as reproductive. Because women in our own culture have also been treated in these reductionist ways, it was not immediately obvious that other interpretations were possible. Now that a space has been opened for alternative views, it can be hoped that women—and men—of the Upper Paleolithic can be sketched in other dimensions as well.

The Neolithic "Religion of the Goddess"

The Neolithic female figures from Europe and southwest Asia have been widely heralded within the Women's Movement as evidence of women's high status in Neolithic, agricultural societies. But simply celebrating the figurines as goddesses is not sufficient for an engendered archaeology. We need to know many other things. How do the figurines fit into the society, and specifically the material culture? Do they represent goddesses, are they public representations of powerful women, or should there be different interpretations for different figures representing different roles or facets of women? What ideology governed the daily lives of the inhabitants of the sites, and to what extent were their activities gendered?

Several Neolithic sites with female representations have been seen as "sanctuaries of the Goddess," including Çatal Hüyük in Turkey, which has already been encountered, as well as Bronze Age discoveries on both Malta and Crete. To be interpreted as The Goddess, these sites are linked with sweeping generalizations that obscure their varied archaeological content. For example, Ann Barstow, using Mellaart's excavations at Çatal Hüyük, assumes that the images are goddesses. "These images give us our earliest known link between the very early cave art, which goes back to 20,000–30,000 B.C., and the fertility cult goddesses from Sumer and later" (1978:8). The linking of the female figurines of the Paleolithic and Neolithic is highly problematical for many reasons, not the least being the large gaps of time between them, during which no figurines are known, and the distances between the places where they are found. The urge to generalize deplorably essentializes women, and obscures the activities of women in the past no less than generalizations of women as sex objects.

Marija Gimbutas proposes that the figurines of "Old Europe," in eastern Europe and particularly in the Balkans, from about 6000 to 3500 B.C., belong to a general cult of goddess worshippers having many different functions with the "religion of the Goddess" (1991, 1989). Yet while this rendering seems to have been satisfying to many modern women, it remains unsatisfactory to archaeologists, for several reasons.

Margaret Conkey and Ruth Tringham have critiqued Gimbutas's interpretations of Old Europe for using "argument by assertion," for treating the whole region and time span as homogeneous, for allowing only one interpretation of the clay figurines, and for applying modern categories such as religion, temples, shrines, and rituals to the past (Conkey and Tringham 1995:216–217). The big picture, they claim, is emphasized at the expense of the details, and the details are selectively presented. "Gimbutas has painted a picture of massive change in European history, from matrifocal to patrifocal society, in which the variability and individuality of men's and women's histories, which are of interest to feminists and postprocessualists alike, are lost in a normative prehistory. She has added women, but her traditional, advocative epistemological framework remains unchanged" (Tringham 1993:197). In other words, Gimbutas utilized the same techniques that had been used to *disparage* women in the past, but she transposed them to *glorify* women. Pamela Russell remarks that "The archaeological evidence is, in some cases, distorted enough to make a careful prehistorian shudder" (1993:95).

If androcentric blinders should be criticized, gynocentric generalizations cannot be accepted either. This is highlighted by Brian Hayden's (1986) critique of Gimbutas, in which he falls into the same trap of attributing prehistoric "religious" meanings—he simply genders them male. His advocacy of ethnography and "common sense" fails to appreciate the degree to which androcentrism has already entered into these areas. He alleges that "similar religious themes occur in the Neolithic farming community of China" (Hayden 1986:24), without giving a reference—a statement that has no archaeological basis. He also alleges incorrectly that force is involved, and that only men have access to it. "On the whole it appears that men hold the critical reins of power in traditional societies, that is, physical and armed force." And males generally appear unwilling to relinquish these "to assume inferior statuses" (p. 26). Of course, *most* males in stratified societies have inferior status and no access to armed force, so this is an elitist as well an androcentric statement. As Lynn Fisher notes, "[A]lthough Hayden criticizes Gimbutas for a lack of methodological rigor and excessive subjectivity, it is hard to see how his own scenario for Paleolithic and Neolithic religions avoids the same problems" (1993:71).

The Question of Fertility

Gimbutas did not shrink from applying the label of fertility goddesses to the figurines she studied, perhaps because the term has been so widely applied in Europe and southwest Asia that it seemed unnecessary to dispute it. The tendency to call all female figurines "fertility figures" is found especially in the Mediterranean region, where many later religions were known to have some goddesses related to fertility. However, the concept is applied in various ways to figurines around the world. Identifying figurines that actually relate to fertility is problematical without written corroboration. In fact, the whole notion of fertility cults is unacceptable as a sweeping generalization. It combines too many times and places into one mythologizing whole. While it may make a coherent story, it is not a story that is archaeologically sound. One of the uses of mythology, in fact, has been to essentialize women as eternal, fecund, and passive, while gendering the hero as individual, active, and male (e.g. Joseph Campbell 1994).

Although this notion of female fertility has been embraced with enthusiasm by some women, the need to examine this notion, whether a positive or a negative spin is applied to it, has been emphasized by Conkey and Tringham. "Neither approach, however, problematizes the notion of 'fertility.' That large breasts or large stomachs are agreed-upon conventions of imagery signifying lactation and the more inclusive concept of fertility has never been demonstrated or considered critically" (Conkey and Tringham 1995:213).

Ann Cyphers Guillén examines a limited population of figurines, in Middle Preclassic deposits in Chalcatzingo, Mexico, around 700 to 500 B.C. She notes that the context of the figurines is not in burials as had occurred earlier, but rather that they are found associated with houses, patios, or trash dumps. Since 92 percent of the figurines represent adult women, Guillén suggests that they represent female transition rites. Some of the figurines carry children or nurse them, and Guillén divides others into three stages of pregnancy, according to the trimester of gestation. However, she identifies as nonpregnant only figurines with small breasts, believed to represent adolescents, because full-figured women seem to her to be pregnant. Thus, while the distribution of figurines is interesting, some of the attributions seem to be based on problematical assumptions (1988). In fact, the stages of pregnancy, especially the early ones, are hard to discriminate from fat or even loose muscles from previous pregnancies. It is a strange notion of our own culture, a kind of *Playboy* mentality, to believe that women have flat abdomens except when they are pregnant. As Pamela Russell (1991) has shown, women in other times and places have been depicted routinely with rounded bellies, as a part of their beauty and their femaleness. Even a physical attribute like pregnancy is difficult to pin down in figurines. And in what sense would pregnancy indicate fertility? Why not depict mothers with infants? These are questions that need to be considered more closely.

The "fertility" figures of the eastern Mediterranean are of a different order. Parts of the Biblical canon were written at a time when a struggle was still rife between the monotheistic, patriarchal religion of Yahweh and the preexisting local religious expressions that included female figurines, representing various aspects of women. Any female figurine was seen as an idol, a challenge to Yahweh, and therefore to be disparaged. But it doesn't follow that if the monotheistic religions that trace their origins to this area are sexist, the religions that were suppressed and superseded by patriarchal religion were better for women, *or* that goddess worship is necessarily a woman's religion. Jo Ann Hackett takes on the general question of fertility goddesses, and asks, "Can a sexist model liberate us?" In dissecting the notion of fertility goddesses, she makes three important points. First, she shows that the concept of "fertility" is a way to essentialize women, implying that "women everywhere have always been the same, and without change and development there can be no history. . . . We have no history because we have always been wives, mothers, and whores; in other words, we are interchangeable" (1989:65–66). Second, Hackett shows that the concept of fertility religion was applied to anything in the eastern Mediterranean that was not Biblical. In Canaanite religion, naked female figures may represent ritual "prostitution," and may not be a model that modern women would find liberating. Finally, the goddesses portrayed had many facets, and indicated much more than fertility. "The fullness and breadth of power these goddesses represented in the ancient world is boiled down to one or two aspects that the scholars doing the boiling are most threatened by" (1989:75).

Diane Bolger studied female figurines from Cyprus, and found interesting changes through time. She suggests that religious rituals were used to legitimate the social hierarchy, and that figurines were symbols manipulated for particular purposes. "With the radical social and economic changes that accompanied the emergence of social complexity during the Bronze Age, women may ultimately have been excluded from important rituals as powerful elites and centralized authorities created structures in which women's roles were increasingly restricted and social and economic inequalities became institutionalized" (1996:371). She is not convinced that the Neolithic figurines were representations of deities, but asserts that the new types of figurines found in the Bronze Age appear in contexts that suggest ritual, and are stylistically new. In particular, a male figure with horns appears, juxtaposed against the disappearance of birthing figures. Bolger does not interpret this as "fertility," but rather as related to the emergence of the patriarchal family (1996:372).

For unrealistic female figurines, the Middle Jomon in Japan (3600–2500 B.C.) provides interesting examples. Occasionally more than one hundred figurines are found at a single site. They stand in a human pose and have small breasts, so they are interpreted as representing female deities or ancestors. Otherwise, they are highly decorated but scarcely human, with bulging eyes that have been variously interpreted as snow goggles, the closed eyes of the dead, cowrie shells, or the facial gear worn by aliens from outer space. Changes in the styles of clay figures are reflected in those of the pottery containers, some of which may also be ritual objects. They tend to be found in large sites, which are interpreted as locations of community ritual. Like the "Pretty Lady" figurines, they were often deposited in trash or left in houses, but sometimes were ritually treated (Nagamine 1986).

Ideology as Mystification

Ideologies are notoriously difficult to interpret, especially as any overt set of symbols may be created to mask where the real power lies (Parker Pearson 1982). The power of symbols often lies in their taken-for-granted nature: their purpose to deflect criticism from the elite who are human onto the supernatural, and to invert social hierarchies and both reinforce and legitimate them. Conkey and Tringham suggest that Marxist explanations, in particular:

> discuss such rituals and their material manifestations as strategies by which, in the context of household-based social differentiation, one group—a household, senior members, or senior males—dominates and even exploits another group. In this kind of interpretation, the figurines are overt symbols that help create and maintain ideologies by which it seems "natural" or acceptable that some people have power over the labor, actions, relations, and property of others or have more access to resources and wealth than others. (1995:222)

I have suggested that the elite of Niuheliang in China may have harnessed the labor of potters and jade workers to produce goods for elite consumption with this kind of mystification of their real purposes (Nelson 1995). My argument involves the increasing scarcity of pigs arising from environmental change and the use of pigs in ritual, as well as large constructions of several kinds. "Thus a managerial class arose, in the guise of filling a need for serving the gods, and at the same time managing the pigs, for the increasing prosperity of the whole society" (1995:13). It seems likely that some women were held in high esteem and were important in the elite culture.

Ian Hodder (1992:49) argues that "the type of house and pottery symbolism identified in the central European early and middle Neolithic is appropriate in a social context where primary social strategies revolve around male-female relationships, which are themselves linked to competition between lineages for control of labor." He suggests that arrangements in living and in death reflect the same ideology. Long mounds and long houses are oriented in roughly the same directions at given sites. Both are divided into three parts, associated with ditches, and made with similar techniques. They are trapezoidal or rectangular shapes, with the entrance at the broad end, and they face the southeast, with elaborate entrances. On the basis of ethnographic studies in Africa, Hodder suggests that "in small-scale lineage-based societies in which the major concern is to increase labor power, the control of women by men and the negotiation of position by women will become the dominant feature of the domestic sphere" (1983:157). The leap from the similarity of architecture to gender arrangements is not fully justified. Hodder warns that a "careful consideration of the contexts involved" is necessary—but then fails to provide it, in the critical question of gender.

Anna Roosevelt (1988) suggests that the "Pretty Lady" figurines were used with intent to manipulate. Roosevelt explains the apparent emphasis on female sexuality by suggesting that they represent the time of the intensification of agriculture, when more offspring would have been desirable and population growth encouraged (1988). But it is not necessarily the case that a pronatal mentality would lead to an emphasis on overt sexuality—consider, for example, the attitudes of the Catholic Church toward both. The reverse could also be said to be true—sexuality can be divorced from procreation, and sexual gestures may have nothing to do with "fertility." Roosevelt suggests that the figurines reflect a "populationalist ideology," which encouraged human reproduction, in order to supply more people for labor, warfare, and colonization. "Thus it may be that at a time of economic and demographic growth, women gained in status due to their roles in reproduction and production. The art may reflect this change" (1988:1). It seems to me that Roosevelt has produced a testable hypothesis, which could be pursued in each of the societies for which there are female figurines, but she has not demonstrated that the figurines play the same role in each society. Improvement in the socioeconomic position of women might be evident in site and house layouts. Demographic patterns and women's health as reflected in skeletal data might show whether reproductive rates increased. Women's roles and prestige can be inferred from domestic arrangements, subsistence remains, and funerary customs. These data are not the point of her paper, but a thoroughly gendered archaeology will need to consider all the available variables. Manrique and Mancos (in Miller 1988) do examine figurines from Valdivia, Ecuador, in this way, showing that changes in the figures co-occur with new forms and sizes of houses, new settlement patterns, and revised social structure.

Depictions of men and women together may allow interpretations of gender relations, whether in west Mexican ceramic figurines where women are present with men in couples but shown as less active (Goldstein 1988), or Moche ceramics, which show a shift from sex and babies to scenes of sacrifice (Benson in Miller 1988). Aztec figurines have also been scrutinized (Brumfiel 1996). These artifacts were used in household ceremonies, and in several styles. Brumfiel examines the frequencies of different styles at various sites, and notes changes in those frequencies through time. This approach provides a rich data set, showing that the site farthest from an Aztec urban center was the least affected by state-level ideology. These household level figurines stand in direct contrast to the monumental public statuary that includes decapitated and dismembered females as part of the iconography.

Other ways to understand ideology include combining ethnographic and archaeological evidence. Patricia O'Brien compared archaeological discoveries at a burial mound associated with the C. C. Witt Lodge with known Pawnee ceremonies of the Morning Star and Evening Star. The excavated earthlodge was aligned with astronomical events. At the equinox, as the sun rose, it "shone into the entrance, crossed the hearth and illuminated a 4-posted altar" (1990:64). Wings of bluejay, woodpecker, and owl were found in a pit near the entrance, as well as a gar jaw and turtle carapace. All of these were important in Pawnee mythology. In the nearby burial mound the scattered bones of a young girl and several projectile points were found, which could be evidence of the sacrifice of a young girl to the Morning Star, probably a girl captured from an enemy group. These and other details of the site demonstrate that careful work can elucidate facets of ideology that might have seemed beyond reach.

Another interesting examination of gendered ideology pertains to the use of weaving implements as symbols for women. Sharisse and Geoffrey McCafferty argue that spinning and weaving are so closely tied to women in Post-Classic Mexico that implements used in these activities became a metaphor for women themselves, and weaving implements were used as part of a complex iconography to indicate femaleness, exactly the way that "spinster" (one who spins) in English came to mean an unmarried woman, and the "distaff side" (distaff being a staff to hold flax in spinning) refers to the wife. In Mexico, the implements were extended into metaphors for sexuality, childbirth, and female life-cycles. The McCaffertys' work began with research on spindle whorls, in which they found symbolic association of patterns, but they soon noted other aspects of the culture in which spindle whorls seemed to have indirect meanings. They suggest that "the symbolism of spinning and weaving acted within an alternative, female discourse, operating apart from, even in resistance to, the dominant male ideology" (1988a:20).

The "materialization" of ideology (DeMarrais et al. 1996) is an important avenue to understanding gender, though gender is often overlooked in these contexts. Referring to the above article, Elizabeth Brumfiel points out the gender flaw:

> The warrior ideology, materialized in the bronze swords, is said to be the basis of chiefly power, but female bronze ornaments are not materializing anything in particular. If power depended on materialization and materialization rested on the manufacture of bronze swords, why waste bronze on ornaments? More likely bronze ornaments also materialized important, nonwarring, dimensions of elite ideology, such as kinship or reciprocity, that allocated resources and structured political loyalties in important ways. (1996:48)

Conclusions

Gendering iconography thus needs considerable development, but it is a promising avenue into understanding the gender of the past. While resisting interpretations that universalize women into notions of "mother goddesses" and "fertility," the iconography can be studied in its specific contexts, helping the richness of prehistoric ideologies to be made manifest.

CHAPTER NINE

GENDER, EVOLUTION, AND MUTED VOICES

A real past, although blurred, can be glimpsed through archaeological materials.

—Philip Kohl (1985:115)

In turn the routine institutional decisions—about awarding research grants and departmental budgets, allocating equipment and information, and employing personnel—produce a template that enables and constrains the knower and thereby structures the knowledge they produce.

—Joan Hartman and Ellen Messer-Davidow (1991:6)

Adding a consciously gendered perspective to archaeology turns much of archaeology-as-usual upside-down. Most of the attributions of gender to the past, before the 1990s, were based on present gender stereotypes. In considering archaeological perspectives on origins, economy, society, political structures, and ideology, it has become clear that the problem is not that archaeology has not been gendered, but rather that it has been *inappropriately* gendered in a way that subverts key questions and makes assumptions we must now regard as problematic. I have argued that by focusing on power and prestige, archaeologists have prevented serious attention to gender. And by creating barriers to women in the field (in both senses), those with a stake in setting the record straight have until recently been kept outside the gates, or kept in line within them.

In other words, there has always been an archaeology of gender, but it has been inadequate because it has been androcentric, essentialist, and/or simplistic. What is needed is a better archaeology of gender, one that removes the androcentric lenses and focuses its gaze intently on gender in the past, allowing the possibility of discovering that the past was different from the present. Instead of seeking cross-cultural generalizations, an improved archaeology of gender will accept each culture on its own terms, with its individual history, and will seek diversity, variations, subtlety, nuances.

Intentionally gendered archaeology can produce better archaeology. This occurs by reexamining the taken-for-granteds. As Alison Wylie points out, "[W]hen a hypothesis is challenged by alternatives, we are compelled to examine the empirical record more carefully to resolve the ambiguity" (1992b:30). Good examples of explicitly gendered archaeology are nuanced, well argued, careful, and based on several strands of evidence. As we have advanced toward this end, not every attempt has been perfect—though each has explored theories and methods, and even writing styles, that will allow a fully gendered archaeology.

Writing Archaeology

Catherine Lutz (1995) discusses writing styles—a topic that resonates with all of us who write. The structure of academic writing, with its passive constructions, tends to obliterate any actors, male or female. Real struggles with consideration of effective ways to present archaeological cultures are particularly evident in the chapters of Gero and Conkey (1991). Many of the authors of chapters in that book venture into new territory in writing styles. Some of the ambiguity thus expressed is resolved by Janet Spector in *What This Awl Means* (1994), by presenting multiple voices in a book-length treatment of her sites, focusing on a specific artifact: a decorated awl. Moving from field situations to site description to story, she has created a medium that goes well beyond the typical archaeological report.

But these innovations are not always well received in the field. While many archaeologists might wish to write for varied audiences, and present their work in accessible ways, the threat of the gatekeepers is potent. The social context in which archaeological work has been done is one that has tended to disadvantage both women in the present and the search for women in the past. At the same time, the intellectual context of the field has left little room for exploring gender issues.

Cultural Evolution and Gender

Many women archaeologists, as well as some men in the field, have become interested in understanding gender in the past. Constraints on developing theory and method to pursue this topic have been legion, and several of them were explored in Chapter 2. Here, I would like to consider how even *theory* has been gendered male, and what might be done to expand theories to allow gender a place.

The arena of cultural evolution makes this context particularly evident. I have left cultural evolutionism to the last chapter, because, as an important presence in archaeology, it has had a pervasive impact on gender studies, or rather the lack of them. Critiquing the impact of evolutionary theory on gender in archaeology also highlights the themes of power and prestige, as well as draws the themes of this book together tightly. Universal histories were the origin of evolutionary theory (Kehoe 1995:23), but universalizing is exactly what obscures the search for gender in the past. The very definitions of bands, tribes, chiefdoms, and states leave no room for gender issues. The (often unstated) belief that women's roles are established by biology causes women and gender interactions, a priori, to be assumed irrelevant to the enterprise of explaining cultural diversity and change.

Evolutionary stages have been criticized on several other grounds, grounds that may equally inhibit removing the androcentric lenses. Philip Kohl notes, "The comparative universal perspective . . . is today generally accepted but increasingly scrutinized as to what is learned by the rote listing of general similarities among cultures classified together at the same broad evolutionary level" (1985:108). Classing sites and cultures together in stages creates generalizations about culture change, which easily become a typology, leading to a shoehorn approach (O'Brien 1995:67). Gendered archaeology aspires to the opposite—to consider historically specific causes and effects.

Daniel Miller and Christopher Tilley wryly note that "[i]n cultural evolutionary theories, societies are treated like football teams with labels on their backs. They compete in the adaptive stakes—ground rules for the game are laid out *a priori*—before any analyses start. The assumed need for societies to adapt . . . becomes a differential measure of success. Some societies develop to the status of civilizations and reach the top of the league, while others are relegated to the lower divisions of bands and chiefdoms" (1984:2).

Suggesting that "neoevolutionism" leads to focusing on "static social types," Blanton et al. (1996) provide an alternative strategy for studying the evolution of "civilization." "Researchers should abandon [evolutionary] static ideal-type stages and instead investigate the varying strategies used by political actors to construct and maintain polities and other sociocultural institutions" (1996:1). This approach is better, but not yet ideal. While the emphasis on agency is laudable, it still will not enable gender issues to be engaged if it only investigates the top players (to extend the sports metaphor above). A focus on heterarchy instead of hierarchy shifts the balance from seeking evidence of male dominance to the possibility of seeing that "women have realms of, or access to economic and/or political power" (White 1995:118). Thus, more than the top players (or those perceived in those roles) become visible, and a more complex dynamic emerges.

The study of evolution as an increase in hierarchy assumes an increasing concentration of power and prestige. But other ways to look at power are created under the spotlight of gender. Alison Wylie notes that power is rarely absolute, and that in fact power may be illusory. "Power is granted to the dominator by hosts of other people, and that power is not unretractable" (1992a:59). As we have seen beginning with nonhuman primates, androcentric conceptions of power exclude women from the possibility even of *having* power. Instead, female power is seen as illegitimate, and women who are able to achieve their goals are manipulative, because legitimate power is not believed to be available to women (1992a:57). Thus the notion of evolutionary stages reifies power and obscures women's contributions to cultures.

For a thoughtfully gendered archaeology to arise, there are a number of additional problems with the standard theories of cultural evolution. Some of these are as follows:

- The tendency to paint with too broad a brush, seeking causes or origins, tends to make gender disappear, or to affix it to biology. Comparison can be a useful tool, though frequently it leads to a focus on similarities, ignoring differences. This usually obscures women's roles in culture change, particularly if women are expected to be doing nothing but the housework of society, conceived of as both unchanging and uninteresting.

- Gender hierarchy seems to be a condition that changes but is not itself perceived as evolutionary. As we have noted in examining such topics as origins, hunting, and social changes that arose with agriculture, and later with the state, a variety of possible gender arrangements can be found at every stage. The evolutionary differences in gender arrangements that have been proposed all dissolve on closer scrutiny. We need to look beyond a notion of "patriarchy," which obscures many other kinds of gender hierarchies. The problem is not so much that "too much" has been written about men, or even that too little notice is taken of women, but that there are too many assumptions about gender itself, unsupported by evidence.

- Grand evolutionary schemes, created by ethnographic analogy without archaeological evidence, usually make essentialist gender assumptions. It is nevertheless the case that any challenge to the grand scheme is rejected, and evidence is demanded. Even grand evolutionary schemes should have empirical grounding.

- The emphasis on power and prestige, their reification, and their location in public places forecloses any discussion of gender. Women are defined out of the public sphere without argument, therefore the origin-of-the-state discussion cannot include women because they have become invisible. All evolutionary stages have invisible women. Examples have been presented of women as invisible gatherers, invisible farmers, invisible artisans, and even invisible rulers.

- Finally, evolution is understood from the viewpoint of the dominant class. Oppression and exploitation of the primary producers are not acknowledged (Gailey 1985), still less the appropriation of women's labor. While the "achievements" of cultural evolution are celebrated, with attention to monumental architecture, art styles, and the like, effects on the lives of ordinary people are usually unexamined. Alice Kehoe points out the "political effect of masking imperialist conquests and exploitation by reading the archaeological record as a story of environmental stimuli and stresses" (1995:23–24).

Agency and Values

Feminist writings supply remedies for these problems by adding agency and values. Agency asks not only "Who does it?" but also "For whom is it done?" Rather than perceiving a whole society as adaptive, considering the constituent parts creates a richer understanding of societal workings and illuminates the tensions from which change arises. An emphasis on values asks "For whom is this good or bad, and in what ways?" To suppose that anything is simply "adaptive" for any total culture is naive. The consequences of change are likely to be different for different groups within the culture.

Feminists are concerned not merely with what happens to women, but with what happens to other groups of "others" as well. There are important similarities between the study of gender in archaeology and other muted groups on the fringes of the archaeological establishment. Examples of marginalized approaches to archaeology are archaeoastronomy and epigraphy. At the Oxford V archaeoastronomy conference in 1996, George Gumerman offered an analogy between the latter two:

> It may well be that the way archaeologists have defined or identified archaeological data has limited the range of questions we ask and thus is self-limiting on what we call data. It appears that archaeoastronomical data suffer from the same syndrome. The questions asked and issues addressed by the archaeoastronomers tend to fall outside the self defined parameters of what archaeologists think are significant. (Gumerman and Warburton 1996:12–13)

Substitute "gendered" for "archaeoastronomical" and the quote still applies. Gumerman concludes his comparison of Mayan epigraphic studies with archaeoastronomy by noting that it took over 150 years of epigraphic and iconographic research before these studies were accepted as relevant to Mayan archaeological research. Perhaps "mainstream" archaeology will not take that long to accept gendered archaeology.

Culture as a system, and in particular the ecosystem approach, have already been critiqued as precluding the study of gender (Brumfiel 1992). A further critique was offered by Gumerman and Warburton: "So there is no question some of us have exaggerated the importance of the role of environment and technology in culture change. We tend to treat the prehistoric peoples almost as a barometer reflecting changes in environment. . . . In other words, we tended to lose sight of some of those very things that made the prehistoric people human—their belief system and their social system" (1996:4). What is needed is the integration of gender (as well as other ideational and social) studies with the rest of archaeology. Although different kinds of question are posed, the effect of those questions and the change they can produce is profound.

Toward a Gendered Archaeology

There is, in the final analysis, no overall agreement about how to engender archaeology. Kelley and Hanen (1988) propose that many and varied voices on gender issues should be heard. One way to incorporate multiple voices on gender is with a social constructivist position. "Social epistemology . . . asks how are knowledges organized and produced? who participates in organizing and producing them? what are the social relations of the producers? what are the social consequences of the knowledges?" (Hartman and Messer-Davidow 1991:2). They continue, "While most [other] models privilege either agents or social structures in explaining the production of knowledge, social constructionism emphasizes their mutual constitution. . . . [F]eminist social constructionism emphasizes both agent-initiated and system-imposed change" (p. 6), and thus may offer a model for a gendered archaeology that is multivocal.

Margaret Conkey and Joan Gero (1991) suggest that we should do more than "add women and stir," and this phrase has become embedded in the literature. But I believe that while adding women may not be enough, a great deal of "stirring" is called for. We need to keep in mind that adding women is not the end point. Suzanne Spencer-Wood reminds us,

> Feminists need to work to ensure that gender is not treated the same way that ethnicity is treated in historical archaeology, as a topic defined, analyzed, and constructed from a white male point of view. . . . The research problems and hypotheses are based on assumed universals, such as a domestic/public sexual division of labor, which are used to classify and interpret the data in ways that support the favored hypothesis, if at all possible. . . . Androcentric assumptions lead to a biased classification scheme

that results in empirically unwarranted interpretations and research conclusions. (Spencer-Wood 1992:103)

Gender has been treated in a very dichotomized, Aristotelian way, in which everything must be "A" or "Not-A," male or not-male. Gendered archaeology should instead employ "fuzzy thinking" (Kosko 1993), which allows shades of meaning and opposites grading into each other, and which is characterized by subtlety rather than precise cleavages between alternate states.

On the basis of my review of gender studies in this book, it is possible to say that while much has been accomplished, more remains to be done. Many topics require new research, but my short list of urgent studies includes: male appropriation of female labor, resistance to or manipulation of power by subordinate groups, kinship groups and women's places within them, the role of women in legitimating men's power, and oppression of primary producers. These and other themes should be at the heart of gender research.

In sum, a gendered archaeology is a more nuanced one, asking new questions, finding new data, and partitioning the old data in new ways. The focus on power and prestige needs to move over and make room for a focus on agency and values.

BIBLIOGRAPHY

Absalom, Karel
1949 The Diluvial Anthropomorphic Statuettes and Drawings, Especially the So-called Venus Statuettes Discovered in Moravia. *Artibus Asiae* 12:201–220.

Albers, Patricia, and Beatrice Medicine, eds.
1993 *The Hidden Half: Studies of Plains Indian Women.* Washington, D.C.: University Press of America.

Alcoff, Linda, and Elizabeth Potter
1993 *Feminist Epistemologies.* London: Routledge.

Allen, W. L., and Richardson, J. B.
1971 The Reconstruction of Kinship from Archaeological Data: The Concepts, the Methods, and the Feasibility. *American Antiquity* 36:41–53.

Anati, Emanuel
1985 The Questions of Fertility Cults. Papers presented at the First Conference on Archaeology of the Ancient Mediterranean. Anthony Bonanno, ed. Amsterdam: B. R. Grüner Publishing Co.

Anderson, Edgar
1956 Man as a Maker of New Plants and New Communities. In *Man's Role of Changing the Face of the Earth.* William L. Thomas, Jr., ed. Pp. 763–777. Chicago: University of Chicago Press.

Anonymous
1977 4,000 Year Old Clan Cemetery Excavated. *China Reconstructs.* June 1977:21–23.

Anonymous
1993 Female Warriors Unearthed. *China Today.* October 1993:64.

Anonymous
1994 Female Anthropologist's Guide to Academic Pitfalls. In *Equity Issues for Women in Archeology.* Margaret C. Nelson, Sarah M. Nelson, and Alison

Wylie, eds. Archeological Papers of the American Anthropological Association 5.

Ardrey, Robert
1963 *African Genesis: A Personal Investigation into the Animal Origins and the Nature of Man.* New York: Atheneum.
1976 *The Hunting Hypothesis: A Personal Conclusion Concerning the Evolutionary Nature of Man.* Pp. 82–90. New York: Bantam Books.

Arnold, Bettina
1991 The Deposed Princess of Vix: The Need for an Engendered European Prehistory. In *The Archaeology of Gender: Proceedings of the Twenty-Second Annual Chacmool Conference of the Archaeological Association of the University of Calgary.* Pp. 366–374. Dale Walde and Noreen D. Willows, eds. Calgary: Archaeological Association, University of Calgary.

Arnold, Karen, Roberta Gilchrist, Pam Graves, and Sarah Taylor, eds.
1988 Women and Archaeology. *Archaeological Review from Cambridge* 7(1):2–8.

Bachofen, Johann J.
1861[1967] *Myth, Religion and Mother Right. Selected Writings.* Ralph Mannheim, trans. Bollingen Series 84. Princeton, N.J.

Bacus, Elisabeth A., Alex W. Barker, Jeffrey D. Bonevich, Sandra L. Dunavan, J. Benjamin Fitzhugh, Debra L. Gold, Nurit S. Goldman-Finn, William Griffin, and Karen M. Mudar
1993 *A Gendered Past: A Critical Bibliography of Gender in Archaeology.* Ann Arbor: University of Michigan Museum of Anthropology.

Bahn, Paul G.
1986 No Sex, Please, We're Aurignacians. *Rock Art Research* 3:99–120.
1991 Where's the Beef? The Myth of Hunting Magic in Paleolithic Art. In *Rock Art and Prehistory: Papers Presented to Symposium G of the AURA Congress, Darwin 1998.* Paul Bahn and Andrée Rosenfeld, eds. Oxbow Monograph 10.
1992 Review of Engendering Archaeology. *Journal of Gender Studies* 1:338–344.

Bahn, Paul G., and Jean Vertut
1988 *Images of the Ice Age.* Milan: New Interlitho.

Balme, Jane, and Wendy Beck
1993 Archaeology and Feminism—Views on the Origins of the Division of Labour. In *Women in Archaeology: A Feminist Critique.* Occasional Papers in Archaeology, No. 23. Hilary du Cros and Laurajane Smith, eds. Pp.

61–74. Canberra: Department of Prehistory, Research School of Pacific Studies, Australian National University.

Barber, Elizabeth Wayland
1994 *Women's Work: The First 20,000 Years.* New York: W. W. Norton and Co.

Barker Alex W.
1993 Introduction. In *A Gendered Past: A Critical Bibliography of Gender in Archaeology.* Elisabeth A. Bacus, et al., eds. Ann Arbor: University of Michigan Museum of Anthropology.

Barstow, Ann
1978 The Uses of Archaeology for Women's History: James Mellaart's Work on the Neolithic Goddess at Çatal Hüyük. *Feminist Studies* 4(3):7–17.

Bem, Sandra L.
1993 *The Lenses of Gender: Transforming the Debate on Sexual Inequality.* New Haven and London: Yale University Press.

Bender, Barbara
1987 The Roots of Inequality. In *Domination and Resistance.* Daniel Miller, Michael Rowlands, and Christopher Tilley, eds. Pp. 83–95. London: Unwin Hyman.

Bender, Susan J.
1991 Towards a History of Women in Northeastern U.S. Archaeology. In *The Archaeology of Gender: Proceedings of the Twenty-Second Annual Chacmool Conference of the Archaeological Association of the University of Calgary.* Dale Walde and Noreen D. Willows, eds. Pp. 211–216. Calgary: Archaeological Association, University of Calgary.

Benedict, James B.
1993 *Excavations at Bode's Draw: A Women's Work Area in the Mountains Near Estes Park, Colorado.* Boulder, Colo.: Westype Publishers.

Berenguer, Magin
1973 *Prehistoric Man and His Art: The Caves of Ribadesella.* London: Souvenir Press.

Bertelsen, Reidar, Arnvid Lillehammer, and Jenny-Rita Naess, eds.
1987 *Were They All Men? An Examination of Sex Roles in Prehistoric Society.* Acts from a workshop held at Ulstein Kloster, Rogaland, November 2–4, 1979. Stavanger, Norway: Arkeologisk Museum i Stavanger.

Binford, Lewis R.
1962 Archaeology as Anthropology. *American Antiquity* 28(2):217–225.

1986   In Pursuit of the Future. In *American Archaeology Past and Future: A Celebration of the Society for American Archaeology 1935–1985*. David J. Meltzer, Don D. Fowler, and Jeremy A. Sabloff, eds. Pp. 459–479. Washington, D.C.: Smithsonian Institution Press.

Bird, C. F. M.
1993   Woman the Toolmaker: Evidence for Women's Use and Manufacture of Flaked Stone Tools in Australia and New Guinea. In *Women in Archaeology: A Feminist Critique*. Occasional Papers in Archaeology, No. 23. Hilary du Cros and Laurajane Smith, eds. Pp. 22–30. Canberra: Department of Prehistory, Research School of Pacific Studies, Australian National University.

Blanton, Richard E., Gary Feinman, Stephen A. Kowalewski, and Peter N. Peregrine
1996   A Dual-Processual Theory for the Evolution of Mesoamerican Civilization. *Current Anthropology* 37(1):1–14.

Bleier, Ruth
1986a   Introduction. In *Feminist Approaches to Science*. Ruth Bleier, ed. Pp. 1–17. New York: Pergamon Press.
1986b   Sex Differences Research: Science or Belief? In *Feminist Approaches to Science*. Ruth Bleier, ed. Pp. 147–164. New York: Pergamon Press.

Boas, Franz
1909   The Mind of Primitive Man. In *Source Book for Social Origins*. W. Thomas, ed. Chicago: University of Chicago Press.

Bogoras, Waldemar
1904   The Chukchee. The Jesup North Pacific Expedition. *American Museum of Natural History Memoir* 7:1. New York: Stechert.

Bolen, Kathleen M.
1992   Prehistoric Construction of Mothering. In *Exploring Gender Through Archaeology*. Cheryl Claassen, ed. Pp. 49–62. Madison, Wisc.: Prehistory Press.

Bolger, Diane
1996   Figurines, Fertility, and the Emergence of Complex Society in Prehistoric Cyprus. *Current Anthropology* 37(2):365–373.

Bordes, Francois
1968   *The Old Stone Age*. New York: McGraw-Hill.

Boserup, Ester
1970   *Women's Role in Economic Development*. New York: St. Martin's Press.

Boulding, Elise
1976 *The Underside of History: A View of Women Through Time.* Boulder, Colo.: Westview Press.

Boye, L., B. Draidy, K. Hvenegaard-Lassen, and V. Odegaard
1984 Towards an Archaeology for Women. S. Holten-Dall, trans. *Archaeological Review from Cambridge* 3(1):82–85.

Braidwood, Robert
1953 Did Man Once Live by Beer Alone? *American Anthropologist* 55:515–526.
1967 *Prehistoric Men.* New York: William Morrow.

Braithwaite, Mary
1984 Ritual and Prestige in the Prehistory of Wessex c. 2200–1400 B.C.: A New Dimension to the Archaeological Evidence. In *Ideology, Power, and Prehistory.* Daniel Miller and Christopher Tilley, eds. Pp. 93–110. Cambridge: Cambridge University Press.

Bridges, Patricia S.
1989 Changes in Activities with the Shift to Agriculture in the Southeastern United States. *Current Anthropology* 30:385–394.

Brown, Betty Ann
1983 Seen but Not Heard: Women in Aztec Ritual—The Sahagun Texts. In *Text and Image in Pre-Columbian Art.* J. C. Berlo, ed. Pp. 119–154. Oxford: BAR International Series 180.

Brown, Judith K.
1970 A Note on the Division of Labor by Sex. *American Anthropologist* 72:1037–1078.
1975 Iroquois Women: An Ethnohistoric Note. In *Towards an Anthropology of Women.* Rayna Reiter, ed. New York: Monthly Review Press.

Bruhns, Karen Olsen
1991 Sexual Activities: Some Thoughts on the Sexual Division of Labor and Archaeological Interpretation. In *The Archaeology of Gender: Proceedings of the Twenty-Second Annual Chacmool Conference of the Archaeological Association of the University of Calgary.* Dale Walde and Noreen D. Willows, eds. Pp. 420–429. Calgary: Archaeological Association, University of Calgary.

Brumfiel, Elizabeth M.
1989 Factional Competition in Complex Society. In *Domination and Resistance.* Daniel Miller, Michael Rowlands, and Christopher Tilley, eds. Pp. 127–139. London: Unwin Hyman.

1991   Weaving and Cooking: Women's Production in Aztec Mexico. In *Engendering Archaeology: Women and Prehistory*. Joan M. Gero and Margaret W. Conkey, eds. Pp. 224–251. Oxford: Basil Blackwell.

1992   Distinguished Lecture in Archaeology: Breaking and Entering the Ecosystem—Gender, Class, and Faction Steal the Show. *American Anthropologist* 94(3):551–567.

1996   Comments on Agency, Ideology, and Power. *Current Anthropology* 37(1):49–50.

Bumsted, Pamela M., Jane E. Booker, Ramon M. Barnes, Thomas W. Boutton, George J. Armelagos, Juan Carlos Lerman, and Klaus Brendel
1990   Recognizing Women in the Archeological Record. In *Powers of Observation: Alternative Views in Archeology*. Sarah M. Nelson and Alice B. Kehoe, eds. Pp. 89–102. Archeological Papers of the American Anthropological Association 2.

Callender, V. G.
1992   Female Officials in Ancient Egypt and Egyptian Historians. In *Stereotypes of Women in Power*. Barbara Garlick, Suzanne Dixon, and Pauline Allen, eds. Pp. 11–35. New York: Greenwood Press.

Campbell, Joseph
1994   *The Power of Myth*. New York: Doubleday.

Casey, Joanna
1997   Just a Formality: The Presence of Fancy Projectile Points in a Basic Tool Assemblage. In *Gender in African Archaeology*. Susan Kent, ed. Walnut Creek, Calif.: AltaMira Press.

Chang Kwang-chih
1986   *The Archaeology of Ancient China*. New Haven: Yale University Press.

Chase, Sabrina M.
1991   Polygyny, Architecture, and Meaning. In *The Archaeology of Gender: Proceedings of the Twenty-Second Annual Chacmool Conference of the Archaeological Association of the University of Calgary*. Dale Walde and Noreen D. Willows, eds. Pp. 150–158. Calgary: Archaeological Association, University of Calgary.

Chiao Chien
1978   Chinese History—Primitive Society. *China Reconstructs*. December 1978.

Childe, V. Gordon
1951   *Man Makes Himself*. New York: New American Library.

Claassen, Cheryl
1991   Gender, Shellfishing and the Shell Mound Archaic. In *Engendering Archaeology: Women and Prehistory*. Joan M. Gero and Margaret W. Conkey, eds. Pp. 276–300. Oxford: Basil Blackwell.
1992   Questioning Gender: An Introduction. In *Exploring Gender Through Archaeology*. Cheryl Claassen, ed. Pp. 1–10. Madison, Wisc.: Prehistory Press.
1993   *Concerns for a Gendered Prehistory*. Paper presented at the 5th International Interdisciplinary Congress on Women. San José, Costa Rica, February 22–26, 1993.
1994   *Women in Archaeology*. Philadelphia: University of Pennsylvania Press.

Cohen, Mark Nathan, and Sharon Bennett
1993   Skeletal Evidence for Sex Roles and Gender Hierarchies in Prehistory. In *Sex and Gender Hierarchies*. Barbara Diane Miller, ed. Pp. 273–296. Cambridge: Cambridge University Press.

Conkey, Margaret
1983   On the Origins of Paleolithic Art: A Review and Some Critical Thoughts. In *The Mousterian Legacy: Human Biocultural Change in the Upper Pleistocene*. Erik Trinkaus, ed. BAR International Series 164. Pp. 201–227.
1991   Does It Make a Difference? Feminist Thinking and Archaeologies of Gender. In *The Archaeology of Gender: Proceedings of the Twenty- Second Annual Chacmool Conference of the Archaeological Association of the University of Calgary*. Dale Walde and Noreen D. Willows, eds. Pp. 24–33. Calgary: Archaeological Association, University of Calgary.
1993   Making the Connections: Feminist Theory and Archaeologies of Gender. In *Women in Archaeology: A Feminist Critique*. Occasional Papers in Archaeology, No. 23. Hilary de Cros and Laurajane Smith, eds. Pp. 3–15. Canberra: Department of Prehistory, Research School of Pacific Studies, Australian National University.

Conkey, Margaret W., and Joan M. Gero
1991   Tensions, Pluralities, and Engendering Archaeology: An Introduction to Women and Prehistory. In *Engendering Archaeology: Women and Prehistory*. Joan M. Gero and Margaret W. Conkey, eds. Pp. 3–30. Oxford: Basil Blackwell.

Conkey, Margaret W., and Janet Spector
1984   Archaeology and the Study of Gender. *Advances in Archaeological Method and Theory* 7:1–38.

Conkey, Margaret W., and Ruth E. Tringham
1995 Archaeology and the Goddess: Exploring the Contours of Feminist Archaeology. In *Feminisms in the Academy*. Domna C. Stanton and Abigail J. Stewart, eds. Pp. 199–247. Ann Arbor: University of Michigan Press.

Conkey, Margaret, with Sarah Williams
1991 Original Narratives: The Political Economy of Gender in Archaeology. In *Gender at the Crossroads of Knowledge: Feminist Anthropology in the Postmodern Era*. Micaela di Leonardo, ed. Pp. 102–139. Berkeley: University of California Press.

Conrad, Geoffrey W.
1981 Cultural Materialism, Split Inheritance, and the Expansion of Ancient Peruvian Empires. *Antiquity* 46(1):2–26.

Coon, Carleton S.
1976 *The Hunting Peoples*. New York: Pelican Books.

Cordell, Linda S.
1993 Women Archaeologists in the Southwest. In *Hidden Scholars: Women Anthropologists and the Native American Southwest*. Nancy J. Parezo, ed. Pp. 202–345. Albuquerque: University of New Mexico Press.

Costin, Cathy Lynne
1996 Exploring the Relationship Between Gender and Craft in Complex Societies: Methodological and Theoretical Issues of Gender Attribution. In *Gender and Archaeology*. Rita Wright, ed. Pp. 111–142. Philadelphia: University of Pennsylvania Press.

Coward, Rosalind
1983 *Patriarchal Precedents*. London: Routledge and Kegan Paul.

Cowgill, George L.
1993 Distinguished Lecture in Archeology: Beyond Criticizing New Archeology. *American Anthropologist* 95(3):551–573.

Crabtree, Pamela
1991 Gender Hierarchies and the Sexual Division of Labor in the Natufian Culture of the Southern Levant. In *The Archaeology of Gender: Proceedings of the Twenty-Second Annual Chacmool Conference of the Archaeological Association of the University of Calgary*. Dale Walde and Noreen D. Willows, eds. Pp. 384–391. Calgary: Archaeological Association, University of Calgary.

Crumley, Carole L.
1979   Three Location Models: An Epistemological Assessment for Anthropology and Archaeology. In *Advances in Archaeological Method and Theory*, vol. 2. Pp. 141–173. M. Schiffer, ed. New York: Academic Press.

Cucchiari, Salvatore
1981   The Gender Revolution and the Transition from Bisexual Horde to Patrilocal Band: The Origins of Gender Hierarchy. In *Sexual Meanings*. Sherry B. Ortner and Harriet Whitehead, eds. Cambridge: Cambridge University Press.

Cullen, Tracey
1995   Women in Archaeology: Perils and Progress. *Antiquity* 69(266):1042–1045.

Da Gen
1988   China's Oldest Dragon Figure. *China Reconstructs*. July 1988.

Dahlberg, Frances
1981   *Woman the Gatherer*. New Haven and London: Yale University Press.

Damm, Charlotte
1991   From Burials to Gender Roles: Problems and Potentials in Postprocessual Archaeology. In *The Archaeology of Gender: Proceedings of the Twenty-Second Annual Chacmool Conference of the Archaeological Association of the University of Calgary*. Dale Walde and Noreen D. Willows, eds. Pp. 130–135. Calgary: Archaeological Association, University of Calgary.

Davis, Elizabeth G.
1971   *The First Sex: The Book that Proves that Woman's Contribution to Civilization Has Been Greater than Man's*. New York: Penguin Books.

Davis-Kimball, Jeannine
n.d.   Sauro-Sarmatian Nomadic Women: New Gender Identities. *Journal of Indo-European Studies*.
1997   Warrior Women of the Eurasian Steppes. *Archaeology*. January/February:44–48.

Deetz, James
1965   *The Dynamics of Stylistic Change in Arikara Ceramics*. Urbana: University of Illinois Press.
1968   The Inference of Residence and Descent Rules from Archaeological Data. In *New Perspectives in Archaeology*. Sally R. Binford and Lewis R. Binford, eds. Pp. 41–48. Chicago: Aldine.

De Beauvoir, Simone
1953   *The Second Sex*. H. M. Parshley, trans. New York: Knopf.

Delporte, H.
1979 *L'Image de la Femme dans l'Art Prehistorique*. Paris: Picard.

DeMarrais, Elizabeth, Luis Jaime Castillo, and Timothy Earle
1996 Ideology, Materialization, and Power Strategies. *Current Anthropology* 37(1):15–31.

DeVore, Irven, and Sherwood L. Washburn
1963 Baboon Ecology and Human Evolution. In *African Ecology and Human Evolution*. F. C. Howell and F. Bourlière, eds. Chicago: Aldine.

di Leonardo, Micaela
1991 Introduction. In *Gender at the Crossroads of Knowledge: Feminist Anthropology in the Postmodern Era*. Micaela di Leonardo, ed. Pp. 1–48. Berkeley: University of California Press.

Dincauze, Dena F.
1992 Exploring Career Styles in Archaeology. In *Rediscovering Our Past: Essays on the History of American Archaeology*. Jonathon E. Reyman, ed. Pp. 131–136. Aldershot, England: Avebury.

Dirks, Nicholas B., Geoff Eley, and Sherry B. Ortner, eds.
1994 Introduction. In *Culture/Power/History: A Reader in Contemporary Social Theory*. Nicholas B. Dirks, Geoff Eley, and Sherry B. Ortner, eds. Pp. 1–45. Princeton: Princeton University Press.

Dobres, Marcia-Anne
1988 Feminist Archaeology and Inquiries into Gender Relations: Some Thoughts on Universals, Origin Stories, and Alternating Paradigms. *Archaeological Review from Cambridge* 7(1):30–44.
1992 Re-Considering Venus Figurines: A Feminist Inspired Re-Analysis. In *Ancient Images, Ancient Thought: The Archaeology of Ideology*. A. S. Goldsmith, S. Garvie, D. Selin, and J. Smith, eds. Pp. 245–262. Calgary: Archaeological Association, University of Calgary.
1995a Beyond Gender Attribution: Some Methodological Issues for Engendering the Past. In *Gendered Archaeology: The Second Australian Women in Archaeology Conference*. Jane Balme and Wendy Beck, eds. Pp. 51–66. Canberra: ANH Publications, RSPAS, Australian National University.
1995b Gender and Prehistoric Technology: On the Social Agency of Technical Strategies. *World Archaeology* 27(1):25–49.

Dommasnes, Liv Helga
1987 Male-female roles and ranks in Late Iron Age Norway. In *Were They All Men? An Examination of Sex Roles in Prehistoric Society*. Acts from a

workshop held at Ulstein Kloster, Rogaland, November 2–4, 1979. Reidar Bertelsen, Arnvid Lillehammer, and Jenny-Rita Naess, eds. Pp. 65–77. Stavanger, Norway: Arkeologisk Museum i Stavanger.

1990 Feminist Archaeology: Critique or Theory Building? In *Writing the Past in the Present*. Frederick Baker and Julian Thomas, eds. Pp. 24–31. Lampeter, Wales: Saint David's University.

Donley, Linda W.

1982 House Power: Swahili Space and Symbolic Markers. In *Symbolic and Structural Archaeology*. Ian Hodder, ed. Cambridge: Cambridge University Press.

1987 Life in the Swahili Town House Reveals the Symbolic Meaning of Places and Artefact Assemblages. *African Archaeological Review* 5:181–192.

Donley-Reid, Linda W.

1990 The Power of Swahili Porcelain, Beads, and Pottery. In *Powers of Observation: Alternative Views in Archeology*. Sarah M. Nelson and Alice B. Kehoe, eds. Pp. 47–60. Archeological Papers of the American Anthropological Association 2.

1996 A Neolithic Culture on the Analytic Couch. Paper prepared for TAG Conference, 1996.

Doumas, Christos C.

1983 *Thera: Pompeii of the Ancient Aegean*. London: Thames and Hudson.

DuBois, Ellen C., Gail P. Kelly, Elizabeth L. Kennedy, Carolyn W. Korsmeyer, and Lillian S. Robinson, eds.

1987 *Feminist Scholarship: Kindling in the Groves of Academe*. Urbana: University of Illinois Press.

du Cros, Hilary, and Laurajane Smith, eds.

1993 *Women in Archaeology: A Feminist Critique*. Occasional Papers in Archaeology, No. 23. Canberra: Department of Prehistory, Research School of Pacific Studies, Australian National University.

Duhard, Jean-Pierre

1991 The Shape of Pleistocene Women. *Antiquity* 65:552–561.

Duke, Philip

1991 *Points in Time: Structure and Event in a Late Northern Plains Hunting Society*. Boulder: University Press of Colorado.

Duke, Philip, and Michael C. Wilson, eds.
1995 *Beyond Subsistence: Plains Archaeology and the Postprocessual Critique.* Tuscaloosa: University of Alabama Press.

Durkheim, Emile
1933[1893] *The Division of Labor in Society.* G. Simpson, trans. New York: Free Press.

Duyvendak, J. J. L.
1928 *The Book of Lord Shang.* Chicago: University of Chicago Press.

Ehrenberg, Margaret
1989 *Women in Prehistory.* Norman: University of Oklahoma Press.

Ehrenreich, Robert, Carole Crumley, and Janet Levy, eds.
1995 *Heterarchy and the Analysis of Complex Societies.* Archeological Papers of the American Anthropological Association 6.

Eisler, Riane
1976 *The Chalice and The Blade: Our History, Our Future.* San Francisco: Harper and Row.

Ellender, Isabel
1993 Gender in Aboriginal Burial Practices: Evidence from Springfield Gorge Cave, Victoria. In *Women in Archaeology: A Feminist Critique.* Occasional Papers in Archaeology, No. 23. Hilary du Cros and Laurajane Smith, eds. Canberra: Department of Prehistory, Research School of Pacific Studies, Australian National University.

Engelbrecht, William
1974 The Iroquois: Archaeological Patterning on the Tribal Land. *World Archaeology* 6(1):52–65.

Engels, Frederic
1972[1881] *The Origin of the Family, Private Property and the State.* New York: International Publishers.

Estioko-Griffin, Agnes, and P. Bion Griffin
1981 Woman the Hunter: The Agta. In *Woman the Gatherer.* Frances Dahlberg, ed. Pp. 121–152. New Haven: Yale University Press.

Evans, Sir Arthur
1930 *The Palace of Minos: A Comparative Account of the Successive Stages of the Early Cretan Civilization as Illustrated by the Discoveries at Knosses,* vol. 3. London: MacMillan and Co.

Fausto-Sterling, Anne
1985 *Myths of Gender: Biological Theories about Women and Men*. New York: Basic Books.

Fedigan, Linda
1986 The Changing Role of Women in Models of Human Evolution. *Annual Review of Anthropology* 15:25–58.

Fee, Elizabeth
1974 The Sexual Politics of Victorian Social Anthropology. In *Clio's Consciousness Raised*. Mary Hartman and Lois W. Banner, eds. Pp. 86–102. New York: Harper Torchbooks.

Fisher, Elizabeth
1979 *Woman's Creation: Sexual Evolution and the Shaping of Society*. New York: Anchor Press/Doubleday.

Fisher, Helen E.
1982 *The Sex Contract*. New York: William Morrow and Co.

Fisher, Lynn E.
1993 Comment on Brian Hayden's Old Europe: Sacred Matriarchy or Complementary Opposition. In *A Gendered Past: A Critical Bibliography of Women in Archaeology*. Elizabeth Bacus, et al., eds. Pp. 70–71. Ann Arbor: University of Michigan Press.

Flannery, Kent V.
1982 The Golden Marshalltown: A Parable for Archeology of the 1980s. *American Anthropologist* 84(2):265–278.

Flannery, Kent V., and Marcus Winter
1976 Analyzing Household Activities. In *The Early Mesoamerican Village*. Kent V. Flannery, ed. Pp. 34–44. New York: Academic Press.

Fowler, Don D.
1987 Uses of the Past: Archaeology in the Service of the State. *American Antiquity* 52(2):229–248.

Fox, Robin
1967 *Kinship and Marriage*. Baltimore: Pelican Books.

Fraser, Antonia
1989 *The Warrior Queens*. New York: Alfred A. Knopf.

French, Marilyn
1985 *Beyond Power: On Women, Men, and Morals*. New York: Ballentine Books.

Freidel, David, and Linda Schele
1997   Maya Royal Women: A Lesson in Precolumbian History. In *Gender in Cross-Cultural Perspective*. Caroline B. Brettell and Carolyn F. Sargent, eds. Pp. 75–78. Englewood Cliffs, N.J.: Prentice Hall.

Fried, Morton H.
1975   *The Notion of Tribe*. Menlo Park, Calif.: Cummings Publishing Co.

Friedl, Ernestine
1975   *Women and Men: An Anthropologist's View*. New York: Holt, Rinehart & Winston.

Frison, G. C., R. L. Andrews, J. M. Adovasio, R. C. Carlisle, and R. Edgar
1986   A Late Prehistoric Animal Trapping Net from Northern Wyoming. *American Antiquity* 51:352–361.

Fuss, Diana
1989   *Essentially Speaking: Feminism, Nature and Difference*. London: Routledge.

Gailey, Christine Ward
1985   The State of the State in Anthropology. *Dialectical Anthropology* 8:65–89.

Garrow, Barbara Avery, Patrick H. Garrow, and Pat A. Thomas
1994   Women in Contract Archaeology. In *Women in Archaeology*. Cheryl Claassen, ed. Pp. 182–201. Philadelphia: University of Pennsylvania Press.

Gero, Joan M.
1983   Gender Bias in Archaeology: A Cross-Cultural Perspective. In *The Socio-Politics of Archaeology*. Joan M. Gero, David M. Lacy, and Michael L. Blakey, eds. Pp. 51–57. Amherst: University of Massachusetts, Department of Anthropology, Research Report No. 23.
1985   Socio-Politics and the Woman-at-Home Ideology. *American Antiquity* 50(2):342–350.
1991a   Genderlithics: Women's Roles in Stone Tool Production. In *Engendering Archaeology: Women and Prehistory*. Joan M. Gero and Margaret W. Conkey, eds. Oxford: Basil Blackwell.
1991b   Gender Divisions of Labor in the Construction of Archaeological Knowledge. In *The Archaeology of Gender: Proceedings of the Twenty-Second Annual Chacmool Conference of the Archaeological Association of the University of Calgary*. Dale Walde and Noreen D. Willows, eds. Pp. 96–102. Calgary: Archaeological Association, University of Calgary.
1992   Feasts and Females: Gender Ideology and Political Meals in the Andes. *Norwegian Archaeological Review* 25(1):15–30.
1993   The Social World of Prehistoric Facts: Gender and Power in Paleoindian Research. In *Women in Archaeology: A Feminist Critique*. Occasional Papers

in Archaeology, No. 23. Hilary du Cros and Laurajane Smith, eds. Pp. 31–40. Canberra: Department of Prehistory, Research School of Pacific Studies, Australian National University.

Gero, Joan M., and Margaret W. Conkey, eds.

1991 *Engendering Archaeology: Women and Prehistory.* Oxford: Basil Blackwell.

Gero, Joan M., David M. Lacy, and Michael L. Blakey

1983 Introduction. In *The Socio-Politics of Archaeology.* Joan M. Gero, David M. Lacy, and Michael L. Blakey, eds. Pp. 1–4. Amherst: University of Massachusetts, Department of Anthropology, Research Report No. 23.

Gero, Joan M., and Dolores Root

1990 Public Presentations and Private Concerns: Archaeology in the Pages of National Geographic. In *The Politics of the Past.* P. Gathercole and D. Lowenthal, eds. London: Unwin Hyman.

Gibbon, Guy

1984 *Anthropological Archaeology.* New York: Columbia University Press.

1990 What Does an Observation Mean? In *Powers of Observation: Alternative Views in Archeology.* Sarah M. Nelson and Alice B. Kehoe, eds. Pp. 5–10. Archeological Papers of the American Anthropological Association 2.

Gifford-Gonzalez, Diane

1993 Gaps in Zooarchaeological Analyses of Butchery: Is Gender an Issue? In *From Bones to Behavior: Ethnoarchaeological and Experimental Contributions to the Interpretation of Faunal Remains.* Jean Hudson, ed. Pp. 181–199. Carbondale: Southern Illinois University at Carbondale Center for Archaeological Investigations.

1997 Gender and Early Pastoralists in East Africa. In *Gender in African Archaeology.* Susan Kent, ed. Walnut Creek, Calif.: AltaMira Press.

Gilchrist, Roberta

1991 Women's Archaeology? Political Feminism, Gender Theory and Historical Revision. *Antiquity* 65:495–501.

Gilligan, Carol

1982 *In a Different Voice.* Cambridge, Mass.: Harvard University Press.

Gimbutas, Marija

1982 *The Goddesses and Gods of Old Europe: Myths and Cult Images.* Berkeley and Los Angeles: University of California Press.

1989 *The Language of the Goddess.* San Franciso: Harper and Row.

1991 *The Civilization of the Goddess: The World of Old Europe.* San Francisco: HarperCollins.

Goldberg, Steven
1974   *The Inevitability of Patriarchy.* New York: William Morrow.

Goldstein, Marilyn
1988   Gesture, Role, and Gender in West Mexican Sculpture. In *The Role of Gender in Precolumbian Art and Architecture.* Virginia Miller, ed. Pp. 53–62. Lanham, Md.: University Press of America.

Goodale, Jane C.
1971   *Tiwi Wives: A Study of the Women of Melville Island, North Australia.* Seattle: University of Washington Press.

Gorman, Alice
1995   Gender, Labour, and Resources: The Female Knappers of the Andaman Islands. In *Gendered Archaeology: The Second Australian Women in Archaeology Conference.* Jane Balme and Wendy Beck, eds. Pp. 87–91. Canberra: Australian National University.

Gould, Stephen J.
1981   *The Mismeasure of Man.* New York: W. W. Norton and Co.

Gross, Michael, and Mary Beth Averill
1983   Evolution and Patriarchal Myths of Scarcity and Competition. In *Discovering Reality: Feminist Perspectives on Epistemology, Metaphysics, Methodology, and Philosophy of Science.* Sandra Harding and Merrill B. Hintikka, eds. Pp. 71–95. London: D. Reidel Publishing Company.

Grove, David C., and Susan D. Gillespie
1984   Chalcatizingo's Portrait Figurines and the Cult of the Ruler. *Archaeology.* July/August:27–33.

Guenther, Todd R.
1991   The Horse Creek Site: Some Evidence for Gender Roles in a Transitional Early to Middle Plains Archaic Base Camp. *Plains Anthropologist* 36(134):9–23.

Guillén, Ann Cyphers
1988   Thematic and Contextual Analyses of Chalcatzingo Figurines. *Mexica* 10(5):98–102.

Gumerman, George J., and Miranda Warburton
1996   The Universe in a Cultural Context. Presented at Oxford V Archaeoastronomy Conference. Santa Fe, New Mexico, August 1996.

Guo Da-Shan
1995   Hongshan and Related Cultures. In *The Archaeology of Northeast China.* Sarah M. Nelson, ed. Pp. 21–64. London: Routledge.

Haag, William G.
1986   Field Methods in Archaeology. In *American Archaeology Past and Future: A Celebration of the Society for American Archaeology 1935–1985*. David J. Meltzer, Don D. Fowler, and Jeremy A. Sabloff, eds. Pp. 63–76. Washington, D.C.: Smithsonian Institution Press.

Haaland, Gunnar, and Randi Haaland
1995   Who Speaks the Goddess's Language? Imagination and Method in Archaeological Research. *Norwegian Archaeological Review* 28(2):105–121.

Hackett, Jo Ann
1989   Can a Sexist Model Liberate Us? Ancient Near Eastern "Fertility" Goddesses. *Journal of Feminist Studies in Religion* 5:65–76.

Hamblin, D. J.
1973   *The First Cities*. New York: Time-Life Books.

Hancar, Franz
1940   Problem Der Venus Statuettin im Eurasiatischen Jung-Palaeolithikum. *Praehistorische Zeitschrift* 30/31.

Hanen, Marsha P., and Jane H. Kelley
1983   Social and Philosophical Frameworks for Archaeology. In *The Socio-Politics of Archaeology*. Joan M. Gero, David M. Lacy, and Michael L. Blakey, eds. Pp. 107–117. Amherst: University of Massachusetts, Department of Anthropology, Research Report No. 23.
1992   Metaarchaeology: Reflections by Archaeologists and Philosophers. In *Boston Studies in the Philosophy of Science*. Robert D. Cohen, ed. Pp. 195–225. Dordrecht, Netherlands: Kluwer Academic Publishers.

Haraway, Donna
1983   Animal Sociology and a Natural Economy of the Body Politic, Part I: A Political Physiology of Dominance. In *The Signs Reader: Women, Gender and Scholarship*. Elizabeth Abel and Emily K. Abel, eds. Pp. 123–139. Chicago: University of Chicago Press.

Harding, Sandra
1986   *The Science Question in Feminism*. Ithaca, N.Y.: Cornell University Press.

Harding, Sandra, and Merrill B. Hintikka, eds.
1983   *Discovering Reality: Feminist Perspectives on Epistemology, Metaphysics, Methodology, and Philosophy of Science*. Dordrecht, Netherlands: D. Reidel Publishing Co.

Harris, Marvin
1993   The Evolution of Human Gender Hierarchies: A Trial Formulation. In *Sex and Gender Hierarchies*. Barbara Diane Miller, ed. Pp. 57–79. Cambridge: Cambridge University Press.

Hartman, Joan E., and Ellen Messer-Davidow
1991   Introduction. In *(En)Gendering Knowledge*. Joan E. Hartman and Ellen Messer-Davidow, eds. Pp. 1–7. Knoxville: University of Tennessee Press.

Hastorf, Christine A.
1991   Gender, Space and Food in Prehistory. In *Engendering Archaeology: Women and Prehistory*. Joan M. Gero and Margaret W. Conkey, eds. Pp. 132–158. Oxford: Basil Blackwell.

Hawkesworth, Mary E.
1989   Knowers, Knowing, Known: Feminist Theory and Claims of Truth. *Signs* 14(3):533–557.

Hayden, Brian
1986   Old Europe: Sacred Matriarchy or Complementary Opposition? In *Archaeology and Fertility Cults in the Ancient Mediterranean: Papers Presented at the First International Conference on Archaeology of the Ancient Mediterranean*. A. Bonanno, ed. Pp. 17–30. Amsterdam: B. R. Grüner Publishing Co.
1990   Nimrods, Pisators, Pluckers, and Planters: The Emergence of Food Production. *Journal of Anthropological Archaeology* 9:31–69.
1992   Observing Prehistoric Women. In *Exploring Gender Through Archaeology*. Cheryl Claassen, ed. Pp. 33–47. Madison, Wisc.: Prehistory Press.

Herschberger, Ruth
1940   *Adam's Rib*. New York: Pellegrini and Cudahy.

Higham, Charles, and Rachanie Bannanurag
1990   The Princess and the Pots. *New Scientist* 26:50–55.

Higham, Charles, and Rachanie Thosarat
1994   Thailand's Good Mound. *Natural History* 12(94):60–66.

Hill, James N.
1968   Broken K Pueblo: Prehistoric Social Organization in the American Southwest. Anthropological Papers of the University of Arizona 18.

Hobbes, Thomas
1958[1642]   *Leviathan*. New York: Liberal Arts Press.

Hodder, Ian

1982 Theoretical Archaeology: A Reactionary View. In *Symbolic and Structural Archaeology*. Ian Hodder, ed. Cambridge: Cambridge University Press.

1983 Burials, Houses, Women and Men in the Mesolithic. In *Ideology, Power and Prehistory*. Daniel Miller and Christopher Tilley, eds. Pp. 51–68. Cambridge: Cambridge University Press.

1987 Contextual Archaeology: An Interpretation of Çatal Hüyük and a Discussion of the Origins of Agriculture. *Bulletin of the Institute of Archaeology* 24:43–56.

1991a Gender Representation and Social Reality. In *The Archaeology of Gender: Proceedings of the Twenty-Second Annual Chacmool Conference of the Archaeological Association of the University of Calgary*. Dale Walde and Noreen D. Willows, eds. Pp. 11–16. Calgary: Archaeological Association, University of Calgary.

1991b Interpretative Archaeology and Its Role. *American Antiquity* 56(1):7–18.

1992 *Theory and Practice in Archaeology*. London: Routledge.

Hollimon, Sandra

1992 Health Consequences of Sexual Division of Labor Among Prehistoric Native Americans: The Chumash of California and the Arikara of the North Plains. In *Exploring Gender Through Archaeology*. Cheryl Claassen, ed. Pp. 81–88. Madison, Wisc.: Prehistory Press.

Hubbard, Ruth

1990 Some Thoughts about the Masculinity of the Natural Sciences. In *Making All the Difference: Inclusion, Exclusion, and American Law*. Martha Minow, ed. Pp. 1–15. Ithaca, N.Y.: Cornell University Press.

Hudson, Mark, and Gina Barnes

1991 Yoshinogari: A Yayoi Settlement in Northern Kyushu. *Monumenta Nipponica* 46(2):211–235.

Hurcombe, Linda

1995 Our Own Engendered Species. *Antiquity* 69(262):88–100.

Isaac, Glynn L.

1968 Traces of Pleistocene Hunters: An East African Example. In *Man the Hunter*. Richard B. Lee and Irven DeVore, eds. Pp. 253–254. Chicago: Aldine.

Jackson, Thomas L.
1991 Pounding Acorn: Women's Production as Social and Economic Focus. In *Engendering Archaeology: Women and Prehistory*. Joan M. Gero and Margaret W. Conkey, eds. Pp. 301–328. Oxford: Basil Blackwell.

Jochim, Michael A.
1988 Optimal Foraging and the Division of Labor. *American Anthropology* 90:130–136.

Johnson, Matthew, and Simon Coleman
1990 Power and Passion in Archaeological Discourse. In *Writing the Past in the Present*. Frederick Baker and Julian Thomas, eds. Pp. 13–17. Lampeter, Wales: Saint David's University.

Joyce, Arthur A., and Marcus Winter
1996 Ideology, Power, and Urban Society in Pre-Hispanic Oaxaca. *Current Anthropology* 37(1):33–86.

Joyce, Rosemary
1992 Images of Gender and Labor Organization in Classic Maya Society. In *Exploring Gender Through Archaeology*. Cheryl Claassen, ed. Pp. 63–70. Madison, Wisc.: Prehistory Press.
1996 The Construction of Gender in Classic Maya Monuments. In *Gender and Archaeology*. Rita Wright, ed. Pp. 167–198. Philadelphia: University of Pennsylvania Press.

Kehoe, Alice B.
1990a Points and Lines. In *Powers of Observation: Alternative Views in Archeology*. Sarah M. Nelson and Alice B. Kehoe, eds. Pp. 23–38. Archeological Papers of the American Anthropological Association 2.
1990b Gender is an Organon. *Zygon* 25(2):139–150.
1990c "In Fourteen Hundred and Ninety-Two, Columbus . . ." The Primacy of the National Myth in US Schools. In *The Excluded Past: Archaeology in Education*. Peter Stone and Robert MacKenzie, eds. Pp. 201–215. London: Unwin Hyman.
1991 No Possible, Probable Shadow of Doubt. *Antiquity* 65:129–131.
1992a The Muted Class, Unshackling Tradition. In *Exploring Gender Through Archaeology*. Cheryl Claassen, ed. Pp. 23–32. Madison, Wisc.: Prehistory Press.
1992b The Paradigmatic Vision of Archaeology: Archaeology as a Bourgeois Science. In *Rediscovering Our Past: Essays on the History of American Archaeology*. Jonathon Reyman, ed. Pp. 3–14. Aldershot, England: Avebury.

1995   Processual and Postprocessual Archaeology: A Critical Review. In *Beyond Subsistence: Plains Archaeology and the Postprocessual Critique*. Philip Duke and Michael C. Wilson, eds. Pp. 19–27. Tuscaloosa: University of Alabama Press.

1996   On Unambiguous Upper Paleolithic Carved Male. *Current Anthropology* 37(4):665–670.

Kehoe, Alice B., and Sarah M. Nelson

1990   Introduction. In *Powers of Observation: Alternative Views in Archeology*. Sarah M. Nelson and Alice B. Kehoe, eds. Pp. 1–4. Archeological Papers of the American Anthropological Association 2.

Keller, Evelyn Fox

1983   *A Feeling for the Organism*. San Francisco: Freeman Press.

1985   *Reflections on Gender and Science*. New Haven, Conn.: Yale University Press.

1986   How Gender Matters or Why It's So Hard for Us to Count Past Two. In *Perspectives on Gender and Science*. Jan Harding, ed. Pp. 168–183. London: The Falmer Press.

1991   The Wo/Man Scientist: Issues of Sex and Gender in the Pursuit of Science. In *The Outer Circle: Women in the Scientific Community*. H. Zuckerman, J. Cole, and J. Bruer, eds. Pp. 227–236. New York: W. W. Norton and Co.

Kelley, Jane H.

1992   Being and Becoming. In *Rediscovering Our Past: Essays on the History of American Archaeology*. Jonathon Reyman, ed. Pp. 81–90. Aldershot, England: Avebury.

Kelley, Jane H., and Marsha P. Hanen

1988   *Archaeology and the Methodology of Science*. Albuquerque: University of New Mexico Press.

Kendall, Laurel

1985   *Shamans, Housewives, and Other Restless Spirits*. Honolulu: University of Hawaii Press.

Kenoyer, Jonathan Mark

1995   Ideology and Legitimization in the Indus State as Revealed through Public and Private Symbols. *Pakistan Archaeologists' Forum* 1995(3).

Kent, Susan

1995   Does Sendentarization Promote Gender Inequality? A Case Study for the Kalahari. *Journal of the Royal Anthropological Institute* 1:513–536.

1996 Hunting Variability at a Recently Sedentary Kalahari Village. In *Cultural Diversity among Twentieth-Century Foragers.* Susan Kent, ed. Cambridge: Cambridge University Press.
1997 Invisible Gender, Invisible Foragers: Late Stone Age Southern African Hunter-Gatherer Prehistory. In *Gender in African Archaeology.* Susan Kent, ed. Walnut Creek, Calif.: AltaMira Press.

Kidder, Alfred V.
1949 Introduction. In *Prehistoric Southwesterners from Basket-Maker to Pueblo.* Charles A. Amsden, ed. Pp. xi–xiv. Los Angeles: Southwest Museum.

Kim Won-yong
1983 Recent Archaeological Discoveries in the Republic of Korea. UNESCO: Centre for East Asian Studies.
1986 *Art and Archaeology of Ancient Korea.* Seoul: Taekwang Publishing Co.

Kingston, Maxine Hong
1975 *The Woman Warrior: Memoirs of a Girlhood Among Ghosts.* New York: Vintage Books.

Koenigswald, von G. H. R.
1972 Early Homo Sapiens as an Artist: The Meaning of Paleolithic Art. In *The Origin of Homo Sapiens, Ecology and Conservation,* vol. 3. F. Bordes, ed. Pp. 133–139. Proceedings of the Paris Symposium 1969.

Kohl, Philip
1985 Symbolic Cognitive Archaeology. *Dialectical Anthropology* 9:105–117.

Kornfeld, Marcel, and Julie Francis
1991 Approaches to Gender Studies in Plains Anthropology: An Introduction. *Plains Anthropologist* 36(134):1–7.

Kosko, Burt
1993 *Fuzzy Thinking.* New York: Hyperion.

Kramer, Carol, and Miriam Stark
1994 The Status of Women in Archeology. In *Equity Issues for Women in Archeology.* Margaret C. Nelson, Sarah M. Nelson, and Alison Wylie, eds. Pp. 17–22. Archeological Papers of the American Anthropological Association 5.

Kristiansen, Kristian
1983 Ideology and Material Culture: An Archaeological Perspective. In *Ideology, Power and Prehistory.* Daniel Miller and Christopher Tilley, eds. Cambridge: Cambridge University Press.

1991 Chiefdoms, States, and Systems of Evolution. In *Chiefdoms, Power, Economy and Ideology*. Timothy Earle, ed. Pp. 16–43. Cambridge: Cambridge University Press.

Landau, Misia
1991 *Narratives of Human Evolution*. New Haven: Yale University Press.

Laughlin, William S.
1968 Hunting: An Integrating Biobehavior System and Its Evolutionary Importance. In *Man the Hunter*. Richard B. Lee and Irven DeVore, eds. Pp. 304–320. Chicago: Aldine.

Laurent
1965 *Heuseuse Préhistoire*. Périguex: Pierre Fanlac.

Leacock, Eleanor B.
1975 Class, Commodity, and the Status of Women. In *Women Cross-Culturally: Change and Challenge*. Ruby Rohrlich-Leavitt, ed. Pp. 601–616. The Hague: Mouton.
1978 Women's Status in Egalitarian Society: Implications for Social Evolution. *Current Anthropology* 19(2):247–275.
1981 *Myths of Male Dominance: Collected Articles on Women Cross-Culturally*. New York: Monthly Review Press.
1983 Interpreting the Origins of Gender Inequality: Conceptual and Historical Problems. *Dialectical Anthropology* 7(4):263–284.
1993 Women in Samoan History: A Further Critique of Derek Freeman. In *Sex and Gender Hierarchies*. Barbara Diane Miller, ed. Pp. 351–365. Cambridge: Cambridge University Press.

Lee, Richard B.
1979 *The !Kung San: Men, Women, and Work in a Foraging Society*. Cambridge: Cambridge University Press.

Lee, Richard B., and Irven DeVore, eds.
1968 *Man the Hunter*. Chicago: Aldine.

Leone, Mark P.
1973 Archaeology as the Science of Technology: Mormon Town Plans and Fences. In *Research and Theory in Current Archaeology*. C. L. Redman, ed. New York: John Wiley & Sons.

Lerner, Gerda
1986 *The Creation of Patriarchy*. Oxford: Oxford University Press.

Leroi-Gourhan, André
1967 *Treasures of Prehistoric Art*. N. Guterman, trans. New York: Harry N. Abrams.

Lévi-Strauss, Claude
1963 *Structural Anthropology*. Claire Jacobson and Brooke Grundfest, trans. New York: Basic Books.
1969 *The Elementary Structures of Kinship*. Rodney Needham, ed. James Harle Bell and John Richard Von Strumer, trans. Pp. 93–119. Boston: Beacon Press.

Levine, Mary Ann
1991 An Historical Overview of Research on Women in Anthropology. In *The Archaeology of Gender: Proceedings of the Twenty-Second Annual Chacmool Conference of the Archaeological Association of the University of Calgary*. Pp. 177–186. Dale Walde and Noreen D. Willows, eds. Calgary: Archaeological Association, University of Calgary.

Levy, Janet E.
1995 Heterarchy in Bronze Age Denmark: Settlement Pattern, Gender, and Ritual. In *Heterarchy and the Analysis of Complex Societies*. Robert M. Ehrenreich, Carole L. Crumley, and Janet E. Levy, eds. Pp. 41–54. Archeological Papers of the American Anthropological Association 6.

Li Ki-baek
1992 *The New History of Korea*. Edward W. Wagner and Edward J. Shultz, trans. Cambridge, Mass.: Harvard University Press.

Lightfoot, Kent G., and Gary M. Feinman
1982 Social Differentiation and Leadership Development in Early Pithouse Villages in the Mogollon Region of the American Southwest. *American Antiquity* 47(1):64–85.

Linnekin, Joyce
1990 *Sacred Queens and Women of Consequence: Rank, Gender, and Colonialism in the Hawaiian Islands*. Ann Arbor: University of Michigan Press.

Linton, Sally
1971 Woman the Gatherer: Male Bias in Anthropology. In *Women in Cross-Cultural Studies*. Sue-Ellen Jacobs, ed. Urbana: University of Illinois Press.

Lloyd, Elisabeth A.
1993 Pre-Theoretical Assumptions in Evolutionary Explanations of Female Sexuality. *Philosophical Studies* 69:139–153.

Longacre, William A.

1966 Changing Patterns of Social Integration: A Prehistoric Example from the American Southwest. *American Anthropologist* 68(1):94–102.

1968 Some Aspects of Prehistoric Society in East-Central Arizona. In *New Perspectives in Archaeology*. Sally R. Binford and Lewis R. Binford, eds. Chicago: Aldine.

Longino, Helen

1987 Can There Be a Feminist Science? *Hypatia* 2(3):51–64.

1990 *Science as Social Knowledge: Values and Objectivity in Scientific Inquiry*. Princeton: Princeton University Press.

1995 To See Feelingly: Reason, Passion, and Dialogue in Feminist Philosophy. In *Feminisms in the Academy*. Domna C. Stanton and Abigail J. Stewart, eds. Pp. 19–45. Ann Arbor: University of Michigan Press.

Lowie, Robert

1915 Proceedings of the American Anthropological Association for 1914. *American Anthropologist* 17(2):357–362.

Lubbock, J.

1870 *The Origin of Civilization and the Primitive Condition of Man*. London: Longmans Green and Co.

Lutz, Catherine

1995 The Gender of Theory. In *Women Writing Culture*. Ruth Behar and Deborah A. Gordon, eds. Pp. 249–266. Berkeley: University of California Press.

Mack, Rainer Towle

1992 Gendered Site: Archaeology, Representation, and the Female Body. In *Ancient Images, Ancient Thought: The Archaeology of Ideology*. A. S. Goldsmith, S. Garvie, D. Selin, and J. Smith, eds. Pp. 235–244. Calgary: Archaeological Association, University of Calgary.

MacKinnon, Catharine A.

1989 *Toward a Feminist Theory of the State*. Cambridge, Mass.: Harvard University Press.

Maine, H. S.

1861 *Ancient Law*. London: J. Murray.

Malinowski, Bronislaw

1922 *Argonauts of the Western Pacific*. London: Routledge and Kegan Paul.

Mandt, Gro
1986   Searching for Female Deities in the Religious Manifestation of the Scandinavian Bronze Age. In *Words and Objects.* G. Steinsand, ed. Pp. 111–126. Oslo: Norwegian University Press.
1987   Female Symbolism in Rock Art. In *Were They All Men? An Examination of Sex Roles in Prehistoric Society.* Acts from a workshop held at Ulstein Kloster, Rogaland, November 2–4, 1979. Reidar Bertelsen, Arnvid Lille-hammer, and Jenny-Rita Naess, eds. Pp. 35–52. Stavanger, Norway: Arkeologisk Museum i Stavanger.

Marcus, Joyce
1974   The Iconography of Power Among the Classic Maya. *World Archaeology* 6(1):83–94.

Marshack, Alexander
1972   *The Roots of Civilization.* New York: McGraw-Hill.

Marshall, Yvonne
1985   Who Made Lapita Pots? A Case Study in Gender Archaeology. *Journal of the Polynesian Society* 94(3):205–233.

Mascia-Lees, Frances E., Patricia Sharpe, and Colleen Ballerino Cohen
1989   The Postmodernist Turn in Anthropology: Cautions from a Feminist Perspective. *Signs* 15(1):7–33.

Mason, Carol I.
1992   From the Other Side of the Looking Glass: Women in American Archaeology in the 1950s. In *Rediscovering Our Past: Essays on the History of American Archaeology.* Jonathon E. Reyman, ed. Pp. 91–101. Aldershot, England: Avebury.

McCafferty, Sharisse D., and Geoffrey G. McCafferty
1988a   Spinning and Weaving as Female Gender Identity in Post-Classic Mexico. In *Textile Traditions of Mesoamerica and the Andes.* Margot B. Schevill, Janet C. Barlo, and Edward B. Dwyer, eds. Pp. 19–48. New York: Garland.
1988b   Powerful Women and the Myth of Male Dominance in Aztec Society. *Archaeological Review from Cambridge* 7(1)45–59.
1994   Engendering Tomb 7 at Monte Albán. *Current Anthropology* 35(2):143–166.

McCoid, C. H., and L. D. McDermott
1996   Toward Decolonizing Gender: Female Vision in the European Upper Paleolithic. *American Anthropologist* 98:54–61.

McDermott, L.
1996   Self-Representation in Upper Paleolithic Female Figurines. In *Current Anthropology* 37:227–75.

McGaw, Judith A.
1996   Reconceiving Technology: Why Feminine Technologies Matter. In *Gender and Archaeology.* Rita Wright, ed. Pp. 53–75. Philadelphia: University of Pennsylvania Press.

McGuire, Kelly R., and W. R. Hildebrandt
1994   The Possibilities of Women and Men: Gender and the California Milling Stone Horizon. *Journal of California and Great Basin Archaeology* 16(1):41–59.

Mead, Margaret
1949   *Male and Female: A Study of the Sexes in a Changing World.* New York: William Morrow and Co.

Mellaart, James
1962   Excavations at Çatal-Hüyük. *Anatolian Studies* 12:41–65.
1963   Excavations at Çatal-Hüyük 1962: 2nd Preliminary Report. *Anatolian Studies* 13:43–103.
1965   *The Earliest Civilizations of the Near East.* London: Thames and Hudson.

Meltzer, David J., Don D. Fowler, and Jeremy A. Sabloff, eds.
1986   *American Archaeology Past and Future: A Celebration of the Society for American Archaeology 1935–1985.* Washington, D.C.: Smithsonian Institution Press.

Miller, Barbara Diane
1993   The Anthropology of Sex and Gender Hierarchies. In *Sex and Gender Hierarchies.* Barbara Diane Miller, ed. Pp. 3–31. Cambridge: Cambridge University Press.

Miller, Daniel, and Christopher Tilley
1984   Ideology, Power and Prehistory. In *Ideology, Power and Prehistory.* Daniel Miller and Christopher Tilley, eds. Pp. 1–15. Cambridge: Cambridge University Press.

Miller, Virginia, ed.
1988   *The Role of Gender in Precolumbian Art and Architecture.* Lanham, Md.: University Press of America.

Minow, Martha
1990 The Emergence of the Social-Relations Approach. In *Making All the Difference: Inclusion, Exclusion, and American Law.* Martha Minow, ed. Pp. 173–224. Ithaca, N.Y.: Cornell University Press.

Mitchell, Christi
1992 Activating Women in Arikara Ceramic Production. In *Exploring Gender Through Archaeology.* Cheryl Claassen, ed. Pp. 89–94. Madison, Wisc.: Prehistory Press.

Moore, Henrietta L.
1988 *Feminism and Anthropology.* Minneapolis: University of Minnesota Press.

Morgan, Elaine
1972 *The Descent of Woman.* New York: Bantam Books.

Morgan, Lewis Henry
1877 *Ancient Society.* New York: World Publishing.

Morris, Desmond
1967 *The Naked Ape: A Study of the Human Animal.* New York: Dell Publishing Co.

Muller, Viana
1985 Origins of Class and Gender Hierarchy in Northwest Europe. *Dialectical Anthropology* 10:93–105.
1987 Kin Reproduction and Elite Accumulation in the Archaic States of Northwest Europe. In *Power Relations and State Formation.* Thomas C. Patterson and Christine W. Gailey, eds. Pp. 81–97. Archeology Section, American Anthropological Association.

Murdock, George Peter
1949 *Social Structure.* New York: Macmillan.
1968 Are the Hunter-Gatherers a Cultural Type? In *Man the Hunter.* Richard B. Lee and Irven DeVore, eds. Pp. 335–339. Chicago: Aldine.

Nagamine, Mitsukazu
1986 Clay Figurines and Jômon Society. In *Windows on the Japanese Past: Studies in Archaeology and Prehistory.* Richard Pearson, ed. Ann Arbor: Center for Japanese Studies, University of Michigan.

Nelson, Margaret, Sarah M. Nelson, and Alison Wylie, eds.
1994 *Equity Issues for Women in Archeology.* Archeological Papers of the American Anthropological Association 5.

Nelson, Sarah M.

n.d. "Venus" Figurines as Evidence of Sedentism in the Upper Paleolithic. On File, Department of Anthropology, University of Denver.

1987 Tribes in the Chulmun Period. In *Papers in Honor of the Retirement of Professor Kim Won-Yong*. Vol. I, Archaeology. Im Hyo-Jai, ed. Pp. 805–813. Seoul: Seoul National University.

1990 Diversity of the Upper Paleolithic "Venus" Figurines and Archeological Reality. In *Powers of Observation: Alternative Views in Archeology*. Sarah M. Nelson and Alice B. Kehoe, eds. Pp. 11–22. Archeological Papers of the American Anthropological Association 2.

1991a The "Goddess Temple" and the Status of Women at Niuheliang, China. In *The Archaeology of Gender: Proceedings of the Twenty-Second Annual Chacmool Conference of the Archaeological Association of the University of Calgary*. Dale Walde and Noreen D. Willows, eds. Calgary: Archaeological Association, University of Calgary.

1991b The Statuses of Women in Ko-Silla: Evidence from Archaeology and Historic Documents. *Korea Journal* 31(2):101–107.

1993 Gender Hierarchy and the Queens of Silla. In *Sex and Gender Hierarchies*. Barbara Diane Miller, ed. Pp. 297–315. Cambridge: Cambridge University Press.

1994 Comment on S. O. Kim, Burials, Pigs, and Political Prestige. *Current Anthropology* 35(2):135–136.

1995 The Politics of Ethnicity in Prehistoric Korea. In *Nationalism, Politics, and the Practice of Archaeology*. P. Kohl and C. Fawcett, eds. Pp. 218–231. Cambridge: Cambridge University Press.

1996a Ideology and the Formation of an Early State in Northeast China. In *Ideology and the Early State*. Henri J. Claasen and Jarich G. Oosten, eds. Pp. 153–69. Leiden: E. J. Brill.

1996b Protohistoric Burial Patterns in Korea. *Korea Journal* 36(2):26–32.

1996c Ritualized Pigs and the Origins of Complex Society: Hypotheses Regarding the Hongshan Culture. *Early China* 20.

1997 Reflections on Gender Studies in African and Asian Archaeology. In *Gender in African Archaeology*. Susan Kent, ed. Walnut Creek, Calif.: AltaMira Press.

Nelson, Sarah M., and Alice B. Kehoe, eds.

1990 *Powers of Observation: Alternative Views in Archeology*. Archeological Papers of the American Anthropological Association 2.

Nelson, Sarah M., and Margaret C. Nelson
1994   Conclusion. In *Equity Issues for Women in Archeology*. Margaret Nelson, Sarah M. Nelson, and Alice Wylie, eds. Archeological Papers of the American Anthropological Association 5.

Nerlove, Sara B.
1974   Women's Workload and Infant Feeding Practices: A Relationship with Demographic Implications. *Ethnology* 13:207–214.

Nielsen, Joyce McCarl
1990   *Sex and Gender in Society: Perspectives on Stratification*. 2d ed. Prospect Heights, Ill.: Waveland Press.

Oakley, Ann
1974   *Women's Work: The Housewife, Past and Present*. New York: Vintage Books.

Oakley, Kenneth P.
1959   *Man the Toolmaker*. Chicago: University of Chicago Press.

O'Brien, Patricia J.
1990   Evidence for the Antiquity of Gender Roles in the Central Plains Tradition. In *The Archaeology of Gender: Proceedings of the Twenty-Second Annual Chacmool Conference of the Archaeological Association of the University of Calgary*. Dale Walde and Noreen D. Willows, eds. Pp. 61–72. Calgary: Archaeological Association, University of Calgary.
1995   Taxonomic Determinism in Evolutionary Theory: Another Model of Multilinear Cultural Evolution with an Example for the Plains. In *Beyond Subsistence: Plains Archaeology and the Postprocessual Critique*. Philip Duke and Michael C. Wilson, eds. Pp. 66–89. Tuscaloosa: University of Alabama Press.

Ortner, Sherry B.
1981   Gender and Sexuality in Hierarchical Societies: The Case of Polynesia and Some Comparative Implications. In *Sexual Meanings: The Cultural Construction of Gender and Sexuality*. Sherry B. Ortner and Harriet Whitehead, eds. Pp. 359–409. Cambridge: Cambridge University Press.

Ortner, Sherry B., and Harriet Whitehead, eds.
1981   *Sexual Meanings: The Cultural Construction of Gender and Sexuality*. Cambridge: Cambridge University Press.

Parezo, Nancy J.
1993a   *Hidden Scholars: Women Anthropologists and the Native American Southwest*. Albuquerque: University of New Mexico Press.

1993b   Conclusion: The Beginning of the Quest. In *Hidden Scholars: Women Anthropologists and the Native American Southwest*. Nancy J. Parezo, ed. Pp. 334–367. Albuquerque: University of New Mexico Press.

Parker Pearson, Michael

1982   Mortuary Practices, Society and Ideology: An Ethnoarchaeological Study. In *Symbolic and Structural Archaeology*. Ian Hodder, ed. Pp. 99–113. Cambridge: Cambridge University Press.

1983   Social Change, Ideology, and the Archaeological Record. In *Ideology, Power and Prehistory*. Daniel Miller and Christopher Tilley, eds. Cambridge: Cambridge University Press.

Parsons, Mary H.

1972   Spindle Whorls from the Teotihuacan Valley, Mexico. In *Miscellaneous Studies in Mexican Prehistory*. M. W. Spence, J. R. Parsons, and M. H. Parsons, eds. Pp. 45–80. Ann Arbor: University of Michigan Museum of Anthropology, Anthropological Papers 45.

Parsons, Roger B.

1962   Indian Mounds of Northwest Iowa as Soil Genesis Benchmarks. *Journal of the Iowa Archaeological Society* 12(2).

Passemard, Luce

1938   *Les Statuettes Feminines Paléolithiques Dites Venus*. St. Nîmes, France: Libraire Teissier.

Patterson, Thomas C.

1993   *Archaeology: The Historical Development of Civilizations*. 2nd ed. Englewood Cliffs, N.J.: Prentice Hall.

1995   *Toward a Social History of Archaeology in the United States*. Fort Worth, Texas: Harcourt Brace College Publishers.

1996   Gender, Class and State Formation in Ancient Japan. In *Alternative Pathways to Early States*. Nikolay N. Kradin and Valerie A. Lynsha, eds. Vladivostok: Russian Academy of Sciences, Far Eastern Division, Institute of History, Archaeology and Ethnology.

Patterson, Thomas C., and Christine W. Gailey, eds.

1987   *Power Relations and State Formation*. Archeology Section, American Anthropological Association.

Pearson, Richard

1981   Social Complexity in Chinese Coastal Neolithic Sites. *Science* 213:1078–1086.

1988   *Chinese Neolithic Burial Patterns: Problems of Method and Interpretation in Early China*. Berkeley: University of California Press.

Pfeiffer, John
1985   *The Emergence of Humankind*. 4th ed. New York: Harper and Row.

Piggott, Joan R.
n.d.   Chieftain Pairs and Co-Rulers: Female Sovereignty in Early Japan. In *Women and Class in Japanese Society*. Hitomi Tonomura and Anne Walthall, eds. Ann Arbor: Center for Japanese Studies, University of Michigan.

Pomeroy, Sarah
1974   *Goddesses, Whores, Wives, and Slaves in Classical Antiquity*. New York: Schocken.

Posposil, Leopold
1963   Kapauku Papuan Economy. *Yale University Publications in Anthropology* 67. New Haven: Department of Anthropology, Yale University.

Powell, Mary Lucas, Patricia Bridges, and Ann Marie Mires, eds.
1991   *What Means These Bones? Studies in Southeastern Bioarchaeology*. Tuscaloosa: University of Alabama Press.

Preucel, Robert, and Rosemary Joyce
1994   Feminism, Fieldwork and the Practice of Archeology. Paper presented at the 93rd Annual Meeting of the American Anthropological Association, Atlanta.

Prideaux, Tom
1973   *The Emergence of Man: Cro-Magnon Man*. New York: Time-Life Books.

Qian Hao
1981a   The Han Tombs at Mawangdui, Changsha: Underground Home of an Aristocratic Family. In *Out of China's Earth: Archaeological Discoveries in the People's Republic of China*. Qian Hao, Chen Heyi, and Ru Suichu, eds. Pp. 87–126. New York: Harry N. Abrams.
1981b   The Yin Ruins and the Tomb of Fu Hao. In *Out of China's Earth: Archaeological Discoveries in the People's Republic of China*. Qian Hao, Chen Heyi, and Ru Suichu, eds. Pp. 9–28. New York: Harry N. Abrams.
1981c   Qin Dynasty Warriors and Horses: A Great Terracotta Army of 220 B.C. In *Out of China's Earth: Archaeological Discoveries in the People's Republic of China*. Qian Hao, Chen Heyi, and Ru Suichu, eds. Pp. 65–85. New York: Harry N. Abrams.

Rapp, Rayna
1977   Gender and Class: An Archaeology of Knowledge Concerning the Origin of State. *Dialectical Anthropology* 2:309–316.

Rappaport, Roy A.
1967 *Pigs for the Ancestors*. New Haven: Yale University Press.

Reiter, Rayna, ed.
1975 *Towards an Anthropology of Women*. New York: Monthly Review Press.

Renaud, Etienne B.
1929 Prehistoric Female Figurines from America and the Old World. *Scientific Monthly* 28:507–512.

Renfrew, Colin
1984 *Approaches to Social Archaeology*. Cambridge, Mass.: Harvard University Press.

Reyman, Jonathon E., ed.
1992 *Rediscovering Our Past: Essays on the History of American Archaeology*. Aldershot, England: Avebury.

Rice, Patricia C.
1981 Prehistoric Venuses: Symbols of Motherhood or Womanhood? *Journal of Anthropological Research* 37(4):402–416.

Rice, Prudence
1991 Women and Prehistoric Pottery Production. In *The Archaeology of Gender: Proceedings of the Twenty-Second Annual Chacmool Conference of the Archaeological Association of the University of Calgary*. Dale Walde and Noreen D. Willows, eds. Pp. 436–443. Calgary: Archaeological Association, University of Calgary.

Rick, John
1969 Man and Superman. *Historic Archaeology* 3:1–2.

Roberts, Catherine
1993 A Critical Approach to Gender as a Category of Analysis in Archaeology. In *Women in Archaeology: A Feminist Critique*. Occasional Papers in Archaeology, No. 23. Hilary du Cros and Laurajane Smith, eds. Pp. 16–21. Canberra: Department of Prehistory, Research School of Pacific Studies, Australian National University.

Rogers, Susan Carol
1978 Woman's Place: A Critical Review of Anthropological Theory. *Comparative Studies in Society and History* 20(1).

Rohrlich, Ruby
1980 State Formation in Sumer and the Subjugation of Women. *Feminist Studies* 61:76–102.

Rohrlich-Leavitt, Ruby
1976 Peaceable Primates and Gentle People: An Anthropological Approach to Women's Studies. In *Women's Studies: The Social Realities.* Barbara Bellow Watson, ed. Pp. 165–202. New York: Harpers College Press.

Roosevelt, Anna C.
1988 Interpreting Certain Female Images in Prehistoric Art. In *The Role of Gender in Precolumbian Art and Architecture.* Virginia Miller, ed. Pp. 1–34. Lanham, Md.: University Press of America.

Roosevelt, A. C., M. Lima da Costa, C. Lopes Machado, M. Michab, N. Mercier, H. Valladas, J. Feathers, W. Barnett, M. Imazio do Silveira, A. Henderson, J. Sliva, B. Chernoff, D. S. Reese, J. A. Holman, N. Toth, and K. Schick
1996 Paleoindian Cave Dwellers in the Amazon: The Peopling of the Americas. *Science* (272):373–384.

Rosaldo, Michelle Zimbalist
1974 Women, Culture and Society: A Theoretical Overview. In *Women, Culture and Society.* Michelle Zimbalist Rosaldo and Louise Lamphere, eds. Pp. 17–42. Stanford: Stanford University Press.
1980 The Use and Misuse of Anthropology: Reflections on Feminism and Cross-Cultural Understanding. *Signs* 5(3):389–414.

Rosaldo, Michelle Zimbalist, and Louise Lamphere, eds.
1974 *Women, Culture and Society.* Stanford: Stanford University Press.

Rossiter, Margaret W.
1982 *Women Scientists in America: Struggles and Strategies to 1940.* Baltimore, Md.: Johns Hopkins Press.

Russell, Pamela
1991 Men Only? The Myths About Paleolithic Artists. In *The Archaeology of Gender: Proceedings of the Twenty-Second Annual Chacmool Conference of the Archaeological Association of the University of Calgary.* Dale Walde and Noreen D. Willows, eds. Pp. 346–351. Calgary: Archaeological Association, University of Calgary.
1993 The Paleolithic Mother-Goddess: Fact or Fiction? In *Women in Archaeology: A Feminist Critique.* Occasional Papers in Archaeology, No. 23. Hilary du Cros and Laurajane Smith, eds. Canberra: Department of Prehistory, Research School of Pacific Studies, Australian National University.

Saccasyn Della Santa, Evelyn
1947 *Les Figures Humaines du Paléolithique Superior Eurasiatique.* Paris: Amberes.

Sacks, Karen
1979 *Sisters and Wives: The Past and Future of Sexual Equality.* Westport, Conn.: Greenwood Press.

Sahlins, Marshall D.
1968 *Tribesmen.* Englewood Cliffs, N.J.: Prentice Hall.

Saitta, Dean J.
1992 Radical Archaeology and Middle-Range Methodology. *Antiquity* 66:253–264.

Sanday, Peggy Reeves
1981 *Female Power and Male Dominance: On the Origins of Sexual Inequality.* Cambridge: Cambridge University Press.
1988 The Reproduction of Patriarchy in Feminist Anthropology. In *Feminist Thought and the Structure of Knowledge.* M. Gergen, ed. Pp. 49–68. New York: New York University Press.

Sandler, Bernice R.
1986 *The Campus Climate Revisited: Chilly for Women Faculty, Administrators, and Graduate Students.* A publication of the Project on the Status and Education of Women. Association of American Colleges.

Sassaman, Kenneth E.
1992 Gender and Technology at the Archaic Woodland Transition. In *Exploring Gender Through Archaeology.* Cheryl Claassen, ed. Pp. 71–79. Madison, Wisc.: Prehistory Press.

Sauer, Carl O.
1952 Agricultural Origins and Dispersals. Bowman Memorial Lectures, Series 2. New York: Geographical Society.

Schlegel, Alice
1972 *Male Dominance and Female Autonomy.* New Haven: HRAF Press.
1977 *Sexual Stratification: A Cross-Cultural View.* New York: Columbia Review Press.

Schoenwetter, James
1990 Lessons from an Alternative View. In *Powers of Observation: Alternative Views in Archeology.* Sarah M. Nelson and Alice B. Kehoe, eds. Pp. 103–112. Archeological Papers of the American Anthropological Association 2.

Sempowski, Martha M.
1986 Differential Mortuary Treatment of Seneca Women: Some Social Inferences. *Archaeology of Eastern North America* 14:35–44.

Service, Elman R.
1962 *Primitive Social Organization: An Evolutionary Perspective.* New York: Random House.
1966 *The Hunters.* Englewood Cliffs, N.J.: Prentice Hall.

Shanks, Michael, and Christopher Tilley
1987 *Re-Constructing Archaeology.* Cambridge: Cambridge University Press.

Shapiro, Judith
1981 Anthropology and the Study of Gender. In *A Feminist Perspective in the Academy: The Difference It Makes.* Elizabeth Langland and Walter Gove, eds. Pp. 110–129. Chicago: University of Chicago Press.

Silverblatt, Irene
1988 Women in States. *Annual Review of Anthropology* 17:427–460.
1991 Interpreting Women in States: New Feminist Ethnohistories. In *Gender at the Crossroads of Knowledge: Feminist Anthropology in the Postmodern Era.* Micaela di Leonardo, ed. Pp. 140–171. Berkeley: University of California Press.

Society for American Archaeology
1991 Archaeology . . . Is Gender Still an Issue? *Bulletin* 9(1):1, 6–10.

Soffer, Olga
1983 Politics of the Paleolithic in the USSR: A Case of Paradigms Lost. In *The Socio-Politics of Archaeology.* Joan M. Gero, David M. Lacy, and Michael L. Blakey, eds. Pp. 91–105. Amherst: University of Massachusetts, Department of Anthropology, Research Report No. 23.

Sorenson, Mary Louise Stig
1988 Is There a Feminist Contribution to Archaeology? *Archaeological Review from Cambridge* 7(1):9–21.

South, Stanley A.
1969 Wanted: An Historical Archaeologist. *Historical Archaeology* 3:75–84.

Spector, Janet D.
1983 Male and Female Task Differentiation Among the Hidatsa: Toward the Development of an Archaeological Approach to the Study of Gender. In *The Hidden Half: Studies of Plains Indian Women.* Patricia Albers and Beatrice Medicine, eds. Pp. 77–100. Washington, D.C.: University Press of America.
1991 What This Awl Means: Towards a Feminist Archaeology. In *Engendering Archaeology: Women and Prehistory.* Joan M. Gero and Margaret W. Conkey, eds. Pp. 388–406. Oxford: Basil Blackwell.

1994 *What This Awl Means: Feminist Archaeology at a Wahpeton Dakota Village.* St. Paul: Minnesota Historical Society Press.

Spencer, Herbert
1895 *The Principles of Sociology.* 3rd ed. New York: D. Appleton and Company.

Spencer-Wood, Suzanne M.
1984 Status, Occupation and Ceramic Indices: A Nineteenth-Century Comparative Analysis. *Man in the Northeast* 2(2):87–110.
1992 A Feminist Program for Nonsexist Archaeology. In *Quandaries and Quests: Visions of Archaeology's Future.* LuAnn Wandsnider, ed. Carbondale: Southern Illinois University at Carbondale, Center for Archaeological Investigations.

Sperling, Susan
1991 Baboons with Briefcases vs. Langurs in Lipstick: Feminism and Functionalism in Primate Studies. In *Gender at the Crossroads of Knowledge: Feminist Anthropology in the Postmodern Era.* Micaela di Leonardo, ed. Pp. 204–234. Berkeley: University of California Press.

Spindler, Konrad
1994 *The Man in the Ice.* E. Osers, trans. New York: Harmony.

Stahl, Ann B., and Maria das Dores Cruz
1997 Men and Women in a Market Economy: Gender and Craft Production in West Central Ghana c 1775–1995. In *Gender in African Archaeology.* Susan Kent, ed. Walnut Creek, Calif.: AltaMira Press.

Stalsberg, Anne
1987 The Interpretation of Women's Objects of Scandinavian Origin from the Viking Period Found in Russia. In *Were They All Men? An Examination of Sex Roles in Prehistoric Society.* Acts from a workshop held at Ulstein Kloster, Rogaland, November 2–4, 1979. Reidar Bertelsen, Arnvid Lillehammer, and Jenny-Rita Naess, eds. Pp. 89–101. Stavanger, Norway: Arkeologisk Museum i Stavanger.

Stanford, Craig B.
1996 The Hunting Ecology of Wild Chimpanzees: Implications for the Evolutionary Ecology of Pliocene Hominids. *American Anthropologist* 98(1):96–113.

Stanislawski, M. B.
1973 Review of Archaeology as Anthropology: A Case Study by William A. Longacre. *American Antiquity* 38:117–122.

Steinem, Gloria
1980   If Men Could Menstruate. In *Pulling Our Own Strings*. Gloria Kaufman and Mary Kay Blakely, eds. Bloomington: Indiana University Press.

Steward, J.
1955   *Theory of Culture Change*. Urbana: University of Illinois Press.

Stiehm, Judith Hicks
1985   A Feminist in Military Academy Land, or Men and their Institutions as Curiosities. In *For Alma Mater: Theory and Practice in Feminist Scholarship*. Paula A. Treichler, Cheris Kramarae, and Beth Stafford, eds. Pp. 377–392. Urbana: University of Illinois Press.

Stone, Merlin
1976   *When God was a Woman: The Story—Archaeologically Documented—of the Most Ancient of Religions, the Religion of the Goddess, and the Role this Ancient Worship Played in Judeo-Christian Attitudes Toward Women*. New York: Dial Press.

Taylor, Sarah
1990   "Brothers" in Arms? Feminism, Post-Structuralism, and the "Rise of Civilisation." In *Writing the Past in the Present*. Frederick Baker and Julian Thomas, eds. Pp. 32–41. Lampeter, Wales: Saint David's University.

Tedlock, Barbara
1995   Works and Wives: On the Sexual Division of Textual Labor. In *Women Writing Culture*. Ruth Behar and Deborah A. Gordon, eds. Pp. 267–286. Berkeley: University of California Press.

Thomas, David Hurst
1983   The Archaeology of Monitor Valley 2. Gatecliff Shelter. Anthropological Papers of the American Museum of Natural History, vol. 59, part 1. New York.
1986   Contemporary Hunter-Gatherer Archaeology in America. In *American Archaeology Past and Future: A Celebration of the Society for American Archaeology 1935–1985*. David J. Meltzer, Don D. Fowler, and Jeremy A. Sabloff, eds. Pp. 237–276. Washington, D.C.: Smithsonian Institution Press.
1989   *Archaeology Second Edition*. Fort Worth, Texas: Holt, Rinehart and Winston.

Thomsen, Christen J.
1836   *Ledetraad til Nordisk Oldkyndigked*. Copenhagen.

Tiffany, Sharon W.
1979   Women, Power, and the Anthropology of Politics: A Review. *International Journal of Women's Studies* 2:430–442.

Tiffany, Sharon, and Kathleen J. Adams
1985   *The Wild Woman: An Inquiry into the Anthropology of an Idea.* Cambridge, Mass.: Schenkman Publishing Co.

Tiger, Lionel, and Robin Fox
1969   *Men in Groups.* New York: Random House.
1971   *The Imperial Animal.* New York: Dell.

Tilley, Christopher
1984   Ideology and the Legitimization of Power in the Middle Neolithic of Southern Sweden. In *Ideology, Power and Prehistory.* Daniel Miller and Christopher Tilley, eds. Pp. 111–146. Cambridge: Cambridge University Press.
1989   Archaeology as Socio-Political Action in the Present. In *Critical Traditions in Contemporary Archaeology.* V. Pinsky and A. Wylie, eds. Pp. 104–115. Cambridge: Cambridge University Press.
1993   *Interpretive Archaeology.* Providence, R.I.: Berg.

Tobach, Ethel, and Betty Rosoff
1994   *Challenging Racism and Sexism: Alternatives to Genetic Explanations.* New York: Feminist Press at the City University of New York.

Trigger, Bruce G.
1986   Prehistoric Archaeology and American Society. In *American Archaeology Past and Future: A Celebration of the Society for American Archaeology 1935–1985.* David J. Meltzer, Don D. Fowler, and Jeremy A. Sabloff, eds. Pp. 187–215. Washington, D.C.: Smithsonian Institution Press.

Tringham, Ruth
1991   Households with Faces: The Challenge of Gender in Prehistoric Architectural Remains. In *Engendering Archaeology: Women and Prehistory.* Joan M. Gero and Margaret W. Conkey, eds. Oxford: Basil Blackwell.
1993   Review of The Civilization of the Goddess. *American Anthropologist* 95(1):196–197.
1994   Engendered Places in Prehistory. *Gender, Place and Culture* 1(2):169–203.

Trocolli, Ruth
1992   Colonization and Women's Production: The Timucua of Florida. In *Exploring Gender Through Archaeology.* Cheryl Claassen, ed. Pp. 95–102. Madison, Wisc.: Prehistory Press.

Trotter, James
1976 God: She's Alive and Well: An Anthropological Study of Mother Goddess Worship in Eastern India Shows How Traditional Symbols Can Function in a Modernizing Society. *Science News* 109(7):97–112.

Tschauner, Hartmut
1996 Middle-Range Theory, Behavioral Archaeology, and Postempiricist Philosophy of Science in Archaeology. *Journal of Archaeological Method and Theory* 3:1–30.

Tylor, E. B.
1865 *Researches into the Early History of Mankind and the Development of Civilization.* London: J. Murray.

Ucko, Peter J., ed.
1995 *Theory in Archaeology: A World Perspective.* London and New York: Routledge.

Ucko, Peter J., and Andree Rosenfeld
1973 *Palaeolithic Cave Art.* New York: McGraw-Hill.

Vincent, Joan
1986 System and Process, 1974–1985. *American Review of Anthropology* 15:99–119.

Vinsrygg, Synnøve
1987 Sex-Roles and the Division of Labour in Hunting-Gathering Societies. In *Were They All Men? An Examination of Sex Roles in Prehistoric Society.* Acts from a workshop held at Ulstein Kloster, Rogaland, November 2–4, 1979. Reidar Bertelsen, Arnvid Lillehammer, and Jenny-Rita Naess, eds. Pp. 23–32. Stavanger, Norway: Arkeologisk Museum i Stavanger.

Voight, Mary M.
1991 The Goddess from Anatolia: An Archaeological Perspective. *Oriental Rug Review.* December 1990/January 1991:33–39.

Wadley, Lyn
1997 The Invisible Meat Providers: Women in the Stone Age of South Africa. In *Gender in African Archaeology.* Susan Kent, ed. Walnut Creek, Calif.: AltaMira Press.

Walde, Dale, and Noreen D. Willows, eds.
1991 *The Archaeology of Gender: Proceedings of the Twenty-Second Annual Chacmool Conference of the Archaeological Association of the University of Calgary.* Calgary: Archaeological Association, University of Calgary.

Wallman, Sandra
1978   The Epistemologies of Sex. In *Female Hierarchies*. Lionel Tiger and Heather T. Fowler, eds. Chicago: Beresford Book Service.

Wandsnider, LuAnn, ed.
1992   *Quandaries and Quests: Visions of Archaeology's Future*. Carbondale: Southern Illinois University at Carbondale, Center for Archaeological Investigations.

Washburn, Sherwood L., and C. S. Lancaster
1968   The Evolution of Hunting. In *Man the Hunter*. Richard B. Lee and Irven DeVore, eds. Chicago: Aldine.

Wason, Paul K.
1994   *The Archaeology of Rank*. Cambridge: Cambridge University Press.

Watson, Patty Jo
1986   Archaeological Interpretation. In *American Archaeology Past and Future: A Celebration of the Society for American Archaeology 1935–1985*. David J. Meltzer, Don D. Fowler, and Jeremy A. Sabloff, eds. Pp. 439–457. Washington, D.C.: Smithsonian Institution Press.

Watson, Patty Jo, and Mary C. Kennedy
1991   The Development of Horticulture in the Eastern Woodlands of North America: Women's Role. In *Engendering Archaeology: Women and Prehistory*. Joan M. Gero and Margaret W. Conkey, eds. Pp. 255–275. Oxford: Basil Blackwell.

Webster, Gary
1990   Labor Control and Emergent Stratification in Prehistoric Europe. *Current Anthropology* 31(4):337–366.

Weiner, Annette B.
1976   *Women of Value, Men of Renown: New Perspectives in Trobriand Exchange*. Austin: University of Texas Press.

Whallon, Robert Jr.
1968   Investigations of Late Prehistoric Social Organizations in New York State. In *New Perspectives in Archaeology*. Sally R. Binford and Lewis R. Binford, eds. Chicago: Aldine.

Whelan, Mary K.
1995   Beyond Hearth and Home on the Range: Feminist Approaches to Plains Archaeology. In *Beyond Subsistence: Plains Archaeology and the Postprocessual Critique*. Philip Duke and Michael C. Wilson, eds. Pp. 46–65. Tuscaloosa: University of Alabama Press.

Whelan, Mary K., R. M. Withrow, and B. H. O'Connell
1989 The Blackdog Burial Site (21 Dk 26). Paper presented at the 54th annual meeting of the Society for American Archaeology.

White, Joyce C.
1995 Incorporating Heterarchy into Theory on Socio-Political Development: The Case from Southeast Asia. In *Heterarchy and the Analysis of Complex Societies*. Robert M. Ehrenreich, Carole L. Crumley, and Janet Levy, eds. Pp. 101–123. Archeological Papers of the American Anthropological Association, No. 6.

White, Leslie
1959 *The Evolution of Culture Change*. New York: McGraw-Hill.

Wilk, Richard R., and William L. Rathje
1982 Household Archaeology. *American Behavioral Scientist* 25(6):317–340.

Wilmsen, Edwin N.
1989 *Land Filled with Flies: A Political Economy of the Kalahari*. Chicago: University of Chicago Press.

Winters, Howard
1968 Value Systems and Trade Cycles in the Late Archaic in the Midwest. In *New Perspectives in Archaeology*. Sally R. Binford and Lewis R. Binford, eds. Chicago: Aldine.

Wobst, H. Martin, and Arthur S. Keene
1983 Archaeological Explanation as Political Economy. In *The Socio-Politics of Archaeology*. Joan M. Gero, David M. Lacy, and Michael L. Blakey, eds. Pp. 79–89. Amherst: University of Massachusetts, Department of Anthropology, Research Report No. 23.

Woodall, J. Ned, and Philip J. Perricone
1981 The Archaeologist as Cowboy: The Consequence of Professional Stereotype. *Journal of Field Archaeology* 8:506–509.

Woodward, Val
1994 Can We Draw Conclusions about Human Societal Behavior from Population Genetics? In *Challenging Racism and Sexism*. Ethel Tobach and Betty Rosoff, eds. Pp. 35–57. New York: The Feminist Press of the City University of New York.

Wormington, H. M.
1957 Ancient Man in North America. *Denver Museum of Natural History Popular Series* 4.

Wright, Patricia Chapple
1993   Variations in Male-Female Dominance and Offspring Care in Non-human Primates. In *Sex and Gender Hierarchies*. Barbara Diane Miller, ed. Pp. 127–145. Cambridge: Cambridge University Press.

Wright, Rita P.
1991   Women's Labor and Pottery Production in Prehistory. In *Engendering Archaeology: Women and Prehistory*. Joan M. Gero and Margaret W. Conkey, eds. Pp. 194–223. Oxford: Basil Blackwell.
1996   Technology, Gender, and Class: World of Difference in Ur III Mesopotamia. In *Gender and Archaeology*. Rita Wright, ed. Pp. 80–110. Philadelphia: University of Pennsylvania Press.

Wurtzburg, Susan J.
1994   Down in the Field in Louisiana: An Historical Perspective on the Role of Women in Louisiana Archaeology. In *Women in Archaeology*. Cheryl Claassen, ed. Pp. 120–137. Philadelphia: University of Pennsylvania Press.

Wylie, Alison
1983   Comments on the "Socio-Politics of Archaeology"; The De-Mystification of the Profession. In *The Socio-Politics of Archaeology*. Joan M. Gero, David M. Lacy, and Michael L. Blakey, eds. Pp. 119–129. Amherst: University of Massachusetts, Department of Anthropology, Research Report No. 23.
1989   The Interpretive Dilemma. In *Critical Traditions in Contemporary Archaeology*. V. Pinsky and A. Wylie, eds. Pp. 18–27. Cambridge: Cambridge University Press.
1991a   Gender Theory and the Archaeological Record: Why Is There No Archaeology of Gender? In *Engendering Archaeology: Women and Prehistory*. Joan M. Gero and Margaret W. Conkey, eds. Pp. 31–54. Oxford: Basil Blackwell.
1991b   Feminist Critiques and Archaeological Challenges. In *The Archaeology of Gender: Proceedings of the Twenty-Second Annual Chacmool Conference of the Archaeological Association of the University of Calgary*. Dale Walde and Noreen D. Willows, eds. Pp. 17–23. Calgary: Archaeological Association, University of Calgary.
1992a   Feminist Theories of Social Power: Some Implications for a Processual Archaeology. *Norwegian Archaeological Review* 25(1):51–67.
1992b   The Interplay of Evidential Constraints and Political Interests. *American Antiquity* 57:15–35.

1993 Introduction: The Complexity of Gender Bias. In *Women in Archaeology: A Feminist Critique*. Occasional Papers in Archaeology, No. 23. Hilary du Cros and Laurajane Smith, eds. Pp. 53–60. Canberra: Department of Prehistory, Research School of Pacific Studies, Australian National University.

1994 Pragmatism and Politics: Understanding the Emergence of Gender Research in Archaeology. Text of a lecture delivered as the 1994 Skomp Lecture, Indiana University.

1997 The Engendering of Archaeology: Reconfiguring Feminist Science Studies. *Osiris*, special issue, *Women, Gender and Science*. S. Kohlstadt and H. Longino, eds.

Yoffee, Norman, and Andrew Sherratt, eds.

1993 *Archaeological Theory: Who Sets the Agenda?* Cambridge: Cambridge University Press.

Zagarell, Allen

1986 Trade, Women, Class, and Society in Ancient Western Asia. *Current Anthropology* 27(5):415–430.

Zhang Zhongpei

1985 The Social Structure Reflected in the Yuanjunmiao Cemetery. *Journal of Anthropological Archaeology* 4:19–33.

Zihlman, Adrienne L.

1978 Women in Evolution: Part II, Subsistence and Social Organization in Early Hominids. *Signs* 4(1):4–20.

1991 Gender: The View from Physical Anthropology. In *The Archaeology of Gender: Proceedings of the Twenty-Second Annual Chacmool Conference of the Archaeological Association of the University of Calgary*. Dale Walde and Noreen D. Willows, eds. Pp. 4–10. Calgary: Archaeological Association, University of Calgary.

1993 Sex Differences and Gender Hierarchies Among Primates: An Evolutionary Perspective. In *Sex and Gender Hierarchies*. Barbara Diane Miller, ed. Pp. 32–56. Cambridge: Cambridge University Press.

Zihlman, Adrienne, and Nancy Tanner

1978 Gathering and the Hominid Adaptation. In *Female Hierarchies*. Lionel Tiger and Heather T. Fowler, eds. Chicago: Beresford Book Service.

NAME INDEX

A

Absalom, K., 157
Albers, P., 57
Alcoff, L., 16
Allen, W. L., 50
Anati, E., 158, 159
Anderson, E., 102
Anonymous, 46, 122, 139
Ardrey, R., 70, 85, 159
Arnold, B., 147
Arnold, K., 43, 142

B

Bachofen, J. J., 65
Bacus, E. A., 18, 52
Bahn, P. G., 83, 84, 156
Bannanurag, R., 124
Barber, E. W., 59, 109
Barker, A. W., 26
Barnes, G., 139
Barnes, R. M., 139
Barstow, A., 34, 115, 160
Bem, S. L., 25, 26
Bender, B., 80, 84
Bender, S. J., 42
Bennett, S., 35, 59, 103
Berenguer, M., 156, 158

Bertelsen, R., 22
Binford, L. R., 22, 58, 80, 118
Bird, C. F. M., 92, 93, 95
Blakey, M. L., 20
Blanton, R. E., 172
Bleier, R., 46
Boas, F., 67, 68
Bogoras, W., 125
Bolen, K. M., 125
Bolger, D., 164
Bordes, F., 94
Boserup, E., 86
Boulding, E., 34
Boye, L. B., 20
Braidwood, R., 108
Bridges, P. S., 103
Brown, B. A., 139
Brown, J. K., 72, 86, 125, 126
Bruhns, K. O., 111
Brumfiel, E. M., 20, 50, 104, 105,
    109, 110, 134, 167, 168, 174
Bumsted, P., 103

C

Campbell, J., 162
Casey, J., 95
Chang Kwang-chih, 121
Chiao Chien, 121

Childe, V. G., 102
Claassen, C., 16, 39, 42, 100, 101
Cohen, C., 31
Cohen, M. N., 35, 59, 103
Coleman, S., 53
Conkey, M., 14, 23, 40, 43, 48, 51,
        54, 65, 67, 69, 74, 80, 131,
        157, 161, 162, 165, 170, 175
Coon, C. S., 71
Cordell, L. S., 42, 43, 45
Costin, C. L., 56, 57, 59
Coward, R., 33, 115
Cowgill, G. L., 50, 53, 152
Crabtree, P., 102, 111
Crumley, C. L., 148
Cruz, M., 106, 108
Cucchiari, S., 126
Cullen, T., 48

D

Da Gen, 123
Dahlberg, F., 33, 71, 72
Damm, C., 147
Davis, E. G., 72, 140
De Beauvoir, S., 25
Deetz, J., 50, 119
Delporte, H., 155, 157, 158
DeMarrais, E., 168
DeVore, I., 75, 90
di Leonardo, M., 17, 50
Dincauze, D. F., 43, 47
Dirks, N. B., 18
Dobres, M., 66, 74, 97, 98, 158
Donley, L. W., 61, 62, 63, 146
Doumas, C. C., 137
Duhard, J., 159
Duke, P., 56
Durkheim, E., 116
Duyvendak, J. J. L., 140

E

Ehrenberg, M., 15
Ehrenreich, R., 148
Eisler, R., 91
Ellender, I., 92
Engelbrecht, W., 120, 136
Engels, F., 34, 52, 127
Evans, A., 137

F

Fedigan, L., 76, 79
Fee, E., 33, 49, 115, 116
Feinman, G. M., 141, 143, 144
Fisher, E., 158
Fisher, H., 77
Fisher, L., 34, 162
Flannery, K. V., 44, 64, 69
Fowler, D. D., 54
Fox, R., 36, 37, 71, 72, 117
Francis, J., 31, 91
Fraser, A., 140
Freidel, D., 148
French, M., 34, 83, 94, 128
Fried, M. H., 69
Friedl, E., 125
Frison, G. C., 57

G

Gailey, C. W., 52, 173
Garrow, B. A., 47
Garrow, P. H., 47
Gero, J. M., 20, 23, 42, 43, 44, 54,
        56, 81, 82, 91, 92, 93, 94,
        95, 96, 145, 146, 170, 175
Gibbon, G., 20
Gilchrist, R., 41, 43
Gilligan, C., 25

Gimbutas, M., 34, 161, 162
Goldberg, S., 71
Goldstein, M., 167
Goodale, J. C., 33
Gorman, A., 92
Gould, S. J., 66, 67, 80
Griffin, P. B., 72, 98
Gross, M., 88
Guenther, T. R., 35
Guillén, A. C., 137, 162, 163
Gumerman, G. J., 174
Guo Da-Shun, 147

H

Haag, W. G., 39
Haaland, G., 146
Haaland, R., 146
Hackett, J. A., 163
Hamblin, D. J., 133, 134
Hancar, F., 158
Hanen, M.P., 15, 20, 41, 47, 48, 175
Haraway, D., 66, 80
Harding, S., 46, 159
Harris, M., 128
Hartman, J. E., 31, 169, 175
Hastorf, C. A., 103, 105, 106, 108
Hayden, B., 34, 135, 140, 141, 142, 161, 162
Herschberger, R., 75
Higham, C., 124, 125
Hildebrandt, W. R., 100
Hobbes, T., 66
Hodder, I., 24, 25, 49, 51, 53, 56, 60, 64, 144, 165, 166
Hubbard, R., 45
Hudson, M., 139
Hurcombe, L., 158

I

Isaac, G. L., 91, 113

J

Jochim, M. A., 111
Johnson, M., 53
Joyce, R., 42, 43, 139, 147, 148

K

Keene, A., 74, 84
Kehoe, A., 15, 18, 23, 39, 40, 50, 52, 69, 88, 89, 94, 95, 96, 109, 157, 171, 173
Keller, E. F., 36, 37
Kelley, J. H., 15, 20, 39, 41, 46, 47, 48, 175
Kendall, L., 102
Kennedy, M., 94, 101, 102, 136
Kenoyer, J. M., 61
Kent, S., 44, 57, 60, 62, 64, 143
Kidder, A.V., 42
Kim Won-yong, 137
Kingston, M. H., 139
Kipling, R., 65
Koenigswald, von G. H. R., 157
Kohl, P., 169, 171
Kornfeld, M., 91
Kosko, B., 176
Kristiansen, K., 51

L

Lacy, D. M., 20
Lamphere, L., 32, 116, 134
Lancaster, C. S., 70
Landau, M., 66, 74
Laughlin, W. S., 71
Laurent, 58, 156

Leacock, E., 34, 73, 87, 98, 116, 135, 139
Lee, R. B., 90, 98
Leone, M., 51
Lerner, G., 34, 72, 73, 128
Levine, M. A., 39, 42
Levy, J. E., 58, 148
Li Ki-baek, 86
Lightfoot, K., 141, 143, 144
Linnekin, J., 132, 134, 135
Linton, S., 71, 98
Lloyd, E., 38, 74
Longacre, W. A., 50, 119
Longino, H., 13, 17, 23, 37, 38
Lowie, R., 67
Lubbock, J., 115
Lutz, C., 170

M

MacKinnon, C. A., 36
Maine, H. S., 65, 115
Malinowski, B., 117
Marcus, J., 64
Marshack, A., 126
Marshall, Y., 153
Mason, C. I., 39
McCafferty, G. G., 134, 136, 137, 167
McCafferty, S. D., 134, 136, 137, 167
McCoid, C. H., 157
McDermott, L. D., 157
McGaw, J. A., 88
McGuire, K. R., 100
Mead, M., 24
Medicine, B., 57, 119, 136
Mellaart, J., 146, 160
Meltzer, D. J., 54
Miller, B. D., 19, 34
Miller, D., 51, 171
Miller, V., 58, 166, 167
Mitchell, C., 119

Moore, H., 35
Morgan, E., 52, 65, 67, 72, 123
Morgan, L. H., 52, 65, 67, 72, 123
Morris, D., 70
Muller, V., 135, 138, 140
Murdock, G. P., 86, 90

N

Nagamine, M., 164
Nelson, M. C., 47, 48, 53
Nelson, S. M., 21, 35, 40, 47, 48, 52,
        53, 88, 120, 123, 127, 128,
        143, 146, 147, 152, 155,
        158, 159, 165
Nerlove, S. B., 125

O

O'Brien, P. J., 15, 63, 95, 96, 167, 171
Oakley, A., 87, 90
Ortner, S. B., 18, 19, 134

P

Parezo, N. J., 39, 42, 45, 46, 47
Parker Pearson, M., 165
Parsons, M., 109
Parsons, R. B., 109
Passemard, L., 159
Patterson, T. C., 39, 52, 54
Pearson, R., 52, 121, 123, 165
Perricone, P. J., 42, 43, 44
Pfeiffer, J., 159
Piggott, J. R., 127
Pomeroy, S., 27
Posposil, L., 86
Potter, E., 16
Preucel, R., 42, 43
Prideaux, T., 83

Q

Qian Hao, 140

R

Rapp, R., 34, 115, 134
Rappaport, R. A., 142
Rathje, W. L., 64
Reiter, R., 32
Renaud, E. B., 151
Renfrew, C., 117, 133
Reyman, J. E., 38, 48
Rice, P. C., 106, 107, 126, 152
Richardson, J. B., 50
Rick, J., 42
Roberts, C., 15
Rogers, S. C., 85, 86, 113, 125
Rohrlich, R., 34, 115, 134, 137
Roosevelt, A. C., 82, 166
Root, D., 44
Rosaldo, M. Z., 32, 65, 73, 116, 132, 134
Rosenfeld, A., 158
Rossiter, M. W., 47
Russell, P., 161, 163

S

Sabloff, J. A., 54
Saccasyn Della Santa, E., 159
Sacks, K., 34, 113, 127, 128, 134
Sahlins, M. D., 153
Saitta, D., 52
Sanday, P. R., 33, 146, 151, 153
Sandler, B. R., 35
Sassaman, K. E., 106
Sauer, C. O., 102
Schele, L., 148
Schlegel, A., 24, 33
Schoenwetter, J., 88, 89

Service, E. R., 32, 68, 69
Shanks, M., 20, 51
Sharpe, P., 31
Silverblatt, I., 13, 35, 128, 135
Soffer, O., 52, 121
South, S. A., 21, 44, 82, 107
Spector, J. D., 40, 43, 51, 54, 97, 131, 170
Spencer, H., 27, 65, 175, 176
Sperling, S., 76, 79
Spindler, K., 92
Stahl, A. B., 106, 108
Stalsberg, A., 62
Stanford, C. B., 77, 78, 79, 80
Stanislawski, M. B., 50
Stark, M., 39
Steinem, G., 127
Steward, J., 68, 69
Stiehm, J. H., 45, 46, 47
Stone, M., 72, 91, 92, 95, 100

T

Tanner, N., 33, 79
Thomas, D. H., 35, 39, 54, 99
Thomas, P. A., 47,
Thomsen, C. J., 68
Thosarat, R., 124, 125
Tiffany, S. W., 33, 125, 141
Tiger, L., 71, 72
Tilley, C., 20, 21, 22, 51, 171
Trigger, B. G., 44, 50, 69
Tringham, R. E., 23, 34, 52, 62, 63, 118, 161, 162, 165
Trocolli, R., 147
Trotter, J., 151
Tschauner, H., 53
Tylor, E. B., 65, 67

U

Ucko, P. J., 54, 158

V

Vertut, J., 83, 84, 156
Vinsrygg, S., 99

W

Wadley, L., 56, 92, 98
Walde, D., 41
Wallman, S., 15, 17
Warburton, M., 174
Washburn, S. L., 70, 75
Wason, P. K., 146
Watson, P. J., 54, 94, 101, 102, 136
Webster, G., 143
Weiner, A. B., 33
Whallon, R., 119, 120
Whelan, M. K., 56, 57, 58, 60
White, J. C., 172
White, L., 66, 68

Whitehead, H., 19
Wilk, R. R., 64
Williams, S., 67, 74
Willows, N. D., 41
Wilmsen, E. N., 56
Wilson, M. C., 56
Winter, M., 64
Wobst, H. M., 74, 84
Woodall, J. N., 42, 43, 44
Woodward, V., 80
Wormington, H. M., 81
Wright, P. C., 76, 77, 125
Wright, R. P., 58, 106, 107, 135
Wurtzburg, S. J., 43
Wylie, A., 18, 19, 20, 21, 35, 38, 41,
    42, 48, 53, 56, 116, 131,
    170, 172

Z

Zagarell, A., 138
Zhang Zhongpei, 121, 122, 123
Zihlman, A. L., 33, 71, 72, 76, 78, 79

SUBJECT INDEX

A

aboriginal Australia, 92
academic prestige, 37, 56
adaptation, 47, 70, 93, 117
adaptive, 171, 174
adiposity, 159 (*see also* fat)
adulthood, 59, 83
Africa, 64, 95, 98, 109, 136, 143, 166;
    African, 70, 98, 99, 127, 143,
    144, 159; African kingdoms,
    127, 143
agency, 50, 51, 120, 143, 172, 174,
    176
ages, 27, 113, 121, 123
agriculture, 68, 69, 74, 110, 121,
    146, 148, 166, 173 (*see also*
    cultivation, domestication,
    and farming)
altars, 140
Amazonian, 117
ambitious, 45, 141, 143
American Anthropological Associa-
    tion, 40
American Antiquity, 144
American Southwest, 42, 143, 144, 151
Americanist archaeology, 39
Americas, 56, 81, 82, 118
Andaman Islands, 92

Andean, 135
androcentric, 17, 19, 20, 25, 27, 29,
    33, 34, 36, 44, 47, 52, 56,
    57, 70, 72, 75, 77, 79, 81,
    84, 91, 132, 142, 158, 161,
    162, 169, 170, 171, 172;
    androcentrism, 22, 25, 31,
    32, 33, 38, 41, 53, 54, 55,
    81, 116, 118, 142, 161
animals, 65, 68, 78, 79, 80, 81, 82,
    83, 84, 88, 89, 92, 93, 95,
    99, 100, 101, 135, 146, 158;
    animal husbandry, 121
anthropological archaeology, 17, 19,
    29, 39
anthropology, 18, 27, 28, 29, 32, 33,
    34, 35, 40, 50, 52, 65, 67,
    68, 70, 71, 73, 77, 84, 85,
    101, 113, 114, 115, 117,
    118, 131, 132, 134, 142, 159
apes, 74, 75, 76
archaeological theory, 14, 28, 30
Archaic, 100, 101, 103, 104
argument by assertion, 161
Aristotelian, 176
Arizona, 119
arrowheads, 140
arrowshafts, 63

art, 27, 68, 69, 75, 82, 83, 84, 99,
   146, 156, 158, 160, 166, 173
art historians, 146
artifact, 21, 29, 55, 57, 58, 60, 61,
   62, 63, 64, 68, 81, 84, 87,
   88, 89, 90, 91, 92, 93, 94,
   96, 97, 99, 100, 102, 105,
   109, 110, 119, 122, 124,
   148, 152, 159, 167, 170
artist, 83, 88, 156, 158
Asia, 64, 69, 102, 107, 128, 138, 160, 162
Australia, 92
authority, 23, 29, 33, 43, 74, 117,
   123, 135, 140, 143
awl, 96, 109
Aztec, 104, 105, 110, 134, 137, 167

B

bag, 92, 96
Balkans, 161
bangle, 61, 124
Banpo, 121
bas relief, 154, 155
base camp, 35, 99
basketry, 88, 90, 96, 99, 109
beads, 61, 122, 124, 139, 140
beans, 101
beer, 46, 105, 106, 143, 144, 145
beliefs, 95, 152
belly, 160
berdache, 15
Big Man, 141–145
biological essentialism, 25, 26, 31
biology, 26, 55, 171, 172
biophysical anthropology, 34
bird, 123
birthing, 164
births, 157
Blackdog Cemetery, 60

bleeding, 82, 83
Boadicea, 140
body, 53, 67, 155, 156, 157, 159
bone tools, 29, 96, 97
bones, engraved, 126; decorated, 126
boundaries, 81, 120
breasts, 56, 123, 146, 152, 154, 156,
   157, 159, 162, 163, 164
Broken K Pueblo, 119
bronze, 68, 93, 137, 140, 168
Bronze Age, 99, 148, 160, 164
Bulgaria, 143
Buret, 109
burials, 29, 58, 59–60, 61, 63, 100,
   101, 103, 105, 109, 118,
   119, 121, 122, 123, 124,
   125, 127, 131, 133, 139,
   140, 146, 147, 148, 162,
   167; flexed, 122 (*see also*
   cemeteries)
buttocks, 159

C

Cahuilla, 100
California, 100
Canaanite, 163
capitalist, 73, 87
care, 64, 76, 77, 85, 87, 95, 102, 111,
   125, 126
career ladder, 37, 48
careers, 40, 42, 45, 47, 48
carnivores, 70
Carter Ranch, 119
carving, 103, 123, 156
Çatal Hüyük, 115, 146, 160
categories, 16, 17, 22, 26, 27, 30, 55,
   60, 65, 69, 92, 94, 100, 119,
   126, 161
Catholic Church, 166

cattle, 148
Cave Man, 82
cave paintings, 68
Celtic, 138, 140, 147
cemeteries, 60, 61
censuses, 59
Central Mexico, 137, 141
centralized authorities, 164
ceramic, 104, 108, 121, 145, 167
ceremonial artifacts, 119, 148
Chacmool Conference, 41
Chalcatzingo, 162
change, 22, 23, 43, 51, 56, 62, 66,
        67, 68, 71, 96, 107, 134,
        161, 163, 165, 171, 172,
        174, 175
chastity belts, 128
chicha, 145
child care, 35, 64, 77, 85, 87, 102, 111, 126
childhood, 59
children, 26, 61, 71, 72, 76, 85, 86,
        87, 88, 100, 116, 117, 118,
        125, 140, 156, 157, 163
chimpanzee, 75, 77, 79, 117
China, 52, 59, 113, 121, 122,
        123, 139, 140, 141, 146,
        147, 161; Chinese, 109,
        121, 122, 123, 132,
        138, 139
chopping tools, 119
cinnabar, 146
civilizations, 171
civilized, 66, 123, 128
clan, 114, 121, 122, 123, 138
class, 15, 17, 32, 34, 52, 61, 67, 85,
        86, 88, 106, 128, 131, 147,
        165, 173; class stratifica-
        tion, 106, 131
Classic Maya, 139, 147, 148

classicists, 27, 32
clay, 106, 107, 108, 124, 140,
        161, 164
cloth, 59, 88, 99, 105, 109, 110, 122
clothing, 42, 62, 82, 87, 88, 89, 101,
        109, 110, 122, 128, 145,
        147, 154
Clovis, 81, 82, 94
cognitive archaeology, 152
colonialism, 34, 56
Colorado, 87, 89
communal center, 121
competition, 37, 46, 142, 165
complex, 22, 24, 52, 68, 88, 90,
        95, 104, 105, 142, 167,
        172; complexity, 134,
        148, 164
constructed, 15, 22, 31, 36, 52, 81,
        94, 111, 175
constructionist, 76
containers, 61, 91, 92, 99, 101, 107,
        108, 164
control, 25, 50, 68, 74, 79, 98,
        115, 117, 132, 133, 135,
        143, 144, 148, 149,
        165, 166
cooking, 61, 82, 103, 104, 107, 108,
        110, 111
copper, 145
copulation, 79, 84, 158
cord, 93, 94, 101, 109, 120
cowboy, 42
cowrie shells, 164
crafts, 88; craft production, 57, 108
creative work, 88, 90
Crete, 109, 137, 160
cultivation, 102, 103, 141
cultural evolution, 19, 67, 171–173

culture, 15, 18, 20, 21, 22, 24, 25, 26, 28,
   30, 31, 42, 43, 55, 56, 57, 58,
   59, 60, 64, 69, 70, 72, 74, 75,
   82, 85, 88, 91, 100, 101, 102,
   107, 133, 138, 140, 141, 151,
   153, 154, 160, 163, 165, 168,
   170, 171, 172, 174, 175; culture
   change, 22, 171, 172, 175

D

daggers, 140
danger, 21, 25, 78, 128
Danish, 109, 147, 148
Darwin, 65
daughters, 50, 113, 120, 122, 127, 140
death, 61, 63, 100, 101, 165
Delphi, 138
demography, 32
Denmark, 148
depictions, 58, 60, 84, 147, 155, 159
despots, 132
diachronic change, 68
diet, 72, 78, 103–105
digging stick, 93, 99
Direct Historical Approach, 14, 56,
   57, 60, 95, 114, 108
disease, 59
division of labor, 29, 55, 60, 67, 70, 72,
   77, 80, 82, 86, 87, 100, 102,
   103, 106, 111, 122, 142, 175
DNA analysis, 59
documents, 21, 58, 110, 127, 134, 137
Dolni Vestonice, 156, 157
domestic, 26, 35, 62, 63, 64, 89, 90,
   96, 131, 132, 166, 175;
   domestic architecture, 62,
   64, 96; domestic arrangements, 166; domestic
   spheres, 131

domestication, 94, 101, 102
dominance, 75, 76, 77, 79, 80, 117,
   133, 135, 149, 172
Don River, 155
dragon, 123
drinking, 43, 144, 145
dualism, 158
dwelling floors, 86 (*see also* houses)

E

Early Intermediate Period, 145
Early Malaka, 108
earth lodges, 95
earth ovens, 107
earth pyramid, 147
East Africa, 136, 143
eastern Europe, 62, 109, 154, 158, 161
ecological, 53, 68, 82, 111, 152; ecology, 50, 68
economic, 17, 37, 64, 90, 103, 114,
   134, 135, 148, 152, 164,
   166, 172
ecosystem, 18, 50, 51
Ecuador, 166
effigy, 145
egalitarian, 73, 122, 123, 148
Egypt, 59, 127
empress, 132
environment, 26, 48, 57, 63, 68, 119, 175
epistemology, 20, 24, 161, 175
equality, 34, 46, 60, 73, 116, 122, 148
erotic, 155, 156, 157
essentialism, 16, 25, 26, 31, 38, 55;
   essentialist, 22, 23, 72, 73,
   76, 169, 173; essentializes,
   66, 161
ethnicity, 15, 16, 17, 28, 175
ethnoarchaeology, 53, 57

ethnographic analogy, 14, 56, 57, 95, 101, 108, 159, 173
ethnography, 16, 33, 57, 67, 113, 116, 142, 143, 161
ethnology, 44, 139
eunuchs, 140
Eurasian steppe, 140
Europe, 60, 62, 64, 69, 93, 108, 109, 128, 135, 143, 154, 155, 158, 160, 161, 162
Evening Star, 167
evil spirits, 61, 62
evolution, 19, 65, 66, 67, 68, 70, 71, 72, 75, 76, 77, 98, 115, 121, 171, 172, 173; evolutionary, 27, 33, 35, 52, 66, 67, 68, 69, 70, 71, 73, 76, 84, 115, 142, 171, 172, 173; evolutionary stage, 27, 67, 69, 142, 172, 173
excavations, 24, 137, 160
exchange of women, 43, 73, 116, 131
exogamy, 73
exotic, 124
exploitation, 121, 173

F

family, 62, 67, 69, 74, 82, 88, 110, 113, 114, 116, 122, 124, 127, 143, 164
fantasy, 156
farmers, 91, 101, 103, 173
farming, 103, 161
fat, 159, 160, 163 (*see also* adiposity)
fathering, 125
feast, 141, 142, 143, 144, 145
female deities, 139, 153, 154, 164

female figurines, 24, 56, 83, 126, 151, 152, 153, 154, 160–165, 166
femaleness, 16, 163, 167
feminist, 14, 15, 16, 17, 18, 19, 20, 23, 25, 27, 28, 30, 31, 32, 33, 34, 35, 37, 38, 39, 40, 41, 45, 49, 50, 51, 52, 53, 54, 56, 73, 80, 114, 115, 116, 131, 132, 134, 142; feminist archaeology, 14, 16, 18, 20, 27, 28, 30, 32, 39, 40, 41, 49, 51, 53, 54; feminist critique, 14, 20, 32, 33, 80, 142; feminist philosophy of science, 28, 32
fertile, 74
fertility, 83, 84, 126, 128, 155, 156, 157, 158, 160, 162, 163, 164, 168; fertility magic, 83, 84, 157; fertility religion, 156, 163; fertility rites, 155
festivals, 106, 144, 145
fidelity, 128
fieldwork, 43, 47
figurines, 109 (*see also* female figurines)
fish, 78, 90, 110, 111
fishing, 90, 92, 107
Florida, 147
food, 35, 61, 62, 70, 72, 75, 77, 78, 82, 87, 88, 92, 93, 94, 98, 99, 100, 101, 102, 103, 104, 105, 107, 108, 142, 144, 145, 158; food preparation, 62, 102–105, 145
forager societies, 69, 70, 87; forager, 69, 70, 87 (*see also* gathering)
force, 21, 24, 88, 105, 149, 161, 162
founding fathers, 42, 116

France, 68, 94, 97, 109, 155
funerary customs, 166
fur clothing, 109
fuzzy thinking, 176

G

Gansu, 122
gardens, 144
gatekeeper, 40, 47, 74, 170
gathering, 40, 72, 79, 80, 86, 99, 101,
    111; gatherers, 86, 90, 91,
    98, 101, 157, 173
gender, assumptions, 50, 53, 118,
    173; gender complementar-
    ily, 116; gender polarization,
    25, 26, 31, 86; gender revo-
    lution, 126
gendered archaeology, 13, 14, 15, 19, 22,
    24, 30, 35, 41, 43, 51, 52, 56,
    166, 170, 172, 174, 175, 176
genderless, 36, 126
genes, 76, 77, 78, 80, 142
genitally mutilated, 128
Germanic, 138, 147
Ghana, 108
goddess worshippers, 146, 161
goddesses, 29, 72, 133, 151, 152,
    153, 154, 159, 160, 162,
    163, 164
gourds, 101, 102, 136
grave goods, 60, 122, 131, 146
gray literature, 40, 48, 52
grinding, 63, 89, 93, 100, 104, 105
Gross Domestic Product, 88
Guila Naquitz, 89
Gusii, 143

H

Harappa, 61, 107, 133
harpoon, 97
harvesting, 102, 111
Hawaii, 127, 135; Hawaiians, 134
headdress, 124, 139
healers, 132, 135, 136–138
herbal medicine, 137
heterarchy, 148, 172
heterosexual, 157
hierarchy of labor, 82
hides, 82; preparing hides, 96
High Plains Archaic, 104
historic archaeology, 39, 82
historiography, 127, 132
history, 18, 27, 32, 35, 41, 73, 74, 76,
    87, 89, 138, 140, 153, 161,
    163, 170
hoards, 148
Holidome, 95
Holocene, 99, 142
homemaking, 131
hominids, 68, 75, 79
Homo sapiens, 155
hormones, 131, 142
horse equipment, 128
horseback, 140
horticultural societies, 73
household architecture, 62
houses, 62, 63, 64, 86, 88, 121, 123,
    124, 133, 139, 143, 162,
    164, 165, 166; house floors,
    63, 64 (*see also* dwelling
    floors); housing, 121, 128
Huaricoto, 96
Human Relations Area Files, 86, 95
human sacrifices, 122

hunting, 16, 33, 57, 58, 68, 69, 70, 71, 72, 77, 78, 79, 80, 81, 82, 83, 84, 86, 89, 90, 92, 93, 94, 95, 98, 99, 100, 104, 111, 159, 173; hunting and gathering, 86, 111; hunting magic, 83

I

Ice Man, 92
iconography, 30, 174
ideal, 155, 158, 172
ideology, 28, 29, 51, 52, 69, 121, 126, 131, 152, 153, 154, 160, 165, 167, 168, 169; ideological, 17, 53, 118, 148, 152
images, 29, 83, 114, 117, 138, 140, 147, 157, 158, 160
Inca, 35, 105, 128, 135, 145
incest taboos, 73
Indian Knoll, 133
infant, 76, 85, 87, 93, 124, 125, 154
influence, 34, 38, 41, 51, 98, 108, 132, 143
inscriptions, 127, 152
invisibility, 52, 88
Ireland, 147
iron, 62, 63, 68, 93, 140; iron nails, 63; iron swords, 93, 140
Iroquois, 120, 136
isotopic values, 105

J

Japan, 93, 127, 138, 139, 154, 164
jewelry, 134, 139, 147, 154
Jomon, 154, 164
journals, 39, 40, 48
juvenile, 126

K

Kansas, 63, 95
Kenya, 63
Khok Phanom Di, 124, 127
kingship, 21, 127
kinship, 28, 29, 60, 62, 65, 109, 113, 114, 115, 116, 117, 120, 121, 127, 128, 168, 176
Kintampo Complex, 95
kiva, 119
knives, 92, 93
Korea, 21, 47, 52, 86, 93, 102, 120, 127, 128, 136, 137, 138, 139
Kyongju, 21
Kyushu, 138

L

La Vache, 97
laboratories, 37
Late Archaic, 101
latrines, 61, 126
leadership, 43, 131, 141, 147
League of the Iroquois, 120
leather, 99, 109
Leizi, 123
Lespuges, 109
linguistics, 34
lithics, 29 (*see also* stone tools)
llama, 106, 145
lunar cycle, 126

M

machismo, 43
Magdalenian, 97
maguey, 109
maize, 101, 104, 105, 106, 145
Majiayao, 122

Malaka, 108
male origin myths, 72
male torso, 133
maleness, 16, 42, 70
Malta, 109, 160
Manhattan, 95
marine shell, 133
marriages, 114
Marxism, 121; Marxist, 34, 51, 52, 53,
     165; Marxist archaeology, 52
mastodon, 103
materialist, 49, 50, 152
materialization, 168
maternal, 125, 154
matriarchy, 33, 114–118, 123, 146,
     154; matriarchal, 33, 52,
     114, 117, 121, 122
matrifocal, 161
matrilineal, 33, 103, 114–118, 121,
     123, 124, 127
matrilocality, 114–118
mats, 96
Mayan, 174
meat, 63, 77, 78, 79, 82, 92, 93,
     94, 96, 98, 103, 104, 106,
     107, 145
medicine, 101, 136, 137
Medicine Crow, 119
medicine women, 136
Mediterranean, 162, 163
Mehrgarh, 107
Melanesia, 141, 144
menstruation, 126–127; menstrual
     calendars, 126; menstral
     huts, 126
Mesopotamia, 58, 135, 138
metals, 68, 148
metaphor, 25, 26, 27, 47, 74, 80,
     167, 172

Mexico, 64, 89, 104, 105, 109, 110,
     134, 137, 154, 162, 167;
     Mexican, 134, 141, 167
Mexico City, 105
midden, 96, 124
Middle Range Theory, 53, 152
militarism, 128
milling stones, 99, 100
Minnesota, 60
Minoan, 137, 141
mirrors, 26, 80, 140
misogyny, 116
Moche, 167
Mogollon, 143, 144
moieties, 123
monkeys, 75–78 (*see also* primates)
monotheistic, 65, 153, 163
monumental architecture, 173
Morning Star, 167
mortuary, 29 (*see also* burial, cemetery)
mother goddess, 133, 151, 154, 168
mother, 26, 50, 72, 76, 85, 91, 113,
     117, 120, 122, 125, 157, 163
motherhood, 87, 113, 125
mudang, 136, 137
mural, 137
myth, 59, 72, 139, 152

N

National Geographic, 44
National Science Foundation, 50, 69
Native American, 118
Natufian, 102
nature, 18, 23, 37, 38, 57, 75, 90,
     104, 107, 116, 142, 158, 165
neoevolutionism, 172

Neolithic, 52, 60, 62, 64, 86, 108, 109, 120, 121, 122, 123, 146, 147, 160, 161, 162, 164, 165
nets, 94, 96, 98, 109, 111
networking, 48
neutron activation, 108
Niuheliang, 146, 165
North American plains, 57
North American southeast, 100
North Korea, 52
nude, 133, 155, 156
nuts, 100, 101

O

objectivity, 37, 38
ocher, 101, 146
Okinawa, 139
Old World, 137
Opovo, 62, 63
oppression, 18, 73, 176
oracles, 138
oral literature, 59
origin, 22, 44, 65, 66, 67, 68, 69, 72, 73, 74, 81, 82, 171, 173; origin myths, 72; origins of art, 68; origins of the state, 75
ornaments, 61, 88, 133, 147, 168

P

paleoanthropologists, 66
Paleoindians, 56
Paleolithic, 82
palynological, 89
panpipes, 145
paradigm, 49, 54
parts, 13, 59, 69, 82, 109, 111, 138, 143, 156, 157, 165, 174

pastoral nomads, 153
patriarchy, 33, 34, 115, 116, 173; patriarchs, 48
patrifocal, 161; patrilineal, 115, 121
patrilocal, 69, 119; patrilocal band, 69
Pawnee, 95, 96, 167
peasants, 105, 153
peer review, 47
pendants, 21, 61
Peru, 35, 96, 105, 145; Peruvian, 109
phenotype, 80
philosophy of science, 28, 32
physical anthropologists, 32, 33 (*see also* biophysical anthropology)
pigs, 142, 148, 165
placenta, 63
planting, 102
plants, 65, 91, 99, 100, 101, 102, 107, 137; domestication, 94, 101; plant food, 72, 78, 87, 100
platforms, 146
Pleistocene, 68, 91, 99, 113
Pliocene, 79
pochteca, 136
political, 17, 26, 28, 37, 41, 42, 54, 68, 69, 74, 79, 84, 108, 135, 141, 143, 147, 148, 152, 168, 169, 172, 173
political economy, 74, 84
pollution, 61
polo players, 141
polygyny, 143, 144
population, 50, 57, 71, 108, 124, 126, 148, 162, 166
porcelain, 61
portable, 58, 105, 159
post hole, 96
postmarital residence, 119

postprocessualism, 51; postproces-
    sual, 20
potters, 91, 106–109, 118, 120, 124, 125, 165
pottery, 29, 50, 61, 86, 88, 95, 106–
    109, 110, 114, 115, 118,
    119, 120, 122, 124, 136,
    139, 140, 148, 164, 165
power, 13, 17–20, 24, 27, 31, 32, 33,
    34, 41, 43, 49, 50, 51, 52,
    53, 68, 76, 80, 82, 84, 90,
    98, 115, 117, 123, 131, 132,
    139, 141–148, 149, 153,
    162, 164, 165, 166, 168,
    169, 171, 172, 173, 176
practices, 17, 20, 38, 42, 51, 74, 81,
    95, 152
precapitalist societies, 73
Preclassic, 137, 162
Precolumbian Art, 58
predators, 78
pregnancy, 126, 160, 163; pregnant,
    126, 154, 159, 163
prehistoric, 18, 19, 20, 21, 26, 27, 29,
    32, 44, 50, 62, 64, 83, 85, 89,
    91, 92, 93, 94, 97, 106, 111,
    114, 120, 125, 126, 132, 138,
    153, 156, 161, 168, 175
presentist, 67, 80
prestige, 13, 17, 18, 19, 20, 24, 32,
    34, 37, 42, 53, 56, 82, 84,
    88, 124, 132, 142, 145, 146,
    147, 166, 169, 171, 172,
    173, 176
Pretty Ladies, 141, 154
priestesses, 135, 138, 140
priesthood, 134, 139
primate, 33, 72, 74, 75, 76, 77, 80,
    81, 92, 117, 125 (*see also*
    apes, monkeys)

primatologists, 32, 76, 113
primitive, 66, 116, 121
private property, 34, 73, 127
processions, 137, 148
processual archaeology, 50, 119
procreation, 166
projectile point, 81, 93, 94, 95, 96,
    99, 140, 167
property, 34, 43, 73, 117, 127, 128,
    131, 132, 165
prophets, 138
protohistory, 35, 127
psychological, 55, 70; psychology, 35
public sphere, 29, 131, 132, 134,
    146, 173
public/private dichotomy, 55, 131, 134
publish, 40, 47, 48, 51
pueblo, 119
Pyrenees, 155

Q

Qin Shihuangdi, 139
Queen Himiko, 138, 139
queens, 21, 135, 139, 140
Queyash Alto, 145
quinoa, 106

R

race, 17, 28
racist, 67, 74
rainfall agriculture, 110
rank, 128, 140, 146, 147, 148; rank-
    ing, 17, 75, 76, 131
rape, 128
reconstructions, 19, 23, 29, 51, 83
red ocher, 101
reductionist, 52, 73, 76, 80, 91, 92, 160
reification, 173

reindeer, 125
religion, 35, 65, 152, 153, 156, 161, 163
religious practitioners, 132
reproduction, 55, 60, 80, 129, 158, 166; reproductive age, 126
research universities, 47
resources, 28, 47, 49, 50, 56, 58, 79, 82, 98, 132, 142, 165, 168
rights of inheritance, 43, 131
ritual, 60, 61, 93, 106, 123, 145, 148, 152, 158, 164, 165
rock carvings, 148
rods with breasts, 156
roles, 15, 16, 19, 22, 23, 24, 25, 26, 27, 29, 31, 32, 33, 34, 35, 42, 51, 53, 55, 60, 62, 85, 86, 97, 113, 114, 125, 131, 132, 133, 134, 135, 137, 138, 139, 141, 142, 145, 148, 149, 160, 164, 166, 171, 172
Rome, 138; Romans, 140
rooms, 119, 146
roots, 14, 18, 28, 33, 36, 41, 73, 74, 76, 115
rulers, 21, 72, 132, 135, 137, 173
Russia, 62, 155

S

SAA (see Society for American Archaeology)
sacrificial victim, 118
salt, 110, 111
Sausa, 105
Scandinavia, 62
scrotum with penis, 157
seashells, 140

sex, 15, 59, 60, 72, 75, 77, 79, 84, 100, 103, 111, 116, 127, 133, 134, 138, 142, 147, 151, 153, 157, 161, 167
sex objects, 157, 161
sexes, 103, 106, 113, 121, 123
sexist, 33, 67, 74, 75, 80, 163
sexless figures, 155
sexual innuendos, 44
sexuality, 34, 70, 84, 133, 134, 144, 156, 157, 166, 168
shamanism, 136, 137
shamans, 102, 136, 137, 139, 158
sheep, 148
shell midden, 124
Shell Mound Archaic, 100
shellfish, 87, 90, 100, 101
Shenyang, 123
Shinto, 139
shrines, 139, 146, 161
Siberia, 109, 138, 139, 155
siblings, 113, 115
Silla, 21, 127, 128; Silla Kingdom, 127
simplistic, 52, 76, 169
sisters, 39, 113, 122, 127
skeletons, 122, 124
slaves, 59
snakes, 83, 137
snares, 94
snowshoes, 96
social, 13, 15, 16, 17, 20, 26, 28, 29, 30, 33, 35, 37, 41, 42, 45, 50, 51, 52, 53, 54, 55, 59, 60, 61, 63, 66, 69, 70, 73, 76, 80, 81, 84, 88, 97, 98, 107, 113, 114, 115, 116, 117, 118, 119, 120, 122, 123, 128, 129, 131, 135, 139, 144, 152, 164, 165, 166, 170, 172, 173, 175

social archaeology, 114, 117
social organization, 29, 69, 114, 118,
    120, 129
social phenomena, 50
social reality, 80
social structure, 26, 29, 33, 63, 88,
    114, 118, 122, 128, 129,
    166, 175
society, 16, 17, 18, 19, 23, 24, 29, 32,
    33, 34, 38, 55, 59, 60, 61,
    64, 65, 66, 69, 70, 72, 73,
    76, 77, 85, 86, 87, 88, 90,
    96, 98, 99, 101, 102, 103,
    107, 108, 109, 113, 114,
    115, 116, 117, 120, 121,
    122, 125, 127, 128, 129,
    132, 133, 134, 135, 136,
    138, 139, 140, 141, 142,
    143, 144, 146, 147, 148,
    154, 155, 157, 158, 160,
    161, 162, 165, 166, 169,
    171, 173, 174
Society for American Archaeology
    (SAA), 39, 44, 54
sociobiology, 76, 80
sociocultural anthropology, 33, 34,
    114, 142
sociology, 18, 28, 35, 39
soil analysis, 126
sorcerers, 158
South America, 82
South Asia, 107
South Korea, 21
southeastern United States, 103
southwest Asia, 69, 102, 128, 160, 162
Soviet Union, 39, 52, 121
Spain, 68; Spaniards, 134
Spanish Conquest, 147
spatial arrangements, 58

spindle whorls, 109, 110, 140, 168
spinning, 109, 122, 167, 168
spirituality, 152, 153
spoons, 140
squash, 101
standpoint theory, 17
state formation, 28
states, 69, 127, 128, 134, 171, 176
statistical, 109, 118, 119, 120
statuettes, 137, 152, 154, 155
status, 34, 36, 41, 59, 60, 61, 98, 115,
    122, 123, 124, 125, 127,
    131, 133, 134, 138, 141,
    142, 143, 145, 146, 147,
    154, 160, 162, 166, 171
steatopygia, 159
stereotyped, 85
stone, 61, 68, 81, 88, 89, 90, 91, 92,
    93, 95, 96, 97, 98, 99, 104,
    111, 114, 122, 140, 145,
    155, 160; stone knapping,
    91; stone tools, bifacial, 81;
    stone tools, technology, 68
stratification, 106, 131, 143
stylistic, 30, 118, 119, 120
stylized figurines, 154
subsistence, 33, 50, 68, 69, 71, 77, 87,
    98, 99, 101, 111, 125, 166;
    subsistence base, 69, 111;
    subsistence remains, 166
Sumer, 137, 160
Superman, 42
supernatural, 153, 165
surplus of food, 142
survivorship, 46, 47
Swahili, 61, 62, 63
Sweden, 99
symbolism, 60, 165, 168

T

Tacitus, 138
tamales, 104
Tanzania, 76
technological, 27, 52, 67, 68, 81, 82, 98, 152
technological ages, 27
teeth, 108, 124, 156
temporal divisions, 27
tenure, 36
territory, 21, 36, 81, 89, 95, 104, 128, 148, 170
textiles, 59, 109
texts, 27, 54, 58, 59, 66
Thailand, 124
Three Kingdoms Korea, 137
throne, 146, 147, 153
tiger, 123
Tikal, 148
Timucua, 147
tomb, 21
tool, 25, 35, 57, 68, 88, 89, 90, 91, 92, 93, 94, 99, 172
tooth removal, 124
torso, 133, 155
tortillas, 104, 105
traders, 57, 132, 135, 136
traits, 44, 67
trancing, 136
traps, 94, 98, 109
trash, 97, 119, 124, 162, 164
trauma, 59
tribes, 69, 120, 122, 171
trivializing, 88
tubers, 106
Turkey, 109, 115, 146, 160
tyranny, 56
tyrants, 132

U

unilinear evolution, 68
universalizing, 16, 23, 36, 53, 85, 159, 171
Upper Paleolithic, 25, 56, 83, 84, 94, 109, 126, 151, 152, 154, 155, 156, 157, 159, 160
Ur, 58, 135, 138
Ur II, 58, 135
Ur III, 58, 135
urban center, 167
utilized flakes, 93, 95, 96
uxorilocal, 117

V

Valdivia, 166
Valley of Mexico, 110, 154
value, 21, 22, 24, 26, 28, 37, 38, 46, 49, 50, 61, 88, 94, 105, 157, 174, 176
vegetal food, 70, 82, 99
Venus, 25, 151, 155, 159
Victorian, 33, 65, 66, 84, 115, 117
Viking, 62
villages, 64, 105, 108, 109, 120, 148
Virgin Mary, 153
virginity, 128, 135
vulvas, 84, 156

W

wall frescoes, 146
wall paintings, 137
Wanka I, 105, 106
Wanka II, 105, 106
war clubs, 99
warfare, 43, 57, 59, 93, 108, 120, 128, 131, 134, 140, 141, 166
warriors, 128, 132, 134, 135, 140

wealth, 58, 118, 122, 124, 125, 133,
    147, 165
weapons, 21, 59, 89, 92, 93, 140, 147
weavers, 58, 59, 91, 110; weaving,
    58, 59, 109, 110, 111, 119,
    122, 167, 168; weaving
    tools, 119
web of relations, 26
weeding, 102
Wei Zhi, 138
West Africa, 95, 109
wifehood, 114, 127
Willendorf, 151, 159
Witt Lodge, 167
wives, 48, 113, 127, 128, 135, 140,
    143, 144, 163
woman warrior, 139
Womankind Museum, 90
wombs, 91, 126
women in science, 36
wooden coffins, 148
wooden tools, 93
Woodland, 106
work, 16, 18, 21, 22, 23, 24, 28, 29,
    31, 32, 35, 36, 37, 40, 42,
    43, 45, 47, 48, 51, 52, 53,
    55, 56, 59, 63, 72, 75, 82,
    85, 86, 87, 88, 89, 90, 91,
    95, 96, 99, 102, 103, 104,
    105, 107, 109, 110, 111,
    114, 115, 119, 122, 143,
    147, 167, 168, 170, 175
workplaces, 111
Wyoming, 57

X

Xaltocan, 105, 110
Xico, 105, 110
Xinjiang region, 59
Xinle, 123
Xuehotla, 105

Y

Yahweh, 163
Yamatai, 138
Yamato, 127
Yangshao, 121
Yellow River, 121
Yoshinogari, 138, 139
Yuanjunmiao, 122, 123
yuta, 139

88 artists